PEARS WORD GAMES

PEARS WORD GAMES

Peter Newby

PELHAM BOOKS

Stephen Greene Press

PELHAM BOOKS/Stephen Greene Press

Published by the Penguin Group
27 Wrights Lane, London W8 5TZ, England
Viking Penguin Inc. 40 West 23rd Street, New York 10010, USA
The Stephen Greene Press, 15 Muzzey Street, Lexington, Massachusetts
02173, USA
Penguin Books Australia Ltd, Ringwood, Victoria, Australia
Penguin Books Canada Ltd, 2801 John Street, Markham, Ontario, Canada L3R 1B4
Penguin Books (NZ) Ltd, 182-190 Wairau Road, Auckland 10, New Zealand

Penguin Books Ltd, Registered Offices: Harmondsworth, Middlesex, England

First published 1990

Copyright © 1990 Peter Newby

Typeset in 10/12 Melior by Goodfellow & Egan Ltd, Cambridge.
Printed and bound by Richard Clay Ltd, Bungay, Suffolk

A CIP catalogue record for this book is available from the British Library

ISBN 0 7207 1883 X

To those for whom Granny's tin of buttons was very special:

Melanie Barton, Maxwell Caulfield, Marcus Maclaine,
Alexandra Lisa Newby, Alexander Newby, Katie Newby.

Contents

Relevant Tables and Commentaries are shown in italic

Foreword

Pears Word Games is no mere survey of traditional word games and word play. It is a compilation of the best entertainment for competitors who use the English language as sporting equipment and the likes of **Charades** and **Hangman** – which would surprise you only if they were omitted – are but a facet of what is probably the most truly original book on this subject yet to be published.

Ancient amusements such as **Hot Cockles** and **Questions and Commands** are revived in a format which will appeal to the players of today and new, genuine, games are appearing in print for the first time. The inventors of these new games are given full credit and it is not vanity which has the author naming himself as the major contributor of original material, simply the truth. If I had adopted a cloak of anonymity to suggest a spurious legitimacy of time-honoured acceptance for these inventions you, the reader, would be the victim of a hoax. Instead, I risk your censure for daring to contrast my own solitaire challenge of **Triplets** with its nearest relative, Lewis Carroll's **Syzygies**.

Pears Word Games is significant not only for what it includes but mention should be made of what it rejects.

Compilers of games books face a genuine dilemma – a dearth of good word games. The choice is stark. Concentrate on word play as opposed to competitive word games and produce a mass of examples of literary wit or else devise your own contests using an easy format. The definitive list game, **Guggenheim**, provides the easiest of all formats and dozens of variations on this theme have filled many a page on books devoted to the subject of word games.

This book follows neither trend set by others. **Palindromes**, **Acronyms** and similar literary wit are consigned to mere paragraphs in a solitaire study entitled **Wordsmithery** and the only list game mentioned is **Guggenheim**.

What, if one eschews the easy options, are the alternatives?

The first is totally new concepts in word play. For example, I knew of no game based on the theme of dominoes so I challenged Charles Clewlow, a fellow member of an international society of code breakers, to produce a game or games of this genre. We set about this task independently and our results are found in the Cross Play series of pencil and paper games. Tom Wright creates word puzzles which are regularly published, what could his fertile imagination produce? He devised a fiendish game with words constructed in a triangular formation but it had one very serious drawback, whoever went first in a contest between equals invariably won. Once he changed the geometric shape he had a little masterpiece, **Square Bashing**.

The other alternative is variations of an existing theme but one which will produce interesting games, not banal literary penances which consist simply of who can produce the greatest number of words in categories reflecting the whim of a writer. *Pears Word Games*, has instead, my own Hangman games which have been devised so that more than two can play and these have a family, adult and even wordsmith appeal.

The result is a book of more than 150 genuine games ranging from the children's **I Spy** to the wordsmith's **Code Breaking**. There are challenges for solo amusement. Games for two competitive word lovers; for a relaxed family gathering; for a kiddies' party; for a crowd of slightly inebriated revellers. Competitions for a classroom or a campus, according to the level of skill desired. Word sport for representative teams. Even two games for playing by post and none require anything more than pencil and paper.

Pears Word Games carries additional features which make a real contribution to both word games and word sport. Television's **What's My Line** cannot be played in the parlour as the family knows everyone else's job – unless they play **Oddjob**. The great classic dictionaries have been consulted to produce the basic material for this new game. An A to H list of curious occupations is provided to whet your appetite if **Oddjob** becomes a family favourite and recommended authorities are named should you require such as zaptieh (a Turkish policeman), zepher (an Algerian light infantrymen) or zymotechnologist (a specialist in the fermentation processes) to complete a full employment register beyond the huers, hurriers and hurters who (apart from having no connection with colours, speed or pain) conclude the given data. Lists of this type, mainly for the spoken games, are for 'drop of a hat' play which dispenses with tedious research. The meanings of unusual words on all of these lists are found in the **Appendix**.

The unique **Bingo Letter-Frequency Table** is not only the basis of a series of games in which Bingo is played with words – another original concept – but features in word sport. The dream game of **Goal!**, word soccer, utilizes it and I genuinely dreamt **Goal!** after having, as I thought, completed the book.

Finally, some personal acknowledgements. The writer Darryl Francis introduced me to a treasure trove of word play contained in the American magazine, *Word Ways*. This has found expression in **Sportmanteaux** and **Alphabet Soup**, two of the paragraphs of Wordsmithery. Geoff Hammerton of the *Derby Evening Telegraph* drew my attention to the word SET which features so significantly in **Newby's Bluff**. Della Thompson of the Oxford University Press kindly sent me two delightful foreign proverbs for **Acid Drop**. Julie Titchener, Elaine Hollingworth-Clarke, Joan Smith, Elisabeth Clewlow, Charles Clewlow, John Wilkinson, Janet Wilkinson and Tom Wright test played my own conceptions and were not afraid to tell me to go back to the drawing board.

An unusual acknowledgement is for the efforts of Barbara Newby. She is a scholar and I turned to her for help when my research led me to a game invented in the twelfth century by a baker of York. The Latin description began *'Fuit inventor cujusdam ludi pestiferi et a jure reprobati'*. When my cousin's wife provided a translation which commenced *'There was an inventor of an evil game which was condemned by law'* I hurriedly abandoned the idea and turned, instead, to the study of **Qwaints**.

Last, but not least, my own grown up children who now beat Dad at his own games except when they are dancing in Japan, filming in Hollywood, co-writing a best-selling book in London or turning heads in Nottingham.

To them and the generations from whom I inherited the tradition of parlour play, my grateful thanks.

Peter Newby

PEARS WORD GAMES

Spoken Games

A mixture of traditional and original games of varying degrees of skill. These include entertainments for two people whether in private or killing time in a public place, sober and slightly inebriated adult party games and public competition. There are also games for children.

The following are inventions of the author and strictly copyright © 1990 Peter Newby for any form of commercial exploitation.

I CAN SEE
WICKED WHISPERS
GOAL!
WHO'S ZOO (All three
 versions)
NEWBY'S BLUFF
JUST A MINUTE
EMBERLUCOCK
BLIND GUE

HOT COCKLES
ODDJOB
TWENTY-ONE QUESTIONS
HORACE'S CAT
WHO'S WHO
LEXICONNERY
THE COMPLETE VERBAL
 TENNIS SERIES
THE COMPLETE BACK TO
 FRONT SERIES

The Household Word Series

Nine games. Numbers 1, 2, 4, 5 and 7 are ideal for children. Number 6 is one of the slightly inebriated adult games. Only numbers 8 and 9 are tests of skill.

1. I SPY

A traditional family favourite and one which Granny uses to keep a child amused by posing such simple questions as:
'I spy with my little eye something beginning with T.'
The letter T will be the initial letter of an obvious domestic item such as a table. The child now guesses and Granny may or may not give additional clues if she sees that frustration has set in after (say) both television set and telephone have been rejected as being incorrect.

The usual rule is that one takes turns posing questions of this type.

2. I CAN SEE

'I can see one of these in the room', says Granny, 'and it's made of wood.'

That is her first clue in a series which, for the younger children, will reveal an obvious object such as a table. The clues she gives are the sort which childen could reproduce for themselves quite easily. These will be such as where it is or is not situated. Its colour or a colour which it is not. Its size and so on. The older the children, the more obscure the object.

She has a flexible attitude to the game, varying it according to numbers present, their ages and how quickly she wishes to take her afternoon nap.

On a one to one basis she and a grandchild take turns to challenge each other. They have a maximum of (say) three guesses. These guesses begin as soon as the one setting the challenge has given a reasonable cryptic definition. Granny's full opening statement might well be, 'I can see one of these in the room. It is made of wood. It is square, but it's not near the window. What is it?'

If the child guesses incorrectly or is baffled, Granny awards herself a point and gives another clue. 'It is very large,' is one for a slightly older child or, if coping with the difficulties of a younger child's attention span, 'It's got the teapot on it.'

Somehow, the child always just manages to score that one extra point than Granny in this game and never seems to notice (as other games will show) how she not only improves with age but has a nasty habit of winning them! When there are more children participating, Granny brings a little drama into the game and, this time, rewards those who guess correctly.

She will say something along the lines of:
'I can see one of these in the room and it's made of wood. Now, who would like to guess what it is? If you are wrong you are *out* and may not have another guess. But, if you are right, you will win a button.'

She pauses and surveys the scene.

'It's my red pencil,' could be an immediate response.

'Now wait a minute,' says Granny, 'before you guess don't forget that if you are wrong you won't win a button. I shall give you more clues in a moment.'

A touch of caution affects the young company.

By the time she has revealed that this object is also square, not near the window and large at least one child should be able to identify the table. The little lad with the red pencil has got the right answer and blurts it out.

Granny still preserves the drama. Her tin of buttons is open and tempting. The honour of being the first to have one of Grandpa's old shirt buttons is at stake. She does not confirm his answer – yet. She knows that the others will follow his lead. All, that is, save the lad's younger brother who will say, 'Chair', just to be different. Granny takes command of the vocal chaos.

She repeats her counsel about incorrect guessing but lays greater emphasis on the winning of one of Grandpa's coveted shirt buttons. When those who wish to say table have clearly indicated their desire, she awards buttons. The stubborn younger brother has to wait for her next mystery object.

(*For the adult version of this game see Dutch Auction page 51.*)

3. CRAMBO

Pepys Diary for the 20th May 1660 carries the following entry:

> '*From thence to the Hague again playing at Crambo in the waggon.*'

Pepys is only one of the great literary figures who has enjoyed this classic spoken word game for two players.

It consists of someone setting a line which the other is to rhyme to, but no word of the first line must occur in the second.

4. DUMB CRAMBO

A rhyme of a given word is mimed until guessed. Unlike Crambo any number can play.

5. CHINESE WHISPERS

The players sit in a circle and a message is whispered round. Each player must pass on what he or she honestly believes was heard. Consequently, a message such as 'Great. Omit anemone', will eventually return to the first player in a form rather like, 'Grey tom ate an enemy.'

6. WICKED WHISPERS

The adult version of *Chinese Whispers* surreptitiously inserted into the basic game. One or two people seated in the circle are made the victims of scurrilous gossip whilst innocently expecting to pass on a normal silly message. The acid test is – will the original gossip return as given, or will tact or some other emotion render a change?

Similarly, messages of various sorts such as one person has part of his clothing embarrassingly unfastened can be introduced into a seemingly innocent circle of adults playing a children's game.

7. SIMPLE ADDITION

This game takes many basic forms but its object is to add so much additional detail to the original sentence that players become confused and have to drop out.

The first player says something along the lines of:-

'I packed my bag and in it I put (whatever).'

Or:

'I went to market and there I obtained (whatever).'

Or even:

'I pulled back the covers of (somebody's) bed and there I discovered (whatever).'

The second player now has to repeat the original sentence but add an additional item which can be as ludicrous or sensible as he or she wishes. Subsequent players following the same pattern.

As more and more items are added, it becomes increasingly difficult to remember everything. Eventually, only the winner remains.

8. GHOST

A two person game in which the object is *not* to say the last letter of a word containing five or more letters. Each player takes turn in giving a letter but can be challenged by the opponent if he or she cannot believe such a word is possible. It is advisable to have a dictionary handy to settle disputes. For example:

JACK: D . . . (he has no particular word in mind)

JILL: Dz . . . (she has DZOBO or DZOMO in mind, she hopes he will challenge.)

JACK: Dzi . . . (he has DZIGGETAI in mind which, even though it would still force him to say the last letter, hopes to get a challenge on the grounds of impossibility)

If a player challenges the last given letter, the other must both spell it out correctly and prove its existence in the agreed reference work. Whoever wins that challenge, wins that particular round. Normally, however, players will stick to everyday words and the D of this example would be followed by (say) an E and the contest would progress to such as DENSITY which Jill would win. DENSELY or DENSENESS are impossible as Jill would win on DENSE.

(*For the meanings of* **dzobo** *and* **dzomo** *see* **zho** *in the Appendix. For* **dziggetai** *see Appendix in normal alphabetical position.*)

9. GOAL!

A minimum of ten players are required to play this fast-moving version of verbal soccer. For convenience of illustration assume that we have a contest of men versus women, they are seated at a long table, Jack and Jill are the respective captains and that the two captains are standing down until the first goal is scored by either team. The eight people in play are seated thus:

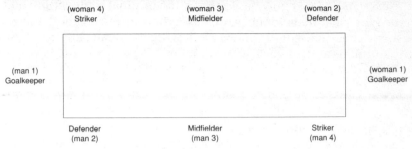

Spins of the coin have Jack acting as the linesman, Jill as the referee and the kick-off is by the women.

The woman midfielder begins by stating vowel or consonant and Jack now consults the **Bingo Letter-Frequency Table** (see page 73) and selects any line of letters commencing with her choice. Assume that she wishes a vowel and Jack chooses line number 2 which reads as follows:

I R Y N I S H A Z U J S E F O V E N G I G R Y T

He announces its first letter, I, and play is deemed to have passed to Woman 2. She has a mere two seconds (judged by the referee, Jill) in which to state a valid 2-letter word containing the letter I. She says (say) IT.

By being successful the 'ball' is passed upfield to Woman 3 who has a similar two seconds in which to get it to her team's striker. She does this by adding another letter to IT in order to produce a valid 3-letter word. She says (say) SIT.

The ball is now at the feet of the woman striker. She has to add another letter within the time limit in order to shoot for a goal. However (say), she overruns her time as she can only think of one word and is too embarrassed to say it.

Jill announces that the ball is loose by saying, 'Go'. The woman striker and the man defender are both free to state a valid 4-letter word. Three possibilities arise:

(a) The striker recovers her equanimity and says (say) SPIT. The male goalkeeper must save the shot if he can. A successful save with (say) SPITS will be discussed below. Failure results in a goal for the women's team.

7

(b) The defender gains control of the ball with (say) SPIT. He passes to the midfielder who, by saying (say) SPITE now has the ball with his striker who, by saying (say) PRIEST, has fired a cannonball shot at the women's goalkeeper.

(c) Neither player can think of a suitable word within the time limit and Jill calls out 'Stop'.

In the event of the goalkeeper saving a shot, the linesman calls out the next letter of the Bingo line. In this example, R. The goalkeeper must now turn this into a 2-letter word for passing forward to his defender. (Some simple letters will prove very tricky for anyone other than a wordsmith. Q is obviously very difficult so too, surprisingly, is C. Abbreviations are not allowed and that rules out, unless you are a wordsmith, CO. An expert wordsmith, however, would not have the slightest problem with either Q or C. The extant words of CA, CE, CO, CU and QI are defined in the Appendix as are the obsolete words CI and QU – both equally valid for play – whereas the remaining 'C words' of AC, CY, IC and OC are not mentioned. The curious case of the non-word CH is also included in the Appendix.)

If the goalkeeper, having saved the shot from the female striker, turns R into such a valid word as OR, play follows its logical progression. But, should he 'fumble' by exceeding the time limit Jill will call out, 'Go'. *Three* players now race for the ball – the woman striker and men's goalkeeper and defender. Whichever is first to say such as ER, OR or RE sends the ball in the logical direction.

A similar situation prevails in the case of the referee saying 'Stop'. The linesman calls out the next letter and the relevant players race for it.

The referee is the sole judge of all matters pertaining to play. Jill, for example, will not need to have a stopwatch for timing but use her commonsense. Similarly, if two players call out words almost simultaneously when going for a loose ball, she decides who was the first. Alternatively, she may call upon the linesman for a fresh letter.

If Jill considers a word is likely to be invalid she is entitled to hold up the game whilst she investigates. For example, SITE is followed by PISTE. Once she is satisfied that the player has correctly used a word meaning a ski slope and that all understand how it is spelt she waves play on. Sometimes, the referee may wish to consult the dictionary in the event of a word about which she has her doubts. This brings into play the concept of fouls and penalties.

A foul is committed by giving an invalid word. A goalkeeper's foul is treated as a penalty.

(a) In the event of a foul, the offending letter is removed and the player directly opposite now has possession of the basic word.
(b) In the event of a penalty, the offending letter is removed and the striker has a free shot with any additional letter at the goal.

Once a goal is scored, Jack and Jill are replaced as officials by other members of their teams. A woman now takes charge of the **Bingo Letter-Frequency Table** and a man is the referee. As with standard football, the team that had the goal scored against it kicks off.

The game lasts either for an agreed period of time or else ends when one side has scored a particular number of goals.

If (say) twelve people are involved this will produce a goal-keeper, a defender, two midfield players and a striker. The kick-off always commences with the midfield player next to the defender.

Goal! is an ideal game for compotition between representatives of different taverns or schools. It is recommended that independent officials be used wherever possible.

The following word rules are for the benefit of serious competitors:

1. All words played must be capable of being confirmed in an agreed dictionary, supplemented by *Pears Advanced Word Puzzler's Dictionary* for such vital categories as 2-letter words and 'Q words without a U'.
2. All words played must be capable of being written in the lower case. For example, **Abba** in the sense of the pop group is invalid whereas **abba** in the sense of a sleeveless outer garment validates that same word.
3. Hyphenated words or compounds are invalid, so too are words which require an apostrophe. It should be noted that one particular popular dictionary, even in its 1988 revised edition, unnecessarily hyphenates many words contrary to the modern practice. This (and similar frustrating curiosities) is discussed in considerable detail on pages 182 to 189 of *Pears Advanced Word-Puzzler's Dictionary*.
4. There is no objection to plurals or sensibly formed verbal inflections or adjectival comparatives and superlatives even though these are often overlooked, for reasons of space, from many dictionaries.

5. Words capable of inference but not given in the agreed reference work may not be used. Essentially this is such as verbs prefixed un- or re- and nouns created by suffixing a verb with -er.

6. There is no objection to such as slang, dialect, Americanisms, obsolete words (but see the commentary on this subject on pages 188–189 of *Pears Advanced Word-Puzzler's Dictionary*), obscenities and words of foreign origin now treated as English. But, words given in a dictionary as foreign are invalid.

Serious competitors should draw up their own rules concerning such matters as substitutes but there is no objection to players, for tactical reasons, changing playing position (i.e. goalkeeper to striker). All changes of this nature may only be made after either team has scored a goal. If a team is a player short and wishes one of its number to fulfil more than one role (i.e. both a midfielder and the striker) this can only be permitted if both the opposing team and the referee agree and the constitution of the competition permits this.

On the question of time for a move, two seconds is ample for wordsmiths but non-wordsmith adults or children may require more time. Time limits are deemed to be two seconds unless otherwise mutually agreed. As an alternative to a stopwatch for a serious contest, chess clocks may be utilized but the organizers must agree suitable penalties for the team which runs out of time first. The penalties should relate to the amount of time by which they are in advance. Penalties can take the form of goals disallowed or else additional free kicks by the team having unused time. Such penalties are left to the discretion of the players.

The Charade Series

Fourteen games to delight the show-off. The children's game is the first version of number 3. The second and third versions are for the slightly inebriated adults, as are numbers 10, 11 and 12.

1. CHARADES

An all-time classic mentioned in the works of such writers as

Sheridan, Thackeray and George Eliot but better known today as television's *Give Us A Clue*.

At its simplest, a multi-syllable word is chosen. Say, CATA-TONIC. A player breaks the word down into sections, not necessarily syllables, and mimes to the company each section separately. For CATATONIC a player might mime:

(a) CAT followed by A followed by TONIC
(b) CAT followed by (H)AT followed by TONIC
(c) CAT followed by (H)AT followed by O followed by NIC(K)

or any other combination which readily suggests itself. The company now has to guess the word.

Played at its best, no finer tuition can be given than watching either of the team captains of *Give Us A Clue* in action. When watching note particularly how Lionel Blair gently leads other members of his team into giving clear information. Some of the celebrities (out of anxiety, arrogance or plain stupidity) fail to give clear signals of what they are attempting to display and, whilst this is sometimes entertaining, it is often downright silly. For example, one celebrity was given the film title, *The Lone Ranger and the lost City of Gold*, to mime.

He immediately launched himself into the role of a rider on horseback. None of his team knew which word or words he was attempting, nor that it was a descriptive name. All naturally assumed that it was the first word and was something like RIDER or JOCKEY. Though Lionel Blair managed to bring order to this chaos with masterly tact, the player ran out of the allotted 2 minutes available for enactment and the men failed to score a point.

Though most readers will know how to play this game, team captains should remind their players of the following basic rules:

1. Give *clear* signals as to which word or syllable you are miming.
2. Listen *carefully* to what your team-mates say. Often the correct word or syllable is stated but missed by an over-anxious performer.
3. If your team-mates are completely baffled by what you are attempting, then stop and reconsider the situation. Could you tell them the same information in a different way, or would it be better to attempt a totally different word?

How could *The Lone Ranger and the lost City of Gold* be mimed?

First of all, give the conventional sign for a film title; which is to mime the action of silent film cameraman using an old hand wound movie camera.

Secondly, hold up nine fingers to represent the nine words of the title.

Thirdly, if you wish to portray *The Lone Ranger* as one item clearly indicate that you are miming the first three words. This is achieved by:

(a) Tapping the top if your head to indicate a name.
(b) Holding up first one finger, then two fingers, then three fingers, to indicate three words.
(c) Pause to see if the point has got across. If it has, then continue.
(d) Mime *not* a man on horseback, but a masked cowboy.
(e) If this fails to get across, stop and take the whole thing word by word. Ensuring that you clearly indicate with your fingers which word is being attempted.

THE The conventional sign for this is the shape of the letter T formed by your index fingers.

LONE If you cannot see a clear way of conveying this word, hold your ear to indicate that what you are about to do 'sounds like' this word. Now choose from BONE, CLONE, CONE, HONE, JOAN, MOAN, PHONE or TONE. Mime one of these.

RANGER You will have to have particularly stupid team-mates if you have to mime this word. As they have already been told that this is the third word of a name and they now know that the first two words are THE LONE, so they should have already said RANGER. Have they? Did you fail to hear it? Listen carefully. If someone says it, touch your nose and point directly at that person and force him or her to say it again so that everyone gets the message.

But, assuming that no one says it. Try the masked cowboy routine again. Still failure. Would 'sounds like' DANGER, MANGER or STRANGER get across? Probably not. So split the word into syllables. RANGE/ER. The conventional sign for this is to place two fingers against the arm. Now place one finger against the arm for the first syllable.

RANGE Mime a cooking range. Alternatively it 'sounds like'

CHANGE (money in the pocket). Once someone says RANGE now try and force him to extend the word. You signify this by holding your hands in the praying position and extending them outwards. Surely someone is going to turn *The Lone Range* into *The Long Ranger*? No?

ER Signify the second syllable by placing two fingers against the arm. Now hold your thumb and index finger close together to indicate a little word or syllable. It 'sounds like' BURR, CUR, FUR, HER, MYRRH, PURR, SIR or WHIRR. Choose and mime. Or point to FUR, point to HER, point to SIR.

AND The conventional sign is to display a wrist with a drooping hand and to move the other hand over the top of it. (H)AND.

THE As before

LOST Mime LOST or 'sounds like' ACCOST, BOSSED, COST, DOSSED, MOSSED or TOSSED.

CITY 'Sounds like' BITTY, DITTY, GRITTY, NITTY, PITY, TITTY, or WITTY.

OF Signify small word.

GOLD Point to some gold in the room. Failing that choose any suitable 'sounds like'.

To play, divide the company into teams (say) men versus women. Now separate into different rooms and devise an agreed number of titles of books, plays, films, television shows and songs. The bookshelf, the show page section of a newspaper will provide plenty of inspiration. Write these titles down on small pieces of paper, which are then folded and put into a hat.

Return to the games room and play. The men have to mime those chosen by the women and vice versa. Impose a time limit and award a single point if a team guesses it correctly. The point is not transferable in event of failure.

Do not be afraid of making a fool of yourself. No one is expecting you to be a second Lionel Blair or Liza Goddard. But, few domestic players will be as stupid as some of the celebrities one could name on the otherwise excellent *Give Us A Clue*. They are expected to maintain a certain degree of professionalism, you and your friends are not.

If neither you nor your company has ever played it before try a session with easy titles to begin with. Something along the lines of THE KING AND I. You will soon wish to progress to the real 'stinkers' that the producer of *Give Us A Clue* reserves for team captains. Charades is one of the all-time great party games.

2. ADVERBS

Divide the company into two teams (say) men versus women. They separate to plan their strategy.

The men write down an agreed number of adverbs (words such as PROUDLY, ANXIOUSLY, STUPIDLY, EMOTIONALLY, RUDELY, ARROGANTLY) all of which are very well known. These are written on separate pieces of paper, folded, and put into a hat. At the same time they write an equal number of activities such as BUYING A LOAF OF BREAD, TAKING THE DOG FOR A WALK, CHATTING UP YOUR FAVOURITE FILM STAR or whatever. These are also put on separate pieces of paper, folded, but put into a *different* hat. The women's team are preparing similar adverbs and activities, for their hats.

When the teams are ready the hats prepared by the men are put side by side at one end of the room and the women's hats are similarly placed at the other end of the room. Or wherever else where they will not be confused. A toss of the coin decides who goes first.

Jill is first. She draws out of the men's 'activity hat' the statement HANGING OUT THE WASHING, this she reads aloud. Next she draws out of the men's 'adverb hat' the word FOOLISHLY. This she does *not* announce but now has to enact the scenario of HANGING OUT THE WASHING, FOOLISHLY to her team-mates. She is allowed to speak *but must not under any circumstances mention the significant adverb.*

The women are permitted a total of five guesses as to the adverb. If they guess it correctly first time they are awarded 5 points, second time 4 points and so on until they have exhausted their guesses. As players will tend to shout all at the same time and disputes could easily arise as to who said what in which sequence, one of the men acts as umpire. Jill gives him her adverb in advance of enactment and his judgement has to be accepted. Similarly, a woman acts as umpire for the men.

The contest is played with teams taking turns to perform and the winners are the team with the greater total at the end of the session.

3. WHO'S ZOO

(a) ANIMAL FARM: *The children's version*
The organizer writes down a number of suitable names of animals – CAT, DOG, HORSE, COW and the like. These are written on separate pieces of paper, folded and put into a hat.

The company is divided into teams (say) boys versus girls.

Suppose that a girl has drawn CAT. She now has to mime the action of a cat to her team. She may not speak or make any sound such as miaow.

Her team has a maximum of five guesses and, as they may well all shout at the same time, the organizer must be in command of the situation until sensible self-discipline prevails after one or two children have had a turn.

This is done by stressing the points which can be won on any scale you consider suitable. For example, 5 points on a first correct guess, 4 points on a second guess and so on. You now ask her team who is going to have that first guess. The ones who said such as CAMEL, GIRAFFE, SPIDER or WHALE are likely to calm down and listen to the more sensible suggestions such as CAT, LION or TIGER. The little girl, meanwhile, must remain as a cat.

You now say, 'Who is going to risk *losing* 5 points for the team by making a wrong guess?' They will soon sort themselves out and appoint their own 'spokesgirl' for that initial guess. Whatever points they win will spur the boys to perform better.

Soon your role will be merely that of a scorekeeper and, perhaps, not even that. They will soon take the game in their stride and be fully aware of the cumulative totals.

(b) ACTING THE GOAT: *The slightly inebriated adult version*
The company divides into teams (say) men versus women and each team is armed with pencil and paper.

A woman writes down (say) GOLDFISH on her team's paper and her colleagues agree. Two men are invited to leave their team-mates, one of them will take the floor and the other will join the women, he is made privy to the secret. The victim on the floor is not.

The victim must now mime a goldfish as directed by his former friend. The director's instructions might well be:

1. Lie on your stomach
2. Have your arms by your side and your feet together.
3. Flap your hands and wriggle your feet.
4. Open and close your mouth.
5. Now go round in circles.

The men have to guess what it is. They are permitted five guesses on a decreasing points scale and the women see that play is fair. They decide which guesses are to be taken seriously!

(c) SUPERGOAT: *A second slightly inebriated adult version*
This time, instead of one victim there are two and the director has to get the message across within 60 seconds (if played seriously and stone cold sober) or from two minutes upwards (according to the state of the participants). There are no limits to guesses and only a single point is at stake.

The women have now selected two very different creatures and the director's instructions to Bill and Ben might take this form:

(To BILL) 1. Stand at a position of attention.

2. Keeping your upper arms still with elbows pressed against your sides, stick your lower arms out as far as you can.

3. Now flap them madly and keep them flapping until I tell you to stop.

4. On the word 'Go' take a very quick step backwards then run around the room.

(To BEN) 1. Get down on all fours.

(To BILL) 1. Go!

(To BEN) 1. Keep perfectly still.

2. Don't laugh or make any other sound.

(To BILL) 1. When I say 'Stop' I want you to stay where you are with your left arm and left leg perfectly still but still keeping your right arm flapping.

2. Stop!

3. Wriggle your right leg and still keep that arm flapping.

(To BEN) 1. Still in a position of all fours, raise yourself to tiptoes.

(To BILL) 1. Slow your movements down.

2. Put your leg down.

3. Stand still.

(To BEN) 1. Rush across and eat him.

In a slightly inebriated minute, could the men have identified a spider and a fly?

Base your timings on a first peformance, making suitable allowances for the skill of the director. If he was particularly good, that will set a high standard for others to follow. But, if he was stupid, and had no idea how to cope with (say) a snake and a mongoose or an elephant and a mouse or whatever, then assume that others will do better and make a reasoned judgement as to what time to allow for all other competitors. Avoid, if possible, having the nurd as the first director.

In this version, players take turns to be the director and they assemble their own cast of victims.

For Acting the Goat or Supergoat it is entirely up to you how specific you wish to be. For example, if you see a way of distinguishing between (say) breeds of dog – Bill *looks* like a bulldog and Ben *looks* like a corgi and you permit one of the women's team to take the floor and stand there looking regal for Ben to play to – that is fair. Otherwise it is better to stick to having Bill as a dog and Ben as (say) a cat. Equally, the ai. This is the three-toed sloth. For a sloth, pure and simple, Bill would have to look like something large and cumbersome hanging upside down from a tree. For the ai, Bill would have to (say) remove his shoes and socks then cover two toes on each foot with a sock and hang upside down from his tree only his thumbs and index fingers visible together with his strangely covered feet.

The two captains should agree ground rules in advance based upon the composition of the company. It would be wise in these circumstances to have at least one of the captains female (however the teams may be divided) so that she can impose limits based upon such practicalities as dress and delicacy of feeling. Mere males are notoriously insensitive.

4. CALL MY (domestic) BLUFF

The delightful BBC 2 programme, *Call My Bluff*, is now firmly established as a parlour game and played in exactly the same way as the television show. The writer has been told of its being played in such diverse locations as a county police headquarters, at a caravan rally, the staff room of a large bingo club, a Rotarian party as well as in private houses. In each case it has necessitated the team leaders undertaking tedious research in order to achieve a fun session.

However, to play the game almost at the drop of a hat proceed as follows. Divide the company into two teams. Ideally three per team but alternative arrangements are discussed below. For the purpose of illustration assume that we have Tom, Dick and Harriet in the 'away' team and Jack, Jill and her mother in the 'home' team.

The visitors are given the first choice of a letter. Suppose they select B and this proves to be completely acceptable as none of the 'home' team has ever studied the entries for B in the Appendix. Jill's team remain with a letter (say) F they had used on a previous occasion.

Basically, the 'away' team now select an agreed number of words beginning with the letter B from the **Allsorts** table opposite. These are written in ignorance of their meanings. The 'home' team also choose an equal number of 'F words' but ones *still unknown to them*.

The teams now withdraw into different rooms and have individual fun devising two false meanings for each selected word, secure in the knowledge that the Appendix will provide some delightfully improbable true meanings for most of their words.

For each word they have three pieces of paper, ideally postcards. Each postcard will now bear the chosen word. Two of them will carry rough notes detailing invented meanings, one will merely say TRUE. They decide the order in which they will offer the words and who, for each individual word, will say what. (A lengthy commentary on strategy and planning will follow this basic outline of play.) Neither team has access to *Pears Word Games* during the period of separation.

When both teams are ready they come together at (say) opposite sides of a table. Each team will then take turns in offering three definitions of a word, challenging the other on a points basis to discover the one which is true.

Normally one would spin a coin to see which team goes first but, as the 'home' team have previous experience, Jill's trio demonstrate the technique of this unrehearsed, unscripted, 'instant', version of a great game. Their order of play is Jack, Jill, Mum. *Pears Word Games* is in the centre of the table and they have their postcards face down in front of them.

Jack takes the book and opens it up at the Appendix on the page where the 'home' team's word is to be found. He takes his postcard and places it in the book. He now defines the word. But, is he reading from his notes or from the book?

Leaving the book open at this page, he removes his postcard and hands the book to Jill. She takes her postcard and places it on that

ALLSORTS

ABAS, ABASSI, ABDEST, ABLAQUEATE, ABLE-WHACKETS,
ACEPHALI, ADAMATE, ADEPS, ADOX, AEL, AFGOD, ALKER,
ALLEGATOR, ALMACLE, ALMUG, ALURK, AMLET, AMMA,
AMPLEX, AMPYX, AMYLLIER, ANATINE, ANDABATE,
ANDERSMEAT, ANKER, ANTEFIX, ANTE-SUPPER, ANTHINE,
ANTHOS, ANTIHELIX, ANTILOPINE, ANTIPARLE, ANTIPHONER,
ANTIPLASTIC, APAN, APOMEL, APRECOX, ARCHEGAY, ARCHET,
ARENOSE, ARFNAME, ARCHHOOD, ARGOLOGY, ARISARD,
ARMAN, ARRHA, ARSEFOOT, ARSEMETRICKE, ASKAPART,
ASSELF, ATTEX, AUGHISKY, AUNTLER, AUSPEX, AUTOLOGY.

BACKBEAR, BACKET, BACKLET, BACKSTRESS, BADDERLOCKS,
BADELYNG, BADLING, BADMASH, BAFF-END, BAGASSE,
BAISEMAIN, BALDUCTUM, BALEYS, BALLMINE, BALZAN,
BANDLE, BANXRING, BARAPICKLET, BARBARA, BARLAFUMBLE,
BARRAT, BASCUANCE, BASELARD, BATFUL, BDELLATOMY,
BEDSISTER, BEDSTAFF, BELLYETTER, BELSIRE, BENDWITH,
BERMOTHER, BIGATE, BIGLOT, BLANKMANGER,
BLOODSTRANGE, BLOODSUPPER, BLUCHER, BLUE DAHLIA,
BLUEHEAD, BLUEMAN, BLUENOSE, BLUE PIPE, BLUNGER,
BODYLET, BONE-ACE, BONE-POLISHER, BONESHAW,
BONGRACE, BOOBRIE, BOROUGH-ENGLISH, BREKEKEKEX,
BROLLACHAN, BROWZE, BRUZZING, BUCRANE, BULBITATE,
BUMBO, BUNGO, BURNEUX, BUSH LAWYER, BUTTERBAG,
BYBLOEMEN, BYRTHYNSAK.

CAFARD, CALEPIN, CALF'S SNOUT, CAMELOPARDEL, CANSTICK,
CAPELOCRACY, CAPHAR, CAPPYHOLE, CARCEL, CASSY,
CASTANE, CASTOCK, CATATHLEBA, CATBRAIN, CATECHU,
CATHEAD, CATSILVER, CATSTICK, CATTLEIST,
CAULIFLOWERING, CAVALET, CAVALLARD, CEBRATANE,
CECILS, CENTRESS, CEPOTAPH, CERVALET, CESTUS,
CHADFARTHING, CHAIRSHIP, CHANNEL BILL, CHAPELESS,
CHAPWOMAN, CHARTALINE, CHASTELING, CHICKER,
CHILDERMAS, CHILDWITE, CHUCKFARTHING, CLAMJAMPHRIE,
CLARENCE, CLAUDE, CLAY-EATER, CLIBBY, CLINAMEN,
CLIPSOME, CLIVE, COCKPENNY, COCK ROSE, CODONOSTOME,
COLT EVIL, COMPTER, CONACRE, CONCEYTATE, CONJOBBLE,
CONNIPTION, CONSEWE, CONTRUDE, CONYGARTH, COO-IN-
NEW, COPART, COPSHEN, CORBICULA, CORDAX, CORDIFORM,

CORPSE CANDLE, CORVY, CORYLET, COSP, COST-CASTLE, COTTABUS, COURSE-A-PARK, COURT CREAM, COVERT-BARON, CRAPPIT-HEID, CREPUSCLE, CRICKET-A-WICKET, CRO, CRONK, CUBBEL, CUBEB, CUBERT, CURTANA, CYNTHIA.

DALT, DAMSAX, DAUKE, DAYESEYE, DEAD TONGUE, DEAD WED, DEARBORN, DEESE, DEESSE, DEMERLAYK, DENDROBATIDAE, DERFLY, DERVERYE, DEVIL'S BOOKS, DEWBIT, DEWBLOWN, DIAMORON, DIDYMATE, DIE-WISE, DIFFODE, DIGENESIS, DILDO, DILLIGROUT, DIMBER, DIMP, DINDERS, DINMONT, DINUS, DIRTY ALLAN, DISPER, DISSELBOOM, DITTON, DOBSON, DODDY, DOG HANGING, DOG POISON, DOG'S GUTS, DOG'S MOUTH, DOG'S TRICK, DOLLY MOP, DOMBA, DONGE, DONGOLA, DOOINNEY-OIE, DOOMSTER, DOPPY, DREE-DRAW, DREMELS, DREPER, DRIBBEK, DRINK-A-PENNY, DROPSTONE, DROVY, DROWSEN, DRUNKENWORT, DRWRY, DRYFAT, DRYINE, DUCK-BILLED CAT, DULBERT, DUNPICKLE, DUSTPOINT, DYSPATHY.

EACH VISAGE, EARTHGRINE, EARTH HORN, EGG-HOT, EIK, EIRACK, EISELL, ELA, ELECTRIX, ELEPHANTA, ELET, ELFCAKE, ELF CUP, ELMEN, ELROQUITE, EMBROYN, EMMET BUT, EMPTINGS, END-AWAY, ENDIAPER, ENDRAPER, ENTER-DEUX, ENTERLOVE, ENTERPART, ENTIA, EPHAH, EPIPHRAGM EPISTAXIS, ERS, ETHEL, EVEJAR, EVVIVA, EWDENDRIFT, EWDER, EXTA, EYE BABY, EYEY.

FAIRESS, FALCON GENT, FAMBLECROP, FANFAN, FANTIGUE, FAP, FARCOST, FARCY HUMOUR, FARDLET, FARDRY, FARSANG, FARTHINGBAG, FASTGONG, FASTLAND, FASTSHIP, FAT HEN, FAWNEY RIG, FAX, FEABERRY, FEARBABE, FEATHERWIFE, FEEBLOSE, FELAPTON, FELONRY, FERBLET, FERFLAX, FERRUP, FETCHLIGHT, FEX, FIANT, FIGDUST, FIGSUE, FILIBEG, FIMBLE, FINEWED, FITSIDES, FIXFAX, FLICKLE, FLIDDER, FLIMPER, FLOCKMEAL, FLODGE, FOG-RACE, FORBYSEN, FORFEX, FORGETT, FORMICANT, FOSTAL, FOX-EVIL, FRAMPOLD, FRASS, FRISTER, FRUTEX, FUFF, FUFU, FUK, FULLHEAD, FUMADE, FUNDUCK, FURCA, FUZZOCK.

For additional words consult a great dictionary such as *Webster's International* or the *Oxford English*; any good encyclopaedia especially *Britannica* or a specialist work such as the *English Dialect Dictionary* or the *Penguin Dictionary of Fairies*.

same page. Is her definition from the notes or from the book?

Jill now passes the book to Mum and she does exactly the same. Who was telling the truth?

Tom, on behalf of the 'away' team, now has to decide. If he is correct they score two points. If he is wrong, the home team have the two points.

Have Jack, Jill and Mum been clever enough to deceive?

Play and scoring continues in this fashion for the agreed period and both techniques will improve and fun grow as expertise develops. Providing that the Appendix is only ever consulted in this fashion for this and similar games so years of fun is available. There is no need to retain rigid teams, but, if you ration the choices of letters wisely, so you keep yourself and regular playing companions in blissful ignorance of the challenge which opponents may offer.

If you have fewer than three people per team, then one player gives two definitions. If you have more than three, then take turns at being dummy. If you have an odd number of participants you have a choice. One team has to operate the dummy aspect or else one person takes the chair, keeps the scores and paraphrases the three definitions.

Call My (domestic) Bluff is great fun with a company of witty people but should be avoided like the plague if you have dullards present. As alternatives you will find that the following game, Jobbery, is quite suitable for most adults, as is the team version of Emberlucock (see page 29).

Note: In order to facilitate the bamboozling of combatants, some of the definitions in the Appendix have extended entries whilst others are extremely terse. This is to enable you to have a wide range of descriptive length for your own false statements. You are recommended to paraphrase the extended entries if they are alien to your natural descriptive style and to colour the terse definitions with examples. In this way your opponents are far less likely to notice the difference between your making a true or false statement.

As your task will be more daunting than that faced by the professionals on television – you have to ad lib your own script – so read on to discover not only how easy you can make it but how stimulating a personal challenge this game is.

(a) True Statements
If you merely read out a terse entry from the Appendix the

contrast between that and natural waffle of your team-mates coping with false descriptions will give the game away each time. So, where you can, waffle.

The word, BARY, is typical of those which normally carry a terse entry had it been included in the listing. It is a 16th century verb describing the cry of an elephant. What else can you say?

Completely off the cuff you could produce something like this:

'As cows moo . . . cats miaow . . . dogs bark or yelp or whine or howl or whimper or make all sorts of other noises so elephants bary – or at least they did do in the 16th century. Now they've changed their tune, they trumpet. Bary is a verb which means to utter the cry peculiar to the elephant.'

If you also happened to know a rare literary usage of the verb, QUACK, then this would have added a delightfully misleading touch as:

' . . . cats miaow . . . dogs bark . . . and frogs quack – but not very often – so elephants . . .'

Alternatively, you might have noticed that BARY is an anagram of BRAY, the noise made by an ass. This fact would be even more likely to render the statement 'false' than the introduction of quacking frogs. By making your contribution as near to that of your team-mates in style and presentation so the more likely you are to bamboozle the opposition.

The same natural waffle is equally vital when presented with a plentitude of facts. For example, one of the words carries the following description:

'A secretion of hardened mucus, sometimes strengthened with carbonate of lime, with which a snail seals the aperture of its shell during hibernation. It contains minute perforations directly opposite the respiratory orifice.'

Unless you would normally speak like that, don't! Instead, paraphrase. An average person might say something on these lines:

'A sort of gunge that a snail produces to seal the aperture of its shell when it hibernates. Sometimes it strengthens this yukky stuff with carbonate of lime but leaves little

holes opposite its nose or whatever else snails breathe
through. In short, snail snoozing gunge.'

So long as you do not amend the facts, this is by far the best
approach to a true statement.

Some entries will carry quotations and these can be either very
funny or deadly dull according to your skill in delivery. The late
Kenneth Williams once instructed a fellow thespian in the art of
humour. 'Emphasise', he advised, 'the significant word or words.'
Consider an Appendix entry such as this:

> FEAK *'When she hath fed, say she feaketh her beak not
> wipeth it'* so a 17th century grammarian instructed. 'She'
> is a hawk and the verb to feak is still used to describe the
> action of a hawk after feeding.

Spoken by a dullard this entry could be as boring as a railway
timetable but a wit would lay great stress on the words **feaketh**
and **wipeth**. **Feaketh** is a command, **wipeth** is beneath contempt.
Quoted in that fashion it becomes funny. Equally significant is the
pause. The wit would end at the word, **instructed**, giving his
audience time to digest his strange statement – nobody yet knows
what he is talking about. Only then would he proceed to the
revelation of the second sentence. Not only does this treatment
render the account interesting it also, by using the pause, suggests
a 'false' definition arising from the need to think aloud.

(b) False Statements.
If you doubt your ability to produce convincing 'false' descriptions then limit your selection to those words which contain a
recognizable element. For example, the word BACKSTRESS.

If this appears to you as BACK-STRESS, then describe the word
as meaning some form of pain in (say) the lower back. To
surmount the difficulty of medical terminology have as the
sufferers of BACK-STRESS the sort of people who use normal
English – miners, sailors or all-in wrestlers. It can then be an
occupational hazard of one of these, such as Cornish tin miners,
Derbyshire lead miners or whatever. Thus, even if the opposing
team are all doctors even they cannot say for certain that your
description is false.

Alternatively it appears to you as BACK'S-TRESS. A tress is a
lock of hair – it is for the back. So, it could be a false hairpiece
worn down the back as a 15th century vanity of the fashionable

women attached to some European court or city. How many of your friends could possibly know how the 'smart set' of Budapest arranged their hair in 1486?

It might even appear as BACKSTR-ESS, a female BACKSTR. If you can define a suitable BACKSTR then she is one of those, only in a frock. And that, believe it or not, is the true definition although, technically, the word is a double feminine form.

Do not forget that between the three of you, only two definitions have to be devised. So, if your friends come up with better ideas than yours for BACKSTRESS, you take the true one. The pre-contest session with your team can be just as much fun as the subsequent battle of wits with the opponents. They, too, are plotting equally wicked ploys to deceive. However, if you wish to have prepared material rather than indulge in the true stimulus of having to think on your feet, then keep the **Allsorts** table as your personal preserve and inflict the tedium of research upon your opponents.

Established groups of devotees have been known to pass on their 'scripts' to others in order to alleviate the boring but essential aspect of pre-session planning – but, on the assumption that you have never played the game before, then such a researched challenge has to be made many days in advance of the competition. Therefore, if you do wish to retain an exclusive access to the **Allsorts** words you will also have to prepare equally good 'false' definitions – your opponents will.

The table ends at the letter F. Pressure on space dictates physical limits and to give you a wide choice from a restricted alphabet rather than have an author's preference from an A–Z table seemed the wiser option.

If you and witty friends wish to indulge in a great game then the 'drop of a hat' version of Call My (domestic) Bluff is recommended. But do restrict play to the witty, this is no entertainment for duller brethren.

5. JOBBERY

A game for six players in two teams of three people. It is played for points over an agreed number of rounds. Essentially, it is a simplified form of Call My (domestic) Bluff in which the less witty may participate.

The **Job Lots** table on page 35 is consulted and (say) the occupation of **apron rogue** is selected. Each member of a team gives a definition, two of which are false and one is true. The opposing team has to decide which is which. The rules are almost the same as those of Call My (domestic) Bluff but, by restricting the subject material to occupations, it is much easier to produce a false concept and to define it.

As with most games of this type, select a letter of the alphabet and make all selections in ignorance of the true meaning. Both teams having different letters. You will find it much simpler to select words that you can readily see possible meanings for, than to find the funny ones and not be able to match them in presentation.

Choose your words, then let the other team select its own. Write down your definitions in brief then copy out the terse statement accompanying most of the Appendix entries for jobs. When both teams are ready then let battle commence. Whilst this method involves additional clerical work and delay it does make the game easier to play.

6. NEWBY'S BLUFF

A game rather like Call My (domestic) Bluff but with a subtle difference – all the statements can be true, or false or a mixture of both!

Few will know that the word, **correspondence**, had a 16th century meaning as sexual intercourse or that the word, **share**, once meant the pubic region. Not that this is a game of dirty words, just that many words we take for granted have or had other meanings. These meanings are easily found in any large diction-ary – simply skim through the pages and stop at an extended entry for any well known word. For example, the word **set** has more meanings that any other word in the English language.

An ideal game for two teams of three adults, it makes a perfect foil for the quiz addicts who organize leagues and knockout tournaments between representatives of public houses.

The teams agree upon a good dictionary. They are told in advance which letter of the alphabet they may make their own selection from but they do not know which letter will be the province of their opponents – merely that it is different. Each side researches its own words. They select (say) a dozen each. They now write down three simple definitions for each word. It is entirely up to the team how many of the meanings are true, the only stipulation is that the word must be well known. For example, in a contest between the Nag's Head and the Royal Oak the 'Nag's Headers' chose the word **set**. How many, if any, of these meanings are true?

TOM:	A noun. A square in the pattern of a tartan
DICK:	A noun. A frame supporting the roof of a mine
HARRIET:	A verb. Of a rabbit, to be resting

If you have a pocket dictionary, none of them. If you have a good family dictionary, only one, Tom's definition. If you have an excellent dictionary, the lot.

To play, it is best to have an independent third party who acts as umpire, scorer, takes the chair for the contest and has previously notified each team in advance which letter they will be using. The third party possesses a copy of the agreed dictionary and he or she takes the ultimate responsibilty for deciding whether or not a particular definition is true or false. For example:

HARRIET: A verb. Of a buck, to be resting.

The male of the rabbit is the buck, but a buck is also a male deer. The verb does not apply to deer. Is this definition true or false? The umpire based upon the evidence to hand, alone decides. Whatever subtleties may have been in Harriet's mind when she phrased it in this form are of no consequence, the umpire has the last word.

If no third party is available, the team agrees in advance that one will select a letter from the first half of the alphabet and the other from the second half. They agree any arbitration procedure amongst themselves.

The game is played for points. Three points being at stake for each round of three definitions of a single word. If those guessing are right, they score a point. If those guessing are wrong, the point goes to the team making the definitions.

In tavern play or any other serious competition between teams who research their own words, it should be made clear to the umpire who is speaking on behalf of the guessing team each time.

For those who would like to play this game on a casual basis using the information given in the Appendix, see the list of **Peculiar Words** (page 223). This details ordinary words having the most peculiar meanings. Unlike the other dictionary-style entries in the Appendix, no indication is given as to the limitation of usage of any particular meaning. Many are obsolete or found only in dialect, American or colonial speech. None of the obvious meanings are given and, for ease of recognition, the headword is written in upper case. If any team wishes to use the word SET they will find that it has a mere 104 of the vastly greater number of meanings possible. As three have been used as examples that still leaves 101 meanings to exploit. The opposing side would have to select the first 24 peculiar words (from ABJECT to ALP) to have an equal number of meanings to hand. All peculiar words contain a minimum of three unusual meanings.

To play on a casual basis, take turns in using the Appendix having previously decided which letter will apply to which team. Unlike Call My (domestic) Bluff you should avoid waffle. Terse bluff is a different art.

7. JUST A MINUTE

An off the cuff public speaking contest which, by being played by teams of two people, is not as daunting as it sounds and far more fun.

The company divides into two-person teams and the whole proceedings are directed by a non-playing organizer. The rules will vary according to the number of participants but as few as six people (three teams) can compete. As the competition requires various officials, so at least one team will be needed to provide these neutral functionaries each round.

The organizer prepares in advance a number of basic subjects for which any reasonable person can readily bring to mind a multitude of examples. These examples are significant as each one mentioned will score a point, but only until the others discover that basic subject. Any subject will do – BOYS' NAMES, GIRLS' NAMES, COLOURS, NUMBERS, COUNTRIES, ANIMALS, HOUSEHOLD OBJECTS are typical examples – and these have been put in a hat without anyone knowing any of the subjects.

It is a contest of both skill and bluff and the officials will be just as involved in the contest as anyone else.

The organizer calls upon two teams. One will compete, the other will provide the officials. A competitor will draw a subject from the hat and all five people (the organizer, the players and the officials) will see what it is. All other teams will be the audience and attempt to discover the subject. A points scoring system will be applied on the following basis:

(a)   1 point for each example mentioned by the players.

(b) A deduction of 2 points from the actual or future score of the team to which any member of the audience belongs who makes a wrong guess at the subject. A guess being made at any time during play with a correct guess ending the round.

(c) A deduction of 5 points is made against the players and the round immediately stopped if, in the opinion of the organizer, the players are being wilfully misleading. This being a matter of fine judgement so the organizer should be a natural leader who commands respect. The circumstances in which players are guilty of being wilfully misleading will become clear once an example, given below, is explored.

First, however, an explanation of the title. In the first minute of public speaking a minimum of four examples must be given. The whole of the time allotted to public speaking is a mediaeval minute (6 minutes in modern reckoning) and, if the speakers are not giving examples at least equal to this same ratio in the remainder of their allotted time, the organizer may call a halt to their activities. This is not necessarily foul play on their part so no points deductions are made. The audience, knowing that the organizer is being fair to all concerned, can concentrate upon isolating the examples. The players are being kept on their toes. A stopwatch is not necessary but a sensible attitude to time is required.

The two officials will act as positive and negative scorers, ideally seated either side of the organizer at a table. Each has a pencil and paper. The negative scorer records the deductions. Each time a member of the audience makes a wrong guess the minus 2 points is noted against his or her team. The negative scorer is *obvious* in his or her actions. By contrast, the positive scorer is very *discreet*. This is essential as the audience must not be made instantly aware of when an example has been given. The positive scorer and the organizer work more closely together to ensure that all examples (and some may be obscure) are correctly recorded.

Let us assume that the subject is COLOURS. The players take centre stage and hold a conversation. Wittily, they mention colours such as ORANGE, LIME, LEMON, ALMOND and PEACH so keeping the negative scorer busy with such audience responses as 'Fruit', 'Trees', 'Flowers', 'Food'. This is excellent gamesmanship.

By contrast, suppose that the players had prefaced each colour with a masculine name, 'William of Orange', 'Harry Lime', 'Fred

Lemon' so misleading the audience into thinking that the subject was NAMES. This is still fair but, if the percentage of names heavily exceeds those of colours, then the organizer may construe this as being wilful and stop the round immediately.

If Just a Minute is being played wth a great number of teams, the organizer should consider having non-playing scorers and limiting the number of responses from the audience. The easiest way of doing this is to stop play every minute and, on a 'hand's up' basis, see how many agree that the subject is (still with this example) fruit or trees or whatever. This way each team has a minimum of a minute in which to record some points. Only the best, or the luckiest, will have the full mediaeval minute.

8. EMBERLUCOCK

Emberlucock is a 17th century verb which means to bewilder or confuse and this is precisely what you are attempting to do to your audience.

They know in advance that you are going to mention a person who performs an activity listed at **Job Lots** on page 35 and they have to spot who it is. You deliberately choose one which suggests something ludicrous, such as a BOOT-CATCHER, a BUTTER BADGER or a DRUDGE PUDDING. Boot catching could be some game, drudge pudding could contain the nastiest of leftovers and buttering badgers might be done for any number of reasons.

Suppose that you decide that, in days of yore, rustics indulged in a rather unkind game which involved the catching of a badger which had been thickly coated with butter. The participants include a goatherd, a dairymaid, an itinerant pedlar of butter, the parish constable or whoever else you weave into your narrative. The prize could be awarded by the medallion clerk of the London Livery Company of Grocers who just happens to become involved in your emberlucocking episode.

The butter badger has now been named, but who is he or she? Award a point to each member of the audience who makes the correct identification. (Each activity listed in **Job Lots** is fully explained in the **Appendix**)

Each player now takes his or her turn and the winner is the one with the greatest number of points at the end of the session.

If, as is usually the case, some people are reluctant to perform divide the comany into two teams. Each team has an equal number of tales to tell and, when it makes a guess, takes the majority opinion of its members. Thus, those who wish to remain totally passive merely vote.

9. FLEXILOQUENCY

Flexiloquent is an old adjective meaning speaking words of double meaning and that is the task facing you.

Each member of the company is challenged to produce an amusing extemporaneous tale without the audience being aware of the punchline. At the simplest level a prefix such as cat- or a suffix such as -ant is chosen and the speaker has to contrive a situation in which the prefix or suffix becomes part of the final comment. For example:

> 'My cat was feeling jaded so I gave the CATATONIC.'
> 'The ants went on a supersonic jet flight. They became known as CONCORDANCE.'

At the highest level a well-known proverb or saying is the subject material and some of these pass into common usage as classic shaggy dog stories.   For example:

> 'The native king collected thrones which he stored in his grass hut. One day they all fell on top of him. The moral of the story is – PEOPLE IN GRASSHOUSES SHOULDN'T STORE THRONES.'

> 'Hiawatha had three wives. One slept on a bed of buffalo skin, one slept on a bed of moose skin whilst his favourite slept on a bed of hippopotomus skin. All gave birth to sons at the same time. The ones on the buffalo and moose hides each had one son but the one on the hippotamus hide had twins. Which proves the old saying that THE SONS OF THE SQUAW ON THE HIPPOPOTAMUS HIDE IS EQUAL TO THE SONS OF THE SQUAWS ON THE OTHER TWO HIDES.'

Even newspapers are not immune to this game. An issue of the *Daily Mail* in June 1988, discussing the testing by potential purchasers of perfumes, carried the headline, SOME THINGS ARE TRIED TO SCENT US. Devotees of the *Daily Telegraph's* simple crossword have cherished the answers to questions 1 and 2 across for many years. For example, 1 across STORIES, 2 across CHEE-TAH. To get the point, say these two answers together – STORIES

CHEETAH! Shakespeare is renowned for his puns but, unfortunately, his best are too bawdy to record in this family volume.

To play, divide the company into two teams. The teams now agree to a basic small word. Examples of ANT and CAT have already been given but such as BE (which can become BEE for punchlines of BEFALL, BEHOLD etc.), SHIP (CENSORSHIP, MEMBERSHIP etc.), NATION (INCARNATION, POLLINATION etc.) and OUT are just some of the suitable choices.

Suppose that ANT is chosen. A player must now construct a tale in which ANT features in the punchline. If he or she succeeds in creating a punchline *which comes as a total surprise* a maximum of three points is awarded by the opposing team. However, the really witty can ask for any multisyllable word or short phrase (CONSTANTINOPLE or TIME FLIES are typical examples) and play for a maximum of five points. The word or phrase being chosen by the opponents. If he or she cannot see any virtue in the particular choice so the option of returning to ANT is still available. Finally, the supreme wit can ask for a proverb and attempt to score a maximum of 10 points, with the ANT option still open.

There is just as much fun in the judgements as in the storytelling. The opponents behaving like a panel of experts and making comments on such as 'groan value', 'yuk quality', 'star potential' and giving advice along the lines of 'I wouldn't give up your day job yet, dearie' or 'Don't call us, we'll call you.' Then, mock-seriously, discussing what points to award.

If you are scared of going first remember that soon you, too, will be a judge and revenge can be very sweet.

10. BLIND GUE

All that is known about Blind Gue, apart from the fact that it is a version of Blindman's Buff, is that in 1604 a charge of sixpence was levied for participation in a session of the game. It would be reasonable to assume, however, that the company was adult, mixed and in all probability, slightly inebriated.

As a modern word game for a similarly extravagant company consider a gue (an old word for a scoundrel) blindfolded and attempting to discover a word or phrase by touching various people and/or objects.

A player pays an agreed fee into a charity tin and leaves the room. The company suggest a word based upon (among other things) their consideration for the feelings of the gue and who amongst them is willing to be touched as an aspect of guessing. Once agreement has been reached, the gue is asked to return then, blindfolded, given the requisite information and led to the person or object providing the first word or syllable. For example:

A male blind gue is told that he is attempting to discover a famous historical personage. He is led to person A, who is male. Person A, on being touched, behaves in a camp fashion. The gue is told that he has touched the first word. He is now led to person B, who is female and her name is Anne. The answer, of course, is Queen Anne – or Victoria or Mary or whoever supplies a suitable name.

A female blind gue might find herself having to decipher a Shakespearean play by touching Henry four times (he keeps moving around the room) then parting two objects for Henry IV Part 2.

If a word like APPLEJOHN is chosen and no John is present, the gue can always be led to an object conveniently sited in the bathroom. Parts of the anatomy can supply aspects of such words as FOOTBALL or THUMBSCREW. Anne could find herself as the first syllable of such as ANTIQUE and Bill, followed by an eye, followed by touching everyone could be BILIOUS.

So long as a forename, nickname or surname or else a specific portion of the anatomy is an aspect of the word or phrase so the gue has a reasonable chance of guessing correctly. You can always have a person identify himself or herself by touching a window BLIND then plunging his or her hands into a bowl of particularly nasty GOO! The game is as funny as you care to make it.

Alternatively, you may prefer to play an equally genuine old game adapted for a modern assembly of word players. Perhaps combining the two games into one session – according to your regard for the current gue. If so, call the portmanteau version 'Blind Cockles' and insert the occasional joker of the following game, Hot Cockles.

To gain the maximum fun from this joker, leave it until volunteers are literally queuing up to be the gue and the ideal mug has just left the room.

11. HOT COCKLES

A very old rustic game, first recorded in a literary work of 1580. Essentially it is Blind Gue played by sadists. This time the hooded person has to kneel down and guess who has hit him.

As a slightly inebriated word game it can be adapted, less painfully, as follows:

A volunteer leaves the room. The remainder of the company agree upon a word or phrase (say) FISHING SMACK.

The volunteer returns, is blindfolded and asked to kneel down. He is told to perform the action of fishing. His task is to identify the two-word description of a mode of transport. He continues to mime the part of a fisherman – then somebody *smacks* him!

Words such as HIT, KICK, BLOW, BUFFET, STRIKE, BOOT, PUNCH, WHIP and the like can be readily adapted for slightly inebriated word fun by hot cocklers.

12. COLD COCKLES

Sloanes are reputed to be masters of amusements which rise to such heights of mental agility as throwing bread at each other. Avid Sloane-watchers have yet to record an example of their involvement in word play.

Especially for Sloanes, Cold Cockles has been devised.

A volunteer has to guess a well-known phrase. He is despatched from the company, whilst they agree the phrase amongst themselves.

On his return to the dining room, everyone throws bread at him. Obviously, *He is well-bred*!

Another example could have him leaving the room in the company of a sweet young thing. They return and he is told to make sense of a well-known phrase concerning his female partner.

The company now smother him in trifle. The sweet young thing is left untouched. Obviously, *she is not to be trifled with*!

(Cold Cockles was suggested by Joan Smith as an up-market version of Hot Cockles.)

The Question and Answer Series

Twenty-five games including the six variations listed under number 14. The children's games are numbers 11, 12, 13 and 14.

1. ODDJOB

An ideal game for a small group of people though it can be played just as easily by two. Essentially it is the same as television's *What's My Line* but with a subtle difference – you have already been told the occupation, but what on earth is it?

Jill selects an occupation from the list opposite and takes a quick glance in the Appendix to find out what it is. She now announces to the others that she is (say) a HOWDY. The definition tells her that the word is extant, Scottish and means a midwife. So, without any knowledge of obstetrics, she can answer any reasonable question even one relating to where the work is done – only Scotland and the north of England should she wish to mislead the others with an honest reply! All the questions must be capable of being answered by a yes or no though replies such as 'Don't know', 'Normally' or 'Possibly' are fair in the circumstances.

As many of the odd jobs will turn out to be historical, foreign or limited to a member of the sex opposite to that of the person being questioned, so such seemingly silly questions as:

'Are you a man?'
'Are you dead?'
'Are you English?'

will prove to be quite sensible in the circumstances.

Each player takes an occupation in turn and attempts to achieve a total of ten replies of 'No' whilst being totally fair. If the location is suitable (i.e. players can move about quite freely) the 'worker' can always commence by giving a mime. Equally helpful to those guessing is to preface a reply of 'Yes' or 'No' with such comments as:

'The studio audience is applauding.'
'The studio audience is laughing its socks off.'

when a question would have provoked such a response in conventional circumstances. Not that it is necessary to help in this fashion but it does make the whole session more fun.

Finally, if the company contains children it might be as well to have a chairman who preselects occupations not only to discover those which would be suitable but also to avoid those which definitely would not. Some jobs will prove to be rather naughty!

2. TWENTY QUESTIONS

Animal, Vegetable or Mineral is the alternative title of this perennial favourite.

JOB LOTS

ABACTOR, ABBA, ABLEGATE, ABUNA, ACCOUCHEUR, ACHATOUR, ACTIONER, ADEPTIST, ADJUTRICE, ADULLAMITE, AEDILE, AGISTOR, AGONISTARCH, ALCALDE, ALE DAME, ALE DRAPER, ALIENIST, ALL-NIGHT MAN, ALMIRANTE, ALNAGER, ALOPECIST, ALTHINGMAN, AMAH, AMBOHT, AMETHODIST ANDREW, ANIMAL MAGNETIST, ANTEMAN, ANTIMASQUER, APIARIAN, APPLE SQUIRE, APRONER, APRON ROGUE, APRON SQUIRE, APTEYKER, ARGENTER, ARIOLE, ARMARIAN, AROMATARY, ASTROMANCER, AURIFEX, AUTOCRATRIX, AVENER, AYNBREKHER.

BABOO, BADGER, BALDYSTROT, BALLISTIER, BARTONER, BASER, BASHAW OF THREE TAILS, BASTON, BATTLEWRIGHT, BAXTER, BEAR LEADER, BED BROKER, BEGLERBEG, BELLYTER, BELSWAGGER, BENET, BERGER, BERGMANN, BERMAN, BERNARD, BETTY, BIBLIOPOLE, BIDSTAND, BIGGAND, BLACKCOAT, BLOCKMAN, BLOOD HUNTER, BLOWEN, BLUNKER, BOMBER, BONAGH, BONDER, BONIFACE, BONZE, DONZESS, BOOKWRIGHT, BOOT-CATCHER, BOOTHALER, BOROUGHHEAD, BORSHOLDER, BOTTLE BOY, BOTTLE HOLDER, BOUQUINIST, BOVICIDE, BOWLER, BOX KEEPERESS, BRACHETOUR, BREADWRIGHT, BREHON, BRIDLE CULL, BRINE SMELLER, BRINJARRY, BROOMDASHER, BROOM SQUIRE, BUDDLER, BUFFO, BUGGESS, BUKSHEE, BULL WHACKER, BURIO, BUSH RANGER, BUTTER BADGER, BUZZGLOAK.

CACHEKOW, CAD, CADGER, CADILESKER, CADUCEATOR, CANTATRICE, CARCOON, CHAIRWOMAN, CHEVISANCER, CHIMNEY PUBLICAN, CLOAMER, CLOSER, COAL WHIPPER, CODDER, COISTREL,COLPORTEUR, CONDER, CONJEE, CONTABILE, COUPLE BEGGAR, COWAN, CROCUS, CROKER, CUB.

DARKER, DATALLER, DEATH HUNTER, DEEMSTER, DEFENSOR, DEMPSTER, DEPARTER, DERRICK, DESTOUR, DESULTOR, DEVELLER, DEXTER, DEY, DIGHTER, DIMBER-DAMBER, DISPORTERESS, DRIFTER, DROIL, DROPPER, DRUDGE PUDDING, DRUNGAR, DUSTYFOOT.

EGGLER, EIRMONGER, ENCHEATER, END-GATHERER, ENFERMER, ENGASTRILOQUE, ERENDRAKE, ESNE, EYEWRIGHT.

A player thinks of any object. It can be as simple as **Africa**, or as bizarre as **Robert the Bruce's spider**. The player now announces whether the object is animal, mineral or vegetable or any combination of all three. Everyone else is allowed a maximum of twenty questions between them in order to discover this mystery object.

The art of the questioner lies in clever elimination by category rather than by asking specific questions. For example, if the object is **France** and it has been established that one is seeking a geographical location, silly players waste questions by making wild guesses such as 'Is it Scunthorpe?' rather than begin an elimination of the globe either by hemisphere or continent.

All the questions must be capable of being answered by a simple yes or no and no clues are given.

3. TWENTY-ONE QUESTIONS

A test of wit between a player and the rest of the company.

The player thinks of any object. Let us suppose Jack chooses a blackbird. He writes blackbird on a piece of paper and conceals this from the rest of the company. They are going to ask him any *general knowledge* questions they wish, each of which must be capable of a single descriptive word answer. At some point he must answer BLACKBIRD to one of these questions. His task is to get away with it. Their task is to catch him out.

This is not a general knowledge quiz, nor a silly question and answer session but a test which is finely balanced between these extremes. As Jack is unlikely to be asked a question to which the absolutely correct answer is BLACKBIRD so he must grab any opportunity which comes his way in order to use it. Obviously if he answered all previous questions correctly, then his BLACK-BIRD is going to stick out like a sore thumb. Therefore, he must answer all questions incorrectly but within a degree of tolerability. What is tolerable?

QUESTION: 'What is the capital of England?'

Intolerable answers are such as BLACKBIRD or ARMPIT. But, BIRMINGHAM, EDINBURGH, SCUNTHORPE or even, at a pinch, MOSCOW could be tolerated.

The company collectively are the judges of what is tolerable. They cannot be too pedantic as each will, in turn, be facing the same test. Certainly they should insist upon a better answer than ARMPIT for England's capital but it is up to them if they are

FAKI, FATILOQUIST, FAYER, FEEDMAN, FELLMONGER, FERASH, FILE, FINGERSMITH, FLAGGER, FLATMAN, FOREMAID, FORSADO, FOSTRILD, FOUJDAR, FRATERER, FRIPIER, FRISEUR, FRUITWIFE, FULKER, FUNAMBULATOR, FURNER, FUSTER.

GABELLER, GALER, GALOPIN, GAMBIST, GAMP, GANNEKER, GARBLER, GARRETEER, GARTHMAN, GENETOR, GENTLEMAN-AT-LARGE, GEODESIAN, GETTER, GILLER, GILT, GIRL, GLIMMERER, GLOTTOGRAPHER, GLUTMAN, GLYPTOGRAPHER, GOMASHTA, GOMBEEN MAN/WOMAN, GOUJAT, GOZZARD, GRABBY, GRASS CAPTAIN, GRASS NURSE, GREFFIER, GREGORY, GRINTER, GRUBBLER, GUBERNATRIX, GUFFY, GUSTER, GY.

HACKBUTTER, HALURGIST, HALVER, HAMMERER, HANDMAN, HANGSTER, HAUBERGIER, HAVENER, HAXTER, HEADSWOMAN, HEAVER, HELLIER, HERETOGA, HEREMENUET, HEWSTER, HIEROMONACH, HILLMAN, HILLWOMAN, HIPPODAME, HISTRION, HOG REEVE, HOPPO, HOUGHER (describe as and see WHIPPER AND HOUGHER); HOUSE FARMER/HOUSE JOBBER/HOUSE KNACKER (select one description and see HOUSE FARMER), HOWDY, HUER, HURRIER, HURTER.

For additional words consult a great dictionary, especially *Webster's International* or the *Oxford English*.

prepared to accept MOSCOW. If, collectively, they reject MOSCOW Jack has to give a more sensible but equally *incorrect* answer.

There is neither need nor purpose in the company taking strict turns to ask questions. Some people will freeze when it is their turn to think of something to ask even when they could ask anything in the world they wished. Let those who have questions, ask them. But, *never* ask a question which can be answered by anything other than a physical object, be it animal, vegetable or mineral or any combination of all three. *Never* accept anything other than a single word answer. Otherwise Jack could have written the word, YES, and be bound to get away with it at some point, or else slip his secret word into a sentence or even a paragraph given in reply to a question.

Jack is facing a maximum of twenty-one questions. He must say his word at some stage. The company, collectively, is only allowed to denounce him once. Once he has got away with it, he has won. The quicker he gets away with it, the more points he will score. 21 points on the first question, 20 points on the second with progressively fewer until a minimum of 5 points can still be won. Only he may win these points, it is up to the company to stop him.

The twenty-first question is unique. He is forced to say his word, no matter what question he is asked. However, if his answer is tolerable (based upon past judgements) then he cannot be denounced. He scores 5 points. If his answer is intolerable, every member of the company receives a bonus of 5 points. It is up to the company to be fair, as they are also going to be in the same situation.

However, the company are not the masters of everything. Suppose they denounce Jack at a stage prior to the twenty-first question. True, if they are right Jack will fail to score, but, if they are wrong, Jack will not only gain the points relevant to the stage at which he is denounced but they deny themselves a possible bonus on the twenty-first question. Dare they denounce?

4. PROVERBS

A great family favourite and fun to play as a team game, though the concept is easier to explain in terms of a one to one contest between Jack and Jill.

Jack has thought of the proverb, TOO MANY COOKS SPOIL THE BROTH, and Jill has the task of discovering it. Jack tells her that there are six words in his proverb but, beyond that, he gives no further information. Jill will now ask him six questions and Jack will include each word of his proverb in turn in each answer. For example:

JILL: 'Have you ever worn purple braces?'
JACK: 'Only TOO often, I'm afraid, but I prefer blue ones.'
JILL: 'Why are you so offensive to Mother?'
JACK: 'I've told you MANY times that she annoys me by putting mothballs in my coffee.'
JILL: 'Will you give me a sensible answer next time?'
JACK: 'Sweetheart, your mother COOKS up the wildest tales about me and you believe her. But, yes, I will give you a sensible answer next time.'
JILL: 'What is six times seven?'
JACK: 'Forty-two, I think. But I won't SPOIL things by saying anything silly.'
JILL: 'Do you like Felicity's new hair-do?'

JACK:	'Not as much as THE old one.'
JILL:	'Do you like *my* new hair do?'
JACK:	'I don't think that you'd consider me a fine BROTH of a boy if I didn't tell you . . .
JILL:	'Too many cooks spoil the broth!'

As will be seen from the above exchanges, some words are much easier to disguise than others and this is where both tact and tactics come into play when the game is played in its traditional form as a contest between teams.

Jill is a great player of word games but Felicity is not and Mother is about average. In a team contest with the men versus the women, Jill is the natural leader of her side and so she contrives to give Felicity the easiest words to answer, Mother the average words, whilst she tackles the most difficult words herself. This is not always possible as one usually arranges for each person to answer in turn and normally goes around the team in a natural clockwise sequence. Suppose that the women select the proverb, PEOPLE IN GLASSHOUSES SHOULDN'T THROW STONES, and the three of them are seated Mother, Jill, Felicity. Felicity is the problem and a word like GLASSHOUSES would give her the vapours. Unfortunately, both she and GLASSHOUSES fall into the third position, to compound the problem she would also have to cope with the last word, STONES, when each of the women face a second question.

If Felicity is honest about her shortcomings the women could always change places but, apart from anything else, the men would know immediately that Felicity has all the easy words such as AND or THE and so concentrate more upon the answers of Mother and, especially, Jill. The best tactics and the most tactful way (Felicity may not think that she is stupid) is for Jill to take the first questions from the men and so have

JILL	PEOPLE
FELICITY	IN
MOTHER	GLASSHOUSES
JILL	SHOULDN'T
FELICITY	THROW
MOTHER	STONES

When it is the women's turn to ask the questions Jill is very likely to be faced with the problem that Felicity will not know what to say. With every question in the world possible, people still freeze up in this situation. Again, players take turns in asking the questions so how does Jill cope?

Before the questioning begins, Jill confides to both Mother and Felicity a 'ploy'. 'One of the cleverest questions one can ask,' says Jill, 'is the same question that someone else has just asked. That always baffles them.' What Jill is *really* saying is, 'Felicity dear, if you can't think of what to ask, just say the same as me.'

The teams may either take turns to choose a proverb or else the winning side continues to choose proverbs until defeated.

As there are both well-known and obscure proverbs available so it is up to the teams to choose as they wish. Do not, however, be pedantic and insist that those guessing must render a word for word accuracy. If they can produce the general sense including the significant words, that is fair enough. In any event, who is to say that the proverb beginning, PEOPLE WHO LIVE IN GLASS-HOUSES etc. should not be THOSE WHO DWELL IN GLASS-HOUSES etc. or any other, similar, phrasing which this proverb can and does take. The same is true for many of the others.

5. BOTTICELLI

A player chooses a famous person, living or dead, fact or fiction and gives the initial letter of the subject's surname. Let us suppose that Granny selects William Shakespeare.

Having only an S on which to base their strategy, everyone else now asks *indirect* questions such as:

JACK: Are you a famous composer?
GRANNY: No, I am not Schubert.
JILL: Are you a famous actress?
GRANNY: No, I am not Sarah Siddons.
MOTHER: Are you a famous writer?
GRANNY: Yes, but I am not Shaw.

Jack, Jill and Mother could continue this elimination process even further by asking if the person is a poet or a playwright but, as yet, may nor ask such *direct* questions as 'Are you a man?' or 'Are you still alive?' One of these may only be asked once Granny fails to produce a suitable name in any particular category. Hence:

JILL: Are you a famous pop star?
GRANNY:
JILL: Are you still living?
GRANNY: No.
JACK: Are you a famous footballer?

PROVERBS

Adversity makes strange bedfellows

All things come to he who waits

Ask no questions and hear no lies

Attack is the best form of defence

A bad excuse is better than none

A barking dog never bites

A bellowing cow soon forgets her calf

The best men are but men at best

The best things come in small packages

Better be an old man's darling, than a young man's slave

Better be envied than pitied

Better one house spoiled than two

It is better to be born lucky than rich

It is better to travel hopefully than to arrive

Better to wear out than rust out

A bleating sheep loses a bite

You cannot get blood from a stone

Blue are the hills that are far away

You can't tell a book by its cover

None but the brave deserve the fair

Brevity is the soul of wit

You cannot make bricks without straw

Every bullet has its billet

A burnt child dreads the fire

A cat in gloves catches no mice

A chain is no stronger than its weakest link

Don't change horses in mid stream

It is as cheap sitting as standing

The child is the father of the man

Children and fools tell the truth

Never choose your women or your linen by candlelight

Let the cobbler stick to his last

Coming events cast their shadows before

A man is known by the company he keeps

Conscience makes cowards of us all

Councils of war never fight

Happy is the country with no history

A creaking door hangs longest

What can't be cured must be endured

Curses like chickens come home to roost

Don't cut off your nose to spite your face

Cut your coat according to your cloth

The darkest hour is just before dawn

Desperate diseases must have desperate remedies

The difficult is done at once the impossible takes a little longer

Throw dirt enough and some will stick

Dirty water will quench fire

Discretion is the better part of valour

Distance lends enchantment to the view

Do right and fear no man

Give a dog a bad name and hang him

Every dog is allowed one bite

What's done cannot be undone

A drowning man will clutch at straws

We must eat a peck of dirt before we die

He that would eat the fruit must climb the tree

Every man for himself and the devil take the hindmost

The exception proves the rule

Experience is the best teacher

Faint heart never won fair lady

GRANNY:
JACK: Did you once live in Stratford upon Avon?
  And now the game is won. But, Granny got her revenge later.
Again she chose an S and it was ages before anyone could
discover that it was an English king. Even then they had to give up
as she was the only person who knew that Edward VII had the
surname Saxe-Coburg-Gotha!

6. GOOD AND BAD

Jack has selected a letter of the alphabet. Mother, Father, Jill and
Felicity are attempting to discover which letter it is. Jack now
proceeds to ask each person a question in turn, replying to the
answer with the word GOOD if it contains his letter and BAD if it
does not. It is a contest amongst the four being questioned to see
who first discovers the significant letter. They either answer a
question sensibly with a single word or else state what the letter
is. However, if they guess incorrectly they are eliminated. A
sample game with R as Jack's choice could proceed as follows:

JACK: What did Granny give you for Christmas?
JILL: Perfume
JACK: Good

JACK: What did you have for breakfast?
FELICITY: Muesli
JACK: Bad

JACK: Give me a word which describes Jill.
FATHER: Precocious
JACK: Brilliant . . . er, I mean good.

JACK: Who is your favourite Shakespearean character?
MOTHER: Portia
JACK: Good

JACK: Where would you like to go on holiday this year?
JILL: Portugal . . . and you're paying!
JACK: My share, sweetheart, my share . . . but, good.

JACK: How old are you?
FELICITY: The letter P.

The female of the species is deadlier than the male

He who fights and runs away lives to fight another day

Fine feathers make fine birds

Fingers were made before forks

First impressions are the most lasting

A fool and his money are soon parted

There's no fool like an old fool

Fortune favours the brave

There's no such thing as a free lunch

Never look a gift horse in the mouth

Go abroad and you'll hear news of home

God made the country and man made the town

God sends meat but the devil sends cooks

Whom the gods love die young

A golden key can open any door

A good Jack makes a good Jill

Good wine needs no bush

A great book is a great evil

The greater the sinner the greater the saint

All is grist that comes to the mill

A guilty conscience needs no accuser

The hand that rocks the cradle rules the world

Handsome is as handsome does

Hard words break no bones

You cannot have your cake and eat it

There is honour among thieves

Hope for the best and prepare for the worst

The husband is always the last to know

It's an ill wind that blows nobody any good

Imitation is the sincerest form of flattery

Jack is as good as his master

Why keep a dog and bark yourself

What you don't know can't hurt you

He who laughs last laughs longest

One law for the rich and another for the poor

A liar ought to have a good memory

Life isn't all beer and skittles

Listeners never hear any good of themselves

Little pitchers have large ears

Little thieves are hanged but great ones escape

Lookers on see most of the game

The age of miracles is past

Where there's muck there's brass

The nearer the bone the sweeter the meat

You can't put new wine in old bottles

Old sins cast long shadows

Opportunity makes a thief

Out of debt out of danger

Things past cannot be recalled

He who pays the piper calls the tune

If you want peace you must prepare for war

One picture is worth ten thousand words

Politics make strange bedfellows

Praise the child and you make love to the mother

Procrastination is the thief of time

It is easier to pull down than to build up

There is always room at the top

The rotten apple injures its neighbours

Save us from our friends

Second thoughts are best

Self preservation is the first law of nature

The sharper the storm the sooner it's over

A short horse is soon curried

Felicity drops out. Both Jill and Mother now know the answer, but will Father get it first?

(*The same game with the GOOD/BAD comments given reverse meanings to those used above can also be found in print. But with a silly, meaningless, name unworthy of repetition.*)

7. QUESTIONS AND COMMANDS

This game is probably as old as Crambo and is recorded in literary works dating back to 1673. Very little is known about it other than it seemed to have enjoyed a life in excess of a hundred years; that one person was the 'king' of a session of the game; kissing came into it in some form; and it appeared to consist of one person addressing ludicrous questions and commands to each member of the company.

A modern equivalent might be a combination of the **Yes/No** challenge which was featured on television in the fifties and to impose forfeits on those people who fail to stand up to the 'king' for 60 seconds of this activity.

The **Yes/No** challenge only works well when one member of the group of games players is outstandingly dominant in mental agility and verbal dexterity and is, in effect, the 'king'. If you have such a 'king' then this is the game.

Each person in turn has to face a barrage of quick fire questions to which he or she may *not* answer 'Yes', 'No', nod or shake his or her head and must reply immediately. Any breach of these rules during the 60 seconds of interrogation by the 'king' results in the paying of a forfeit. In addition to the 'king', a timekeeper is needed together with a referee. For the sake of illustration let us assume that the referee has a gong which he bangs once a player falls victim to the 'king'.

KING:	What is your name?
CONTESTANT:	Felicity
KING:	Felicity?
CONTESTANT:	Yes **BONG!!!**

KING:	What is your name?
CONTESTANT:	Jill.
KING:	Jill?
CONTESTANT:	It is.

Shrouds have no pockets
Silence is a woman's best garment
A slice off a cut loaf isn't missed
A soft answer turneth away wrath
Speech is silver but silence is golden
The squeaking wheel gets the grease
A still tongue makes a wise head
Never give a sucker an even break
Stretch your arm no further than your sleeve will reach
From the sublime to the ridiculous is only a step
From the sweetest wine the tartest vinegar
A tale never loses in the telling
Talk of the devil and he is bound to appear
If a thing's worth doing it's worth doing well

Think first and speak afterwards
Three may keep a secret if two of them are dead
He that will thrive must first ask his wife
He travels fastest who travels alone
The tree is known by its fruit
Two of a trade never agree
The unexpected always happens
Virtue is its own reward
One volunteer is worth two pressed men
Wanton kittens make sober cats
When the wine is in the wit is out
It is easy to be wise after the event
All work and no play make Jack a dull boy
It is not work that kills but worry

KING:	I like your dress.
CONTESTANT:	Thank you.
KING:	Did you buy it at Top Shop?
CONTESTANT:	I did not.
KING:	Your nodded your head then.
CONTESTANT:	I doubt it.
KING:	Not Top Shop?
CONTESTANT:	Correct.
KING:	Where?
CONTESTANT:	I made it myself.
KING:	You did?
CONTESTANT:	I did.
	etc.

The successful merely bask in their own glory but the victims have to pay their forfeits and the following are, despite appearances to the contrary, not only socially acceptable but also exceedingly simple. The first one is a very old test of nerve – could it be as old as the original Questions and Commands?

1. Kiss four bare legs and one bare bottom.
2. Kiss the ugliest person in the room.
3. Bite an inch off the end of that teddy bear's nose.
4. Jump higher than the table.
5. Recite a nursery rhyme whilst standing on your head.
6. Throw this brick through the window.
7. Knock back half a bottle of whisky in one go.
8. Put a match to Mother's new curtains.
9. Display unbridled lust.
10. Remove all of your clothes.
11. Spit on the carpet.
12. Wash the pots.

How are these done?

1. Kiss the legs and the bottom of a chair
2. Tactfully, kiss the back of your own hand.
3. Make a biting motion an inch *away from the end of* the teddy bear's nose.
4. Merely jump – the table cannot.
5. Simply say, 'A nursery rhyme whilst standing on your head.'
6. Open the window first!
7. Tap the bottle so that it moves backwards.
8. Merely put a matchstick against the curtains. You don't have to light it.
9. Open the book at this page and display the following words – UNBRIDLED LUST.
10. Walk out of the room – you take your clothes with you!
11. A spit is a sword, it is also a type of cooking implement and the same word also once described a straight horizontal mark used as a sign in a book. If you can obtain any of these simply put one of them on the carpet.
12. A *real* forfeit – wash the pots!

8. STOPPARD'S QUESTIONS

The first professional performance of Tom Stoppard's *Rosencrantz and Guildenstern Are Dead* was given at the Old Vic Theatre, London, by the National Theatre Company on 11th April, 1967, and the work contains a classic sequence of word play. This word play is similar to the Yes/No aspect of Questions and Commands discussed above except that instead of one person trying to trick another, both are trying to trick each other.

The game is simply to answer a question with a question and failure to do this results in a point being given away, the first to three points wins.

The rules, as revealed in this sequence of witty dialogue, are

(a) No repetitions.
(b) No grunts such as a questioning exclamation (i.e. 'Hah?').
(c) No synonyms. The question in reply must not be the equivalent of a repetition.
(d) No rhetoric.
(e) No *non sequiturs*.

However, played as a game, the rules are essentially what you make them.

9. SPELLBOUND

Spelling competitions were once quite popular, especially in Victorian times when Spelling Bees (as these contests are called) were a common public diversion.

If a simple spelling test does not appeal to you and, let's face it, they are a bit of a bore, try a similar challenge – spelling ordinary everyday words *backwards*.

Providing that you allow no hesitations, corrections of spelling and insist upon a reply the moment the word has been given so even the family's acknowledged expert on spelling can fail with the simplest of words.

Play it as a team game on an elimination basis, with teams taking turns to test each other. The final player unbeaten wins on behalf of the team.

There are two different fun ways of organizing the contest, both of which are fair and involve no tedious delays.

(a) Open up any book or newspaper and whoever is testing each member of the opposing team merely states words in the order of occurrence on the page. Some will get easy words, some will get difficult words but, most importantly, an instant spelling check is to hand. Obviously, the 1-letter, 2-letter and 3-letter words are ignored.
(b) Begin with 4-letter words and ignore all others for that round. The next round is 5-letter words. All subsequent rounds are more than five. To try and find 6-letter and 7-letter words etc.

in sequence is both time consuming and boring. The categories of 4-letter, 5-letter and more than 5 are easy to recognize.

If the game is to be played as a formal competition rather like a Victorian Spelling Bee then the organizer should acquire one of the various crossword-solving books which list words in alphabetical order by numbers of letters. Under these circumstances a completely fair 4-letter, 5-letter, 6-letter, 7-letter etc. sequence of tests can be conducted with the minimum of difficulty.

10. BEE TEAM

A team spelling contest played for points. Long or tricky words such as PARALLELOGRAM or YACHT are selected. Any ordinary words will do, providing that they are likely to cause problems. In fact, a team can object to a word if they have never heard of it.

Each member of the team being challenged has to give a letter in turn. Thus, with a three person team and a word such as PARALLELOGRAM the first player says 'P', the second 'A', the third 'R', the first now has to give the fourth letter (A), the second has to give the fifth letter (L) and so on until the world is either correctly spelt for one point; or an error, a hesitation or a change of mind gives the point away to the opposing side. Select an umpire who has a dictionary handy.

11. JUNIOR BEE TEAM

The same game as Bee Team except that a different physical action or a different number is substituted for each of the five vowels. Easy words are chosen and the children have to, in the case of numbers, say 'One' if the letter is an A, 'Two' for an E, 'Three' for an I, 'Four' for O, 'Five' for U. The fun lies in the confusion, especially if you have them performing silly actions for the vowels.

12. HORACE'S CAT

A children's game but fun for all. Everyone knows someone who owns a cat and that owner's name is chosen for the purpose of the action. For the sake of illustration assume that everyone knows Horace and knows that he has a cat. It is a team contest with each member of a team coming under the spotlight in turn.

One team fires questions at the youngster in the spotlight and he or she has a minute in which to survive the interrogation without making an error, hesitating or changing his or her mind. With success a point is scored for his or her team, failure gives the point away.

Any questions are asked, without bothering to take turns, but only four answers are given:

1. If the answer to a question concerns any person or any creature the reply is *always* 'Horace's cat'. For example:
    'Who is the president of the U.S.A.?' 'Horace's cat'
    'Who did you kiss last night?' 'Horace's cat'
2. If the answer is 'No', the reply is *always* 'Yes'
3. If the answer is 'Yes', the reply is *always* 'No'
4. The answer to *everything else* is 'Cucumbers'.

The faster the questions are asked, the more likely the youngster will be caught out and a team that wastes time arguing over a matter of opinion:

   'Are you stupid?'
   'Are you pretty?'

the less chance they have of catching a player over a point of accepted fact:

   'Is Washington the capital of the U.S.A?

as they only have one minute.

13. HORACE'S KITTEN

The kiddywinkies' version of Horace's Cat. The answer to *every* question is 'cucumbers' or any other word that is liable to make them giggle. If the child in the one minute spotlight smiles, giggles, laughs or has anything but a completely straight face he or she loses. For extra fun have a gong handy for striking on failure.

14. CUT IT OUT

A competition for a children's party – and variations on this theme for adults as well as children.

The organizer chooses such as a dozen newspaper advertisements for well known brands. These are removed from the newspaper and the brand names cut out.

The advertisements are mounted on card and each is numbered, these are placed around the room in a random order.

There are various options now available.

(a) A simple contest to see who can get the most correct. Answers being written on paper.

(b) Two sets of the twelve brand names are written on stiff card. One is in the possession of (say) the hostess and the other of the host. The two are widely separated but adjacent to tables or other clear surfaces.

　　The children are divided into teams (say) boys versus girls. After they have had time to study the adverts, the competitors are called to their corners. The girls to the hostess, the boys to the host.

　　The task is to see which team gets all twelve names in the correct numerical sequence first.

(c) The (say) boys' team have to name all twelve in the correct order. They call the answers from the positions where the advertisements are sited. They are allowed a limited number of guesses according to the way you wish to play it.

　　You may, for example, split them into pairs and have pairs standing by each advert and permit them just one guess, recording the results without comment.

　　A second way of doing it is to have a relay, each boy, in turn, dashes from the starting position and finds his assigned number and is permitted up to three guesses, (3 points for a correct reply on the first guess, 2 points for the second, 1 point for the third).

　　Under this option, you have two further choices. Either a fresh set of advertisements for the girls or else (say) boys have odd numbers and girls have even numbers.

Essentially, the options are governed by circumstances. Such as numbers participating and how suitable the location for children to run around. You could easily turn the above into four different games, depending upon how much advanced planning you care to undertake. One subject could be adverts. Another, photographs of pop stars taken from a specialist fan magazine. A third might even be pictures of Rupert the Bear and the like. (This would be perfect for adults if you decided to play one of these options at a party for grown-ups!) Any subject which you think will appeal and give each game a different name such as 'Adverts', 'Pop Stars' or whatever.

For the older children and/or adults option (b) can be converted into a true word game. This time picture number 4 has to be identified not as RUPERT THE BEAR but an anagram such as PETER A. R. HUBERT which is written on a *separate* answer-card.

The anagram version of option (b) can be made even more devilish if you wish, Suppose that the subject is adverts and PERSIL is one of the items to be discerned. Apart from making its anagram (select from LISPER, PERILS, PILERS, PLIERS or PRILES) available on a card also have some red herrings such as MOO(OMO), DIET (TIDE), ADZ (DAZ) or ENROL (LENOR) shuffled amongst the cards and you will be able to slip away for a quiet cup of tea that has been very well earned.

Six games for the price of your time and ingenuity.

15. DUTCH AUCTION

A quiz on the meanings of words but with a delightful difference – everybody knows the word but few, if any, know the meanings. For example:

'The word I've chosen has 5 letters and begins with the letter A. I'll award you 10 points if you can tell me what it is. It means a large size of drawing paper.'

Assuming no one volunteers an answer, a second clue is given.

'For 9 points, I can tell you that the same word also means the bone which supports the skull.'

Still no takers.

'8 points. It is also an Eastern silk-satin.'

The company is still baffled.

'7 points. This word is a verb which means to carry on one's shoulders.'

Perhaps someone now has a glimmer of an idea but is keeping quiet.

'6 points. Its other meaning as a verb is to prop up.'

This is all the information given in the Appendix. From now on the clues are up to you.

'5 points. The name of a god.'

> '4 points. A range of mountains in North Africa.'

> '3 points. A book of maps.

If the company still has no idea, then you reveal the remaining letters one at a time. A total of twelve clues before the final letter of ATLAS is exposed.

That presentation is easily achieved by any quiz master, However if you have a natural flair for anagrams then, for ATLAS, a first clue could be:

> 'Sat oddly around the French for a large size of drawing paper.'

or, easier ones:

> 'Salt a palindrome for a large size of drawing paper.'
> 'A last anagram describes a large size of drawing paper.

To play the game at a drop of the hat, choose any of the **Peculiar Words** detailed opposite. In each case a minimum of three unusual meanings is given but none of the obvious ones. Many have six or more unusual meanings and these words are clearly designated. Therefore, it is comparatively simple for anyone to be the quiz master and produce at least ten clues which get progressively easier.

Limit clues to ten. The game can be an individual or team contest according to the number present. Twelve participants being (say) four teams of three people. Alternatively, if you have a large crowd in a hall, teams select their own representatives. You can limit individuals or teams to just one guess so that once a wrong guess is given they are eliminated. Once you are down to the easy clues you can say such as:

> 'This next clue is worth 4 points. Who wishes to give an answer?'

You now consider only those people prepared to risk elimination on the unknown. No volunteers, so do not pose that easy question, instead say:

> 'This clue is even easier than the last one would have been. Are there any volunteers for 3 points?'

If there are still no takers you can, if you wish, bring back into the game any person or team having been frozen out for a previous wrong guess. Surely someone is going to risk being eliminated on

PECULIAR WORDS

Players of NEWBY'S BLUFF can use any of these words without difficulty. Players of DUTCH AUCTION, however, may feel they require a certain minimum number of given meanings. The numbers in brackets refer to the number of unusual facts detailed in the Appendix for each particular word. Thus, those who would prefer at least six items of basic information should ignore words marked (3), (4) or (5).

ABJECT (4), ABODE (3), ACCESS (3), ACCIDENT (4), ACCOMPANY (3), ACHE (3), ACTOR (3), ADAMANT (3), ADAM'S APPLE (3), ADDER (6), ADDRESS (5), ADVANCE (4), ADVENTURE (4), ADVERT (3), ADVICE (3), AFFAIR (3), AGAIN (7), AGATE (3), AIR (8), ALBUM (4), ALLAY (10), ALLOWANCE (4), ALMOND (5), ALP (3), AMBER (5), AMOUNT (5), AMUSE (4), ANCHOR (4), ANCIENT (9), APPARITION (6), APPROVE (6), APRON (6), ARBOUR (6), ARM (7), ARREST (4), ARROW (7), ARTICLE (7), ASSAY (9), ASSEMBLE (3), ASSENT (5), ATLAS (5), ATTEND (5), ATTIRE (7), AUNT (4), AUTHENTIC (5), AUTHOR (6), AUTO (3), AVER (6), AWARD (4), AWE (6), AXES (5).

BACKSIDE (3), BACON (6), BAGPIPE (4), BAIL (10), BALD (6), BALE (7), BALK (14), BAN (6), BANK (7), BARB (6), BARGAIN (4), BARK (6), BARKER (3), BARON (5), BARROW (8), BASE (6), BASIL (3), BASS (6), BAT (6), BATH (5), BATTERY (6), BAY (12), BEAM (6), BEAR (6), BEARD (6), BEAT (6), BELL (9), BEN (6), BEND (12), BENEDICT (5), BENEFIT (6), BENT (6), BERRY (10), BESTIAL (3), BICKER (8), BIG (7), BIKE (6), BILL (14), BILLY (4), BIN (4), BIND (6), BING (9), BIRD (6), BISHOP (6), BIT (7), BIZARRE (3), BLACKGUARD (6), BLEACH (3), BLESS (3), BLINK (10), BLOCK (6), BLOOD (6), BLUE (3), BLUNT (6), BLUSH (3), BOB (8), BOG (4), BOLD (6), BOMBAST (3), BONNET (9), BOOT (9), BOROUGH (3), BORROW (4), BOSS (12), BOTTLE (3), BOTTOM (3), BOUGH (3), BOUGHT (8), BOUNCE (3), BOUNDER (3), BOW (3), BRAG (3), BRAID (3), BRAKE (11), BRANCH (3), BRAND (3), BRASH (4), BRAT (6), BRAVE (3), BREAD (3), BREAM (3), BREECH (3), BREEZE (3), BREW (3), BRICK (3), BRIDE (3), BRIDGE (3), BRIEF (3), BRIGHT (3), BRIM (3), BRISK (3), BRIT (4), BROTHEL (3), BROWN (4), BRUTE (3), BUBBLE (5), BUCK (6), BUDGE (8), BUFF (12), BUFFET (3), BUG (3), BULK (4), BULL (3), BULLET (3), BUMBLE (7), BUMP (3), BUN (3), BUNG (3), BURN (3), BURROW (3), BUTT (21), BUTTER (3), BUTTON (9), BUTTONS (3), BUXOM (4), BUZZ (11), BUZZARD (3).

the 2 points question? Admittedly, everyone is baffled as you have been giving them the most peculiar definitions but there has to be a brave soul somewhere. If not, make a final statement:

> 'This final clue is the easiest of the lot. One point for anyone prepared to have a go and guess it correctly. Minus one point for anyone who is wrong.'

This is necessary otherwise everyone will shout at once as they cannot lose anyway.

(**Note:** *Some of these words have ten or more unusual meanings. Select no more than six meanings which appeal to your taste and provide easy clues for the remainder. You can always use that same word again!*)

16. KOLODNY'S GAME

A very bizarre game. One person decides upon a rule, Everyone now questions him, asking anything they wish. Whatever he is asked, he will only answer with a Yes or a No. Yes, if the question complies with his secret rule. No, if it does not. The task is to discover that secret rule.

The rule can be anything, For example:

(a) If the first word of the question begins with a vowel the answer is 'Yes'.
(b) If the questioner is female the answer is 'Yes'.
(c) Every third question is answered 'Yes'.
(d) Every question containing the word YOU is answered 'Yes'.
(e) Every question which I answer when rubbing my chin is answered 'Yes'.

There is no need to take strict turns in posing questions – some people kill games by being slow-witted over such a simple task as thinking of a question to ask – but the skill lies in seeing a pattern then posing a question which complies with it. If the answer to that *considered* question is 'No' then some other rule must apply.

As with all games, some people never understand them and much of the fun will arise from a sequence such as this:

MISS BROWN: Have you ever been unfaithful to your wife?
MR SMITH: Yes.
MRS SMITH: Henry!

17. WHO'S WHO

A game of skill and fun for three or four players, all of whom possess not only a good general knowledge but are experienced games players. Who's Who has a wickedly unique tactical aspect which puts it, in deduction games, in a class by itself.

Players establish a rota which they maintain throughout the whole session. With four players numbered 1, 2, 3 and 4 this means that if (say) player number 3 takes the first turn to set a challenge for the others, then the order of questioning will be players 4, 1, 2; 4, 1, 2; etc. By adhering to a strict rota and with each player taking his or her turn to set the challenge so all have an equal opportunity of winning the whole, points-based, contest.

The person who will set the challenge (hereafter called the tester) has no vested interest in deception but the remaining players (the questioners) are the ones who need to employ subtle tactics. The tester has nothing to gain, the questioners are battling for the point awarded to the one who wins the particular round.

A sample game with Granny as the tester has Tom, Dick and Harriet as the questioners.

Granny has chosen a famous person who may be living or dead, male or female, fact or fiction. Tom, Dick and Harriet may ask any questions they wish providing that Granny can give a simple Yes or No answer. She may, at times, be forced to say such as 'Don't know', or 'Probably' but her fellow competitors are no longer the grandchildren of the days when they played *I Spy* and they respect her encyclopaedic knowledge which makes her such a devastating opponent in any game of this type.

Now for the subtle part.

Any player may ask as many questions as he or she wishes in any one particular turn. But, having asked a question that player may no longer guess at the identity. A player may *either* question at any length or else make a single guess.

The skills will be revealed in this sample game with the rota having the order, Tom, Dick and Harriet.

TOM:	Is this personal fictional?
GRANNY:	No.
TOM:	Female?
GRANNY:	No.
TOM:	British?
GRANNY:	Yes.
TOM:	Living?

GRANNY:	No.
TOM:	Alive this century?
GRANNY:	No.
TOM:	After 1066?
GRANNY:	Yes
TOM:	Before 1800?
GRANNY:	Yes.
TOM:	16th century?
GRANNY:	Yes.
TOM:	Royal?
GRANNY:	Yes.

Tom considers the possibilities. Very likely to be a king, most probably Henry VIII. But could be Henry VII, Edward VI or even James I (who ascended the English throne in the 17th century (1603) but was certainly alive in the 16th century, apart from being James VI of Scotland during that time). Should he eliminate still further? Or should he pass? He decides to pass.

Dick also considers that Granny has chosen a king. He decides to test this in a subtle way which, simultaneously, eliminates the boy king, Edward VI.

DICK:	Was this person's father a monarch?
GRANNY:	Yes.
DICK:	Did this person father a monarch?
GRANNY:	Yes.

Dick dare not eliminate any further as both Harriet and Tom now have the opportunities of guessing before he does. Dick passes.

Harriet, equally versed in the history of the period and equally certain that it is a king, must either make a guess at the three remaining logical choices or is Charles I still possible? In which century was he born? 16th? 17th? Granny would know. Harriet understood Dick's ploy but can she contrive one which will eliminate the most obvious monarch, Henry VIII. Only a fool would ask if he had six wives and Harriet is no fool. But, Granny is very well read. Guess or eliminate? Harriet gambles on an eliminator.

HARRIET:	Did this person marry a lady with three thumbs?
GRANNY:	Yes.

Harriet passes. She knows for certain that it is Henry VIII (the lady being Anne Boleyn) but will Tom or Dick pick up the inference? Whatever happens she knows that Granny will be the major rival in the whole contest as none of them dare select pop stars when Granny is around. Fred Astaire or Ginger Rogers by all means – but a Sex Pistol, never! The days when she allowed them to win in the nursery have long since passed. When Granny plays, she makes the rules. Only the fourth generation, when it competes with Granny, is permitted to tamper with established practice.

18. LEXICONNERY

There is no such word as LEXICONNERY, but it sounds as though it might be real. In the context of this game it can be defined as the art of creating a word which others can be duped into believing is true.

The following words can be found elsewhere in this book – which are genuine?

AMSTERDAMP   a wet odorous smog peculiar to the industrial region of Amsterdam.

BEDSISTER   a mistress or concubine viewed in relationship to a man's lawful wife.

RANGOONERY   Burmese politics.

Two teams challenge each other, on a points basis, to state which of the above are true and which are false. Unfortunately, it does require research in order to provide a correct blend of true and false words but teams prepared to undertake this task can lay the foundations for a fun session.

One member of a team scours the dictionary for a word or compound such as GREGORIAN TREE which is a genuine name for a gallows whilst another coins a term such as GRILL SERGEANT for defining as 'the N.C.O. in charge of the cookhouse'.

The format can vary according to circumstances and at (say) a large gathering of slightly inebriated adults forfeits can be introduced for anyone who was 'lexiconned'. In this company (as opposed to a serious contest between two small teams of sober wordsmiths) the organiser has a prepared list of words and definitions and invites members of the 'audience' to score (say) ten out of ten for a prize or else pay a forfeit on failure. For extra fun a gong is handy, which the assistant strikes as soon as a mistake is made.

For the genuineness or otherwise of the words AMSTERDAMP, BEDSISTER and RANGOONERY see the Appendix. Any which fail to appear are discussed in example (h) of Wordsmithery, page 199.

19. GRIPHS

The word griph was current in the 17th and 18th centuries and was used to describe a serious, philosophical riddle or enigma which would have little appeal today. However, a delightful new type of riddle which is currently in circulation takes this form:

Q.   What is Rupert Bear's middle name?
A.   The.

Other examples take the form of shapes made with the hand or hands.

Q.   What is one of these? (The palm of the hand is held with the fingers separated and pointing upwards.)
A.   A dead one of these. (The hand is now reversed.)
Q.   What is one of these? (The hand makes a looping manoeuvre from right to left.)
A.   I don't know, but here comes another. (The identical action is repeated.)

Yet a third modern griph poses a serious challenge.

Q.   In thirty seconds, name thirty words none of which contain the letter A.
A.   One, two, three, four, five, etc . . .

Yours truly has no idea who coined them, he simply fell foul of them in conversation and was beaten each time. If you know of any others, please send them to me c/o the publisher as I'd love to get my revenge on the swines who posed them.

The Verbal Tennis Series

Three games of which only the third is suitable for children even though it is essentially an adult game.

1. WIMBLEDON

A subject such as COUNTRIES, CITIES, BOY'S NAMES, GIRL'S NAMES, ANIMALS, BIRDS, 2-LETTER WORDS VALID FOR SCRABBLE or whatever is chosen and the first player begins by naming any relevant word within that category. The second player has to reply with an equally valid word but one which begins with the last letter of the one just given. A verbal tennis match ensues until a player is unable to respond, makes an error or repeats a word already used. With ANIMALS as the subject a typical exchange could go as follows:

JACK:	doG	JACK:	EarthworM
JILL:	GiraffE	JILL:	MoosE
JACK:	ElephanT	JACK:	EyrA
JILL:	TitmousE	JILL:	Addax

with Jill winning this particular rally as Jack was unable to think of an animal beginning with the letter X.

This small exchange illustrates three of the skill factors in the game. In each of Jill's replies she has chosen animals which end with an E. This pressurizes her opponent and could easily trap him into repeating himself or making his mind go blank. The choice of GIRAFFE could have led to the simple error of Jack replying wth a word beginning with an F, though such an error is more likely at a later stage in a rally. Finally, she played the killer stroke of a word ending with an X,

The X factor is one of the great tactical ploys in this super game. Players, *who must reply within an agreed time limit*, have to be beware of saying such as WOLF (FOX is the killer reply) or POTTO (OX) as well as trying to force such errors themselves.

Obviously the first rule is that one cannot begin a rally with a word ending X and the other rules are:

(b) No word may be repeated in a rally.
(c) Each word must be acceptable. Had, in the above example, Jill disputed EYRA and no dictionary was available to confirm that it is a South American wild cat so Jack would be forced to give another word in its place. Had Jack replied to Jill's ADDAX with XIPH or XENOPUS then these could be disallowed as the former is an obsolete name for a swordfish and the latter a technical term for a genus of frogs. It is wise to establish ground-rules in advance as, for example, with COUNTRIES being the subject of a rally many players will say 'Africa' when attempting to name a *country* beginning with an 'A'!

The game is normally played over a number of rallies with the server nominating a different subject each time and players taking turns to serve. With four people it can be a verbal tennis doubles and with three people upwards it can be played on a round robin basis eliminating one person each time.

2. NO!

A Wimbledon-type game only this time a 2-letter word is selected
and players have to supply words which begin and end with the
same letters of that original word. There are no category limitations but players obviously cannot repeat words, take too long to
reply or make errors. Some of the 2-letter words can produce long
rallies but such as NO will quickly end after

JACK:	NunciO	JACK:	NerO
JILL:	NeO	JILL:	NatO
JACK:	NegrO	JACK:	NiellO
JILL:	NelumbO	JILL:	NovellO

has produced disputes galore. Is NATO a real word? Can you
believe that NELUMBO is a genus of water lilies? Isn't NEO
merely a prefix not a genuine word? Do we allow surnames such
as NOVELLO?

For a list of 2-letter words see 2-LETTER WORDS (page 95).

3. IVAN THE TERRIBLE

A third form of verbal tennis. Any category is chosen and a
monarch's lengthy name is selected. Suppose that players have to
provide the names of (say) cities which begin with (say) each
letter of IVAN THE TERRIBLE. The rally ends either with failure
during play or by being able to provide the last word. Both the
long name and/or the subject can be changed at the commence-
ment of each rally. To end the monarch's name successfully
results in a tie but most rallies will break down at some stage,
especially if you have a reasonable time limit for replies.

A sample exchange with cities as the subject and Ivan the
Terrible as the basis might proceed as follows:

JACK:	Istanbul	JILL:	Toronto
JILL:	Venice	JACK:	Exeter
JACK:	Antwerp	JILL:	Rome
JILL:	Nice	JACK:	Rangoon
JACK:	Turin	JILL:	Istanbul
JILL:	Hamburg	JACK:	*challenge!*
JACK:	Edinburgh		

Jack wins on the basis of repetition and so avoids not only a tied
game but the prospect of his having to think of a third city
beginning with the letter E.

EUROPEAN MONARCHS

This list of delightfully named monarchs can be readily extended by the ploy of adding a numeral to a name such as Elizabeth the Second, James the Sixth, Louis the Eighteenth or whatever.

THE HOLY ROMAN EMPIRE
Louis the Pious
Charles the Bald
Charles the Fat
Louis the Child
Henry the Fowler
Henry the Saint
Conrad the Salic
Henry the Black
Rudolf of Hapsburg
Adolf of Nassau
Albert of Hapsburg
Henry of Luxemburg
Wenzel of Luxemburg
Rupert of the Palatinate
Sigismund of Luxemburg

SCOTLAND
William the Lion
The Maid of Norway
Robert the Bruce

PORTUGAL
Alfonso the Fat
Pedro the Severe
Maria the Mad

THE EASTERN ROMAN EMPIRE
Julian the Apostate
Leo the Isaurian
Leo the Chazar
Michael the Amorian
Michael the Drunkard
Leo the Wise
Michael the Caulker
Matthew Cantacuzene

SWEDEN
Eric the Victorious
Olaf Scatt-King
Inge the Good

NORWAY
Halfdan the Black
Harald Fairhair
Erik Bloodaxe
Haakon the Good
Harald Greyskin
Haakon of Lade
Olaf Tryggvason
Svein Knutsson
Magnus the Good
Harald the Stern
Olaf the Quiet
Magnus Barelegs
Sigurd the Pilgrim
Haakon the Broadshouldered

ENGLAND
Ethelred the Unready
Edward the Confessor
Richard the Lionheart

RUSSIA
Ivan the Terrible

DENMARK
Gorm the Old
Harald Bluetooth
Svein Forkbeard
Eric the Evergood
Olaf Hunger
Valdemar the Victorious
Eric Ploughpenny
Valdemar Atterdag

FRANCE
Louis the Saint

POLAND
Boleslaw the Wry-Mouthed
Boleslaw the Modest
Wladislaw the Dwarf

The Back to Front Series

There are eight games in this series, all of which are based on the principle of logical word association. The children's games are numbers 2 and 3.

Essentially one will be going on verbal journeys such as from FATHER to SON. A suffix is added to FATHER such as FATHER-HOOD, FATHERLESS, FATHER FIGURE, FATHERLAND, FATHER THAMES, FATHER BROWN, FATHER TIME etc . . . The suffix *must* be a genuine word. The following examples all lead, perfectly logically, from FATHER to SON. Note especially the word OUT. This is one of a number of keywords which are essential ingredients of viability and will be discussed below.

FATHER FIGURE	FATHER TIME
FIGURE OUT	TIME OUT
OUTACT	OUTACT
ACT ONE	ACT ONE
ONE STEP	ONE STEP
STEPSON	STEPSON
FATHERLAND	FATHERLESS
LANDFALL	LESSON
FALLOUT	ONGOING
OUTACT	GOING OUT
ACT ONE	OUTACT
ONE STEP	ACT ONE
STEPSON	ONE STEP
	STEPSON

As many of these games will depend upon the ability to reach a particular destination so the destination needs to be chosen with care.

However, if you can see that this particular destination can be reached from any one of four highly flexible keywords, IN, OFF, OUT or UP, you can almost take it for granted that you can reach that destination from any word your choose.

Thus, knowing that SON can be traced *back* to OUT you can then choose *any* starting word.

The reverse is *not* the same. The fact that FATHER leads to OUT does *not* mean that FATHER can lead to any word you choose. If (say) you wish to go from FATHER to MOTHER you need to be certain that MOTHER can be reached from IN, OFF, OUT or UP.

Therefore, can such as GRANDMOTHER or DEN MOTHER be traced *back* to one of these keywords? If you cannot see this happening (unless, of course, you tried STEPMOTHER which has the same progression as STEPSON) forget MOTHER as the destination.

The simplest way is to take any of the (say) 'OUT' words trace it *forwards* for a few words until you reach a word which appeals to your taste. That word is a proven destination. Now add any starting word and you are assured of success. For example:

```
OUTBACK-DROP-OFF-SIDE-LINE-UP-
OUTBACK-OFF-GUARD-DOG-WATCH-OUT-
OUTBACK-COMB-OUT-LET-OFF-LOAD-
OUTBACK-FIRE-WORK-OUT-RUN-DOWN-
OUTBACK-SPACE-OUT-WORK-MAN-FRIDAY-
```

Now you are certain of reaching any of these words. You can, for the first game discussed below, easily go BACK to BACK, SIDE to SIDE, ROOM to ROOM, MAN to MAN, or, for other games, FRONT to BACK, BOY to MAN, WOMAN to MAN or any other combination which appeals.

Note that correct spelling, not similarity of sound, is the rule concerning continuation. Also note that O is a genuine word in its own right and that such as the suffix -ful is invalid (it is *not* a word) whereas full, as in SPOONFULL or CUPFULL, is perfectly acceptable. This also means that WIND can take either pronunciation in the same sequence – DOWNWIND/WIND DOWN.

1. BACK TO BACK

A two-person game in which you attempt to repeat the chosen word. Select any word which appeals and is known to be attainable from a keyword. For example, BACK. Make BACK the first element in a compound word or logical two-word phrase such as BACKACHE, BACKBENCHER, BACKBITE, BACKBONE. BACKBREAKER, BACKCHAT etc . . . the game is to take turns with your opponent in creating equally valid words or phrases from each second element of the word in play. If BACKBONE had been chosen, then the next word could be such as BONE CHINA, BONE DRY or BONE UP. The winner will be the first person who

can get back to BACK in such forms as DRAWBACK, HALF BACK
or SETBACK.

JACK:	BACK DOOR	JILL:	DATE PALM
JILL:	DOORMAN	JACK:	PALM SUNDAY
JACK:	MANCHESTER	JILL:	SUNDAY SCHOOL
JILL:	CHESTERFIELD	JACK:	SCHOOL WORK
JACK:	FIELD WORK	JILL:	WORK OUT
JILL:	WORKMAN	JACK:	OUTBACK!
JACK:	MANDATE		

Jack wins. However, not all games proceed as smoothly.
For example:

JACK:	BACK DOOR
JILL:	DOORMAN
JACK:	MANIPULATION
JILL:	???

IPULATION? Jill now challenges Jack to produce a word or phrase
which begins with this element. If Jack succeeds then he wins the
game – providing that he produces a compound word or phrase
capable of normal continuation.

Similarly with the sequence:

JACK:	BACK DOOR
JILL:	DOORMAN
JACK:	MANCHESTER
JILL:	CHESTERFIELD
JACK:	FIELD ???

Jill gives him reasonable thinking time, then states that she has
assumed a challenge as he could have said such as FIELD DAY,
FIELD EVENT, FIELDMOUSE etc. and so she wins that particular
contest.

But, suppose that the following happened:

JACK:	BACK DOOR
JILL:	DOORMAN
JACK:	MANCHESTER
JILL:	CHESTER-DRAWS (chest of drawers)

Jack can either laugh it off and continue with such as DRAWS IN,
DRAWS OUT, DRAWS UP etc. or else insist that Jill produce a
reasonable reply within the agreed time limit. Jill, by giving an

answer of sorts, has forfeited the right to challenge his previous word, MANCHESTER. Jack does not have to prove that MANCHESTER is capable of continuation under these circumstances. She must answer sensibly or else he wins.

2. FORE AND AFT

A childen's quiz. The leader selects words and awards points to the child who can make pairings both fore and/or aft of the given word as:

> bank ACCOUNT, ACCOUNT book
> sulphuric ACID, ACID test
> first ACT, ACT out

3. FORE AND AFTER

A children's solo challenge. Any word is chosen and the child has to make the longest possible logical word chain in (say) 60 seconds. The winner being the one who makes the longest chain.

4. BACK TO FRONT

An adult's solo challenge. Logical or witty pairings are selected from consideration of a keyword and the contestant has to make the connection within (say) 60 seconds. Some will prove exceptionally simple such as

BACK to FRONT	*BLACK to WHITE*
BACK UP	BLACKOUT
UP FRONT	OUTBREAK
	BREAK OFF
LEFT to RIGHT	OFF WHITE
LEFT OUT	
OUTRIGHT	*HOT to COLD*
	HOT SPRING
WORK to PLAY	SPRING OUT
WORKOUT	OUTGROW
OUTPLAY	GROW COLD

SCHOOL to COLLEGE	PLAIN to COLOUR
SCHOOL TIME	PLAIN SPEAKING
TIME LOST	SPEAKING OUT
LOST ART	OUTFLOW
ART COLLEGE	FLOW OFF
	OFF COLOUR

FULL TO EMPTY	
FULL MEASURE	LAND to SEA
MEASURE UP	LANDLINE
UPRIGHT	LINEAGE
RIGHT HALF	AGE-LONG
HALF EMPTY	LONG DEAD
	DEAD SEA

Others will take a more complex route such as turning a FROG into a PRINCE but once these have been mastered then the 5 minutes super challenge can be undertaken. For example:

Name a complete pack of cards from ACE to TWO in order

ACEROSE	CAR **JACK**	SEVENFOLD
ROSE-RED	JACKPOT	FOLD OUT
RED **KING**	POT ROAST	OUTSIZE
KING HENRY	ROAST DUCK	SIZE **SIX**
HENRY COTTON	DUCK POND	SIXFOLD
COTTON MILL	PONDAGE	FOLD UP
MILL HAND	AGE **TEN**	UPWIND
HANDOUT	TENPIN	WINDAGE
OUTRIGHT	PINPOINT	AGE **FIVE**
RIGHT ROYAL	POINT **NINE**	FIVEPIN
ROYAL BLUE	NINETEEN	PIN-UP
BLUE MOVIE	TEENAGE	UPGRADE
MOVIE **QUEEN**	AGE **EIGHT**	GRADE **FOUR**
QUEEN BEE	EIGHTFOLD	FOUR-PART
BEEHIVE	FOLDER	PART **THREE**
HIVE OFF	ERGOT	THREESCORE
OFF HAND	GOT LUCKY	SCORE **TWO**!
HANDCAR	LUCKY **SEVEN**	

5. BACK TO FRONT SNOOKER

The basic BACK to BACK game with players making alternative statements only, this time, you score points each time one of a particular group of words is mentioned. Suppose that you have 'colours' as the group and score points on the snooker basis of RED 1 point, YELLOW 2 points, GREEN 3 points, BROWN 4 points, BLUE 5 points, PINK 6 points and BLACK 7 points with WHITE enabling you to have another turn. As with snooker once you mention a colour this allows you to continue the break thus scoring twice for each colour mentioned. Choose a logical pairing, such as FROG to PRINCE, and see what happens:

JACK:	FROGMARCH	
JILL:	MARCH OFF	
JACK:	OFF WHITE	Jack now goes again
JACK:	WHITE FLAG	
JILL:	FLAGSTONE	
JACK:	STONEWALL	
JILL:	WALLPAPER	
JACK:	PAPER TIGER	
JILL:	TIGER RAG	
JACK:	RAG MERCHANT	
JILL:	MERCHANT NAVY	
JACK:	NAVY BLUE	Jack scores 5 points, goes again
JACK:	BLUE-BLACK	Jack scores 12 points, goes again
JACK:	BLACK PRINCE	Jack scores 7 points, game over.

The result? Jill decides she wants to play a different game.

6. OUTPLAY

Choose any logical pair of words as the basis of a verbal journey. At the same time select a particularly popular element of play such as the word OUT. The contest is not to finish the journey but to score a point each time you mention the word OUT. However, once you are ahead on points that is the time to attempt to end the game as you will then emerge the winner. In order to bring the game to such an advantageous conclusion choose an end to the journey with a word capable of being prefixed by such equally popular elements as IN, OFF or UP. Not that this is necessary but it does make a definite ending more likely in a game where the skills are directed towards forcing play in a different direction.

As with Back to Front Snooker it is essential that a player making a score must continue with the next statement otherwise no advantage can be gained. In the sample contest below, the chosen journey is from SCHOOL to MARKET, the scoring word is OUT and the rules are the same as those given in Back to Back page 63.

JACK:	SCHOOL TIME	
JILL:	TIME OUT	Jill scores 1 point for OUT
JILL:	OUTCLASS	Jill scores 1 point for OUT
JACK:	CLASSWORK	
JILL:	WORK OUT	Jill scores 1 point for OUT
JILL:	OUTFALL	Jill scores 1 point for OUT
JACK:	FALL OUT	Jack scores 1 point for OUT
JACK:	OUTCOME	Jack scores 1 point for OUT
JILL:	COME OUT	Jill scores 1 point for OUT
JILL:	OUTCOME	
JACK:	challenge!	

The challenge is on the basis of repetition of the word OUTCOME as it is essential to avoid a stalemate situation of a permanent COME OUT/OUTCOME play. Jill must now give another word and forfeit all of her score. Whilst she loses those points, Jack does not gain them. Play continues

JILL:	OUTLET	Jill scores 1 point for OUT
JACK:	LET OUT	Jack scores 1 point for OUT
JACK:	OUTSIDE	Jack scores 1 point for OUT
JILL:	SIDEBOARD	
JACK:	BOARD GAME	
JILL:	GAME POINT	
JACK:	POINT OUT	Jack scores 1 point for OUT
JACK:	OUTWIT	Jack scores 1 point for OUT
JILL:	WITTICISM	
JACK:	challenge!	

and Jack wins the game by 6 points to 1 as Jill cannot provide a word beginning with TICISM.

Note how many times in the above exchanges the word UP could have featured, so producing the conclusion with the statement UP-MARKET. Jill could have said TIME UP, WORK UP and COME UP. Jack could have said LET UP, BOARD UP and POINT UP. Not that this particular ploy is essential but it does demonstrate how easy it is to ensure a definite ending.

7. DROPOUT

A round robin Back to Front type game only it has no stated ending element. It is an elimination game played at speed with players dropping out for mentioning certain taboo words such as IN, OFF or OUT. A player must reply instantly and the usual challenge and validity rules apply (see Back to Front page 65). To set the game in motion deliberately choose a combination such as COUGH DROP to which the unwary will say such as DROP IN, DROP OFF or DROPOUT but the skilful will say DROPLET or DROPKICK so pressurizing the next player into saying LET IN, LET OFF, LET OUT or KICK IN, KICK OFF or KICK OUT.

Suitable starting combinations of this type include:

ACID DROP, SIT BACK, LOW BLOW, LUNCH BREAK, DOWNCAST, BUILDING CONTRACT, WATERFALL, KEEP FIT, STEADY FLOW, EASY GOING, LEFT HAND, UNDERHAND, RANCH HAND, FOREPLAY, BALLPOINT, FINE PRINT, OVERREACH, TURN RIGHT, LONG RUN, UNDERSELL, HALF SHARE, DEEP SLEEP, ASSORT, TIDY SPREAD, BEDSPREAD, BED SPRING, LONG STANDING, LONG STAY, DOORSTEP, PRISON STRETCH, MINER'S STRIKE, ASSET STRIP, OCEAN SWELL, UPSWING, GO THROUGH, UPTHROW, MARK TIME, TIP TOP, WRISTWATCH, MY WAY, MEN'S WEAR, WATERWEED, HOMEWORK.

8. VOWEL PLAY

A Back to Front points scoring game but without the double and triple goes essential to Outplay and Back to Front Snooker. The skill lies in avoiding the use of a second element beginning with a vowel as your opponent will automatically score with his or her next play. For example:

JACK: DROPOUT
JILL: OUTCOME   Jill scores 1 point

Choose any logical journey and have a bonus of 10 points for whoever can complete it. Impose a strict time limit so that it forces the opponent to say the first thing that comes into his head as

JACK   (*thinking*) COME IN, COME OFF, COME OUT, COME UP . . .

so having to choose between giving away another point or else surrendering the whole game and its 10 points.

Section Two

Pencil and Paper Games

A mixture of traditional and original games of varying degrees of skill.

These include solitaire games, games for two people whether in private or killing time in a public place, games for three or more people, postal games and public competition. Most are adult games with some of these only for the true wordsmith. But, there are also some for children.

The following are inventions of the author and strictly copyright © 1990 Peter Newby for any form of commercial exploitation.

THE COMPLETE BINGO
    SERIES
THE COMPLETE FAN-TAN
    SERIES
DOUBLE EXECUTION
MASS EXECUTION
REPRISALS
SELECTIVE REPRISALS
ACID DROP
ACID PROD
PENTERY WEB
CHINESE CROSSWORDS
CROSSWORD
GETAWAY
SUPERWORDS
LITTLE DOMINOES
SIMON DOE
CHESTERFIELD
THE WAR GAME
CONFERENCE
SECRET SNAKES AND
    LADDERS
LITERARY BATTLESHIPS

JACK
JILL
FORE SCORE
BASEWORDS
DOUBLE BASE
FOXO
NASTIER WORDS
SEVEN UP
FIVES
GREAT FIVES
PANIC
GOLOMBOES
BUILD UP
CLASSROOM BACK TO
    FRONT
SQUARING UP
STRIKE
SHOT PUTTING
DENBY DALE PIE
TRIPLETS
SUMWORDS
SUBJECTIVE DISCOVERIES

71

The Bingo Series

A small series of games which are ideal for a large number of people. As it is pathetically easy to cheat you are counselled against gambling on the results unless you are prepared to check the winner's claim against the letters called. Children, as well as adults, will enjoy game number 1. One person stands down each game and takes the office of bingo caller. The caller is in charge of play. The specific children's game is number 4.

1. BINGO

Three standard subjects are chosen, (say) ANIMALS, COUNTRIES and GIRLS' NAMES. The players write down three 5-letter words one being an animal, one a country and one the name of a girl.

The caller reads from the **Bingo Letter-Frequency Table** opposite and the winner is the first person to mark off all of his or her fifteen letters.

A player is not permitted to mark more than one letter at a time. Thus, if one's words contain a total of seven E's only one of these may be deleted on the calling of that letter.

Misspellings do not matter unless you decide otherwise.

2. OGNIB

Bingo spelt backwards and that is the game. This time the players start off with a blank sheet and build up the three 5-letter words of the chosen subjects.

Players may *not* change their minds about individual letters or the positions these occupy on their paper. This is a more skilful game than Bingo, described above, and all words must be correctly spelt.

3. SUPER OGNIB

A standard subject is chosen, (say) ANIMALS. The caller announces in advance how many letters he or she intends to call. As each line of the **Bingo Letter-Frequency Table** contains 24 letters so the number will be a multiple of 24. However, a mimimum of five lines of the table (120 letters) is required if every

THE BINGO LETTER-FREQUENCY TABLE

Commence at any point and call out letters in a standard left to right, top to bottom sequence.

```
R S A R A C N E E D L R E P D O O R T W U L N U
I R Y N I S H A Z U J S E F O V E N G I G R Y T
A C D E S I L A M I N O R N I F E R K T A T E D
H O G A X I O B E I E W A I R T C M E L U B G S
T Q E P A S Z E L N O A R E S O F E Q A I R T L
O E R A R I S A R E U N I R E C V F I R E S A J
T O S E P I D I D N U T A R K W E N T Y M N U G
E N U R M L T H E C A W B I X A G Y G I T D H S
P B O O G L E S S A D E N T I N D E D I N U R B
E S A T I P A D J E S O R O P I R L Y A G I T A
T E G U G E Z M U N G I S Y M E R A S U R I F S
E A R X E B V E Q O F E W K A R N O W L N E S H
O D A S T L R L T O R C I H A C R P G E H S C U
K I M E R S I T E S O D Q V E E B X A O R O I P
R E Y U S G L S E U B L E R L C A I T N A Y I T
L N I D O A S F T O R Z E O G J T T A G D E N N
A H A S I R A N W E N I R U M R W A F E D Q E A
U N N D I G S E A H T I S A R A R S E N A I O L
B E S R O A M F C H O I G I T V T J Y B A I R S
D A E P U N D E G U L Y E S P O O W A E E N O L
N E R I S R E X T G R W T M I K T F U Z R L R E
D C R S E T U I E R P S I L G E O D P D E E D A
I R O Q O T K E R Y U V E U T G E A H I C F A Y
R S I X I L O A R O L E R O S A E R J A T A N W
N N I Z A F R G S C D S G B N B L S E W M I T M
U T A N H E N N O T A G C E N B G O I C H I T Y
M E S P R A B L I G E L A I N Z U F D S N W S O
O L N A H L E O T T E I W E T I Q U E E R T A V
U R K I R J R R E S R A P I D A M N E S A S E A
G O X U Y S R F E D D R N E S R Y S U O A R J E
R K A R L G H E W A I T A C E G L I B U R A F E
X Z S E G U I S E S I N M E D O P R R E A D D O
O F U P Q T B N C G T M T H A N E L I A S W E N
Y I I S O D V E T R N A T O L R N Q P U F D I D
M E N E S S A U G I N O O D L N W A E S L O N A
H E S Y X E B A T R F I G E E R T W I O H U Y G
A I R R A G E R K C N J R A E S S A O T M T S Z
E A R R R U B L E C O T I V D L E I T P E T E R
```

letter of the alphabet is to be mentioned at least once.

The players attempt to use as many of these letters as they can, the winner being the one who utilizes the greatest number. Thus OX scores 2 points whereas the creature known as a THIRTEEN-LINED GROUND SQUIRREL will score 27 points.

The caller will not slow down despite any pleas from the company and will maintain a steady flow of letters at a pace of:

A and a B and a C and a D and etc.

The players use either graph paper or lined paper with it turned sideways so that it produces vertical lines. At worst, blank paper with numbers running across the top to indicate the position of letters. Thus, one cannot have already written OX and subsequently added an F to turn this into FOX. To gamble on FOX one must have such as

1	2	3	4	5	6	7	8
.	O	X					
F	.	X					
F	O	.					

already written down on paper.

Players may *not* write down letters at the side or bottom of the page for subsequent use. The letters have to be utilized as called or else ignored. For example:

1	2	3	4	5	6	7	8	
T		G	E	R				(hoping to make TIGER)
	O	X						(hoping to make FOX)
B	U	L	L					(with the options of such as BULLS and BULLOCK readily available)

Once calling has finished, the scores are totted up. In the above example only BULL will count, not OX. Similarly, had the player extended BULL as BULL. . KS (hoping for BULLOCKS) there would be no score for BULL.

To enable players to judge the situation it is recommended that the caller indicate every 24th letter. Thus, if 96 letters are going to be used then the caller should say

'. . . N and letter number 24 is U'
'. . . Y and letter number 48 is T'
'. . . E and letter number 72 is D'

In family play one assumes that every player will be honest but, if the game is played as a serious competition amongst strangers, special rules need to be adopted.

1. The caller adopts a different method of announcing letters. Not just 'R . . . S . . . A . . .' but 'R, repeat R; S, repeat S; A, repeat, A . . .'
2. The players draw a line near the bottom of the page under which they write every letter they do *not* wish to use.
3. The winning submissions are checked by officials to ensure:
   (a) That every letter called appears on the paper either above or below the scoring line. If any letter is adrift (omitted, repeated, illegible, crossed out or possessing any other sign of being a possible second thought) the submission is void.
   (b) That every animal (or whatever) claimed for score is valid. Under these circumstances it must appear in a previously named dictionary.

This means that if the top three players are to be honoured, then the top six submissions are taken. Firstly the words are checked for validity then all (say) 96 letters are privately re-called and marked off bingo fashion.

By having the letters originally called 'competition style' no player can complain that he thought that, for example, a V was a B. Equally, if a caller made an error (even though he or she was being monitored by an official during calling) that same error would show up on all submissions. It would be wise in competition play to have the clearest voiced speaker as the caller.

Finally, when stating a subject make absolutely clear what is required. 'Animals' is vague. That could mean words such as cod, American, cowlike can all be claimed as being within the boundaries of acceptability. If you mean 'Descriptive terms for mammals excluding man' say so. Obviously, all words have to be correctly spelt.

4. BINGO CRICKET

A little bit of fun for a couple of youngsters who support different cricket teams. Suppose one favours England and the other enthuses over the West Indies. Each writes down the surnames of the players of his or her choice. If we assume that England is to bat first, then it would probably be Gooch to face the West Indian attack.

The West Indian supporter now reads from the **Bingo Letter-**

Frequency Table. Every letter, other than G, O, C or H, scores a run. As each letter of the surname, Gooch, is read out so that letter is crossed off. The England opening batsman will, therefore, survive four appeals for dismissal before the last letter of his name (be it G, O, C or H) is read out and he is dismissed. Two O's have to be called, not just one for him to lose his wicket.

When England bowl and (say) Richards is facing the attack, then he will score runs for all letters other than those of his surname. The fact that the letter A will be called out quite a number of times before he is finally dismissed is of no consequence other than that first time, all repetitions being treated as non-scoring deliveries.

There is no need to have full teams of eleven players, otherwise boredom can creep in. Three or four might be sufficient, after which the team is presumed to have declared.

If Mum finds herself roped into play, choose Pakistan and have Qadir on your side. With luck, he will score you a lot of runs!

If Dad finds himself facing a roomful of budding cricketers all wanting to bat at the same time, the answer is simple. A limited overs World Cup contest.

Each participant writes down three or four surnames and, as each one is dismissed, so the next batsman takes his place. Each different surname produces different results and my money is still on Mum's Pakistan if she does a little quiet research in advance.

Players shoud be seated in an arrangement which inhibits cheating and enables errors to be corrected. Bowl in overs of six letters, taking a short break between them.

As each line of the table has 24 letters so that represents 4 overs. It is up to Dad how many overs he is prepared to call.

The Fan-Tan Series

The Chinese gambling game of Fan-tan involves the placing of a number of small coins under an upturned bowl and wagering on the value of the remainder after that number has been divided by four.

This small series is based on that principle. Only the first game is suitable for children.

1. FAN-TANSY

Choose any simple subject such as FLOWERS. Each player now

writes the name of any flower on a piece of paper and places it face down in the centre of the table.

Players now guess at the remainder (0, 1, 2 or 3) after the total number of letters of all the words has been divided by four. The winners collect points appropriate to that remainder. If, however, they correctly identify a nil remainder they receive 4 points.

There will be no need to write out names of (say) flowers more than twice, as players can permutate these two flowers as often as they wish. Others, however, may wish to do so in order to baffle opponents. If you choose longer names, such as MICHAELMAS DAISY, write the total number of letters after it (15) to make the mathematics easier.

Misspellings can be amended on checking, if this affects the mathematics. Obviously, a dyslexic rendering of DAISY as 'DIASY' does not affect the outcome of play but ANTIRRHINUM is quite capable of being produced with a different numerical value.

2. FAN-TANGLE

The expert's version of Fan-tansy.

Each player in turn selects a particularly restrictive subject, such as ANIMALS WITH NAMES BEGINNING WITH THE LETTER Z.

ZEBRA is obvious, but are any of the other players likely to produce ZEBU or ZHO? If not, you can be fairly sure that they will all have ZEBRA and you control the total. Admittedly, they have a free guess at the remainder and will suspect you of having produced a wicked example but they have no idea what.

To prevent them bamboozling you, reject plurals. ZEBRAS will change the mathematics and your probable control. Plurals do not have to be an automatic rejection as a different subject might be A SINGLE WORD MEANING THE PLURAL OF DOMESTIC COWS AND BULLS BUT NOT COLLECTIVE NOUNS SUCH AS 'HERD'. The obvious answer is CATTLE. Can you think of another?

This is the point of the game. The person who suggests the subject imposes all the rules. He or she ideally selects a subject having only one very obvious example but which has at least one other, rather obscure, acceptable answer.

Whoever poses the subject is the last person to state his or her guess at the remainder.

All other rules are the same as Fan-tansy.

3. FAN-TANAGRAM

A game for two people without a choice of subject. Both players tell each other which everyday 3-letter word he or she has selected. The race is on to be the first to produce a genuine 6-letter word out of the two words.

4. FAN-TANDAGRAM

An andagram is an anagram of a word plus an additional letter. For example CAT + S can be such as ACTS, CAST, CATS and SCAT. By contrast CAT + H gives CHAT.

Some words have an amazing potential for andagrams. *Pears Advanced Word-Puzzler's Dictionary* gives no fewer than 126 andagrams for the word STAINER, 121 for SATINE, 132 for SATIRE and a mind-boggling 270 for ASTER. If you choose a basic 5-letter word containing two different high-frequency vowels (A, E or I) together with three different high-frequency consonants (L, N, P, R, S or T) it is almost impossible not to have the basis of a set of andagrams.

One player selects a suitable 5-letter word produced as given above. He or she remains the scorer and umpire for that particular word. The other players (a minimum of two are required) in ignorance of the scorer's word choose any letter they wish apart from S. Plurals are perfectly acceptable but only the scorer is permitted to include an S in the playing pool.

The scorer's word is placed face down in the centre of the table. Each player now places his or her individual letter face down beside it. When this has been accomplished the scorer's word is revealed together with any one letter.

The race is on to produce andagrams within a brief spell of time. Not necessarily a minute or any other arbitrary limit but as judged reasonable by the scorer. As a fair rule of thumb once most people have signified that they have finished, the round ends. It is just hard luck on the busy little body who begs for more time.

Any players who have produced andagrams, which they write down on paper, now hand these to the scorer. He or she checks them whilst play continues with the next letter.

At the end of the rounds based on that particular word, the scoresheet is passed to the next player who assumes the responsibilities of the scorer. The former scorer is now a player. The whole game has each player acting as scorer an equal number of times.

(For a fifth Fan-Tan game see Shelling Peas with Gramps which is more conveniently placed in the Classroom Series. Gramps (page 170) is the Fan-Tan version of the contest, Shelling Peas. The many examples of word play in Shelling Peas are perfect for Gramps.)

The Hangman Series

Nine games, of which only the first is suitable for children.

1. HANGMAN

A popular pencil and paper game for two people, be they children with simple words or adults using the more horrendous constructions distilled from such as *Pears Advanced Word-Puzzler's Dictionary.*

A word is chosen by one player and the other has to discover it, letter by letter, within a limit of eleven errors graphically represented by the progressive drawing of a man being hanged.

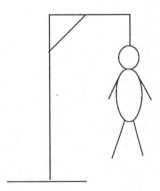

In this example of failure to discover the word, CATHEDRAL, eight dots were drawn to represent each individual letter.

As letters were nominated so the correct ones were placed over their corresponding dots (*both* A's going down simultaneously) or else part of the drawing was made, either a line or a circle.

A T E D R A
. . . .

Hangman is the perfect game to hone one's skills in word recognition which will be of subsequent value in the aristocrat of word play, Code Breaking.

2. DOUBLE EXECUTION

Hangman for three people, two of whom attempt to discover the same word in ignorance of the other's situation.

To play it simply and effectively, have the two contestants seated at opposite ends of a table with the taskmaster seated in the middle. *Each person's playing area is carefully concealed*, all have paper and pencil and the taskmaster has a pack of playing cards. A full round of play will comprise six games with each person being the taskmaster for two consecutive games, so that all will attempt four words and the winner will emerge at the end of an agreed number of full rounds. In the following example, Tom, Dick and Harriet are the players with Tom as the taskmaster,.

Tom, having chosen the word CATHEDRAL, sets out two rows of cards from ace to nine to represent the nine letters of his word. He chooses clubs for Dick and hearts for Harriet. He announces that his word contains nine letters so Dick and Harriet place nine dots on their respective pieces of paper. He tells Dick to have the first choice of a letter.

Dick, very sensibly, goes for the vowels beginning with E the most widely used letter in the English language. As E is the fifth letter of the chosen word, CATHEDRAL, so Tom hands him the five of clubs.

Harriet, equally sensibly, chooses A. Tom now picks up both the two and the eight of hearts taking care to conceal from Dick the fact that two cards are being passed to Harriet. (A simple method of perfect concealment will be given below.)

Dick now selects the letter I, so Tom hands him the first spade or diamond from the top of the pack of 'dead' cards. Dick now has to begin the drawing of his own execution, Harriet chooses E and so she receives the five of hearts.

In lieu of a letter, a player may guess at the word. Failure results in immediate execution. But the player still at 'liberty' now continues without the need for secrecy. The game can still be tied if he or she is subsequently hanged.

Award a point to the winner. The outright winner emerges at the end of an agreed session.

As the player going second is at a nominal disadvantage so two games are played before (say) Tom and Dick change places. Dick having the first choice of letter in game one, Harriet having the first choice in game two.

To ensure perfect concealment, if you are not especially adept at handling cards, always pass on two or sometime three cards each time. The contestant ignoring (say) the four of spades when a relevant two of hearts is included.

It is not the responsibility of the taskmaster to remember who has previously mentioned a particular letter. If a player foolishly mentions the same letter twice that is his misfortune.

3. MASS EXECUTION

T   THE   TH

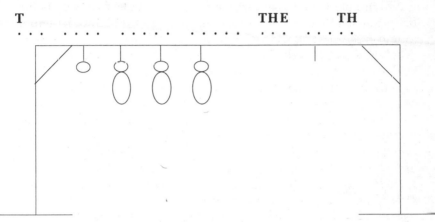

A proverb has been selected. In the above example it is TOO MANY COOKS SPOIL THE BROTH.

Play began with the ground and the gallows already drawn so, unlike Hangman, the maximum errors possible is only seven.

The person guessing chose letters in the order E, T and H. So, THE is complete. However, for the words where these letters are not present we have started drawing the hanged men, for instance, for the word MANY the rope, the head and the body have been drawn as none of the three letters are present.

The object of the game is to discover the proverb before any one man is hanged.

(For a list of proverbs see page 000)

4. REPRISALS

Mass execution in which both players take turns to hang as many of their opponent's men as they can.

This time each hanged man is a victory and scores a point. However, as each man is hanged no additional letters may be placed on the dots which he represented.

No points are gained for partial executions.

5. SELECTIVE REPRISALS

In this version of Mass Execution, the person guessing selects the word he or she wishes to attempt. Thus with the same example of TOO MANY COOKS SPOIL THE BROTH, the art lies in clever selection of words to attempt. The first word could be such as ALL, THE or YOU but AND is virtually impossible. However, the fifth word could easily be AND.

Alternatively, one may attempt one of the longer words. As the letter E is the most widely used of all letters so it may well feature in one of these.

Winning is either on the basis of Mass Execution (as soon as any one man is hanged, the game is over) or else on the basis of Reprisals (scoring points for hanged men).

6. CONFESS

The name derives from the proverb, CONFESS AND BE HANGED. It is a form of Hangman, played with proverbs, in which confession brings about your own execution.

Two players select proverbs containing the same number of words. (See page 41 for a wide selection, all of a similar half a dozen words length).

Jack chooses TOO MANY COOKS SPOIL THE BROTH.

Jill chooses A STITCH IN TIME SAVES NINE.

On the same playing sheet, they represent their proverbs with dots spacing them in word formation thus:

```
JACK   . . .    . . . .      . . . . .    . . . . .    . . .    . . . . .
JILL   .   . . . . . .    . .    . . . . .    . . . . .    . . . .
```

Jack is to go first and it is fairly obvious to him that Jill's first word is A. But, if he is wrong, he will then have to reveal any of the letters in *his* first word. Either the T or else both of the O's. As he cannot think of any possible proverb which begins with either of the words I or O (the only two other possibilities) so he is fairly safe. His guess of A is correct.

Jill considers Jack's proverb. The first word could well be THE. She has nothing to lose anyway, Jack has already robbed himself of the chance of forcing her to reveal the A. She can attack his first word with abandon. Does she wish to do that? What about his fifth word, is it THE or could it be AND? If she attacks it, which of the letters in SAVES is the best one to reveal if she is wrong? She decides to expose the E if she is wrong and must now choose a letter from either THE or AND in order to make her play.

A wrong guess at the complete proverb and a player hangs himself or herself. It must be correct in every particular.

A player who makes an error in numbers of dots must, on revealing that error, put himself at the mercy of his opponent.

7. ACID DROP

Sharp acids corrode their own containers is an Albanian proverb and, as the basis of a Hangman game, its significance lies not only in the fact that few will ever have heard of it but that it is an entertaining statement capable of deduction from partial evidence.

The game can be played by teams or individuals and, at its most pleasing, uses such delights of wit and wisdom as:

(a) English proverbs: *When an ass climbs a ladder, you may find wisdom in women.*
(b) Quotations: Kipling's *The silliest women can manage the cleverest man.*
(c) Classic graffiti: *Snoopy has fleas.*
(d) Famous last words: Lord Palmerston's '*Die, my dear doctor, that's the last thing I'll do.*'
(e) Devilish definitions: *Acorn, an oak in a nutshell.*
(f) Acidic observations: Jules Feiffer's '*I know she's alive. I saw her lips curl.*'
(g) Picturesque phrasings: Woody Allen's '*Her figure described a set of parabolas that would cause cardiac arrest in a yak.*'

In Acid Drop, each word is guessed at individually but, no matter which word is being attempted, the hanging is a collective result of those guesses. The object of the game, therefore, is to hang as many men as possible.

Consider the example of a team being told that they are attempting to discover a Turkish proverb containing six words. The first word has three letters, the second has six letters, the third has six, the fourth has four, the fifth has three and the sixth has eleven.

That team may now apportion words amongst itself or, if it prefers, work collectively using a single sheet of paper. The team decides how it will tackle the problem.

The 'executioners' merely record the hangings.

At some point, the guessing team will face a partial revelation something like this:

ONE AR..IT CANNOT .OLD T.O .ATER.ELONS

and the executioners will have scored (say) one complete hanging and a partial hanging.

The guessing team now has the option of 'reprieving' the partially hanged man, If it can now state what the Turkish proverb is, only the first hanging scores a success for the executioners. However, if it is wrong in any one particular, then a full execution of the second man is made and they must now face the prospect of beginning a third hanging.

The rule is, a wrong guess with a letter builds a hanging and a wrong guess at the full statement produces a full execution.

The winning team is the one with the greater number of hangings over the session of play.

That proverb? *One armpit cannot hold two watermelons.*

Only full stops and commas are given as part of the basic information. Apostrophes give away too much information and are not revealed. Thus, a word such as SHE'S is merely described as a 4-letter word. However, when answering, the guessing team is told that the first letter is S and the fourth letter is apostrophe S – but only if both teams agree in advance to this particular kindness.

However, one type of punctuation can be delightfully confusing and I am grateful to New Zealander Jeff Grant (see Pears Word Games Society page 216) for pointing this out to me. Hyphens.

The *English Dialect Dictionary* contains the names of the following two flowers:

1. KITTY-COME-DOWN-THE-LANE-JUMP-UP-AND-KISS-ME
2. MEET-HER-IN-THE-ENTRY-KISS-HER-IN-THE-BUTTERY

The first is a Kentish term for the cuckoo-pint or wild arum whilst the second is a Lincolnshire expression for the pansy and both of these share the unusual distinction of having nine hyphens.

8. ACID PROD

A variation of Acid Drop which brings a touch of bedevilment when playing with 'easy' statements such as the proverb, *Too many cooks spoil the broth.*

This time you write the words as anagrams (or as near to a true anagram as you can devise) thus:

and reply to guesses with your anagrammed sequence.

The rules are otherwise the same as for Acid Drop.

9. PENTERY WEB

The game of Pentery Web, was first described in *Pears Advanced Word-Puzzler's Dictionary* as that is the ideal reference work for this game.

Pentery Web is a form of Hangman played with a pair of anagrams and that book contains 35,000 words all of which have at least one perfect anagram readily displayed. Thus, the tedium of advance planning is unnecessary. However, if you have the facility for constructing perfect anagrams (a complete word from another complete word) so this game may be for you. In the following example of play, Jack has set Jill the task.

Jack has chosen the pair, PINITE and TIEPIN fully aware that Jill will know TIEPIN but is unlikely to know that PINITE is a chemical substance. Not that this will matter as Jill is such a good wordsmith she will still be able to cope.

Jack displays the two words in a cryptic mixture of dots with the same letter revealed in both. There are ten dots so 10 points can be scored if she could guess the pair.

```
    I
 .  .  .  .  .
             I
 .  .  .  .  .
```

She cannot, so he now adds another matched pair to his display. Eight dots, 8 points.

```
 I     I
 .  .  .  .  .
 I        I
 .  .  .  .  .
```

Still baffled, he adds another pair. Six dots, 6 points. At this stage Jill might well come up with TIEPIN even though she is at a loss for the other word. Jack *makes no comment* as his opponent must be correct with *both* words. She fails. He adds another matched pair of letters.

```
 I  N  I
 .  .  .  .  .
 I        I  N
 .  .  .  .  .
```

```
 I  N  I     E
 .  .  .  .  .
 I  E     I  N
 .  .  .  .  .
```

Once again she fails.

Jill knew the answer before Jack placed the matching T's in the display, but they were given for fun and Jill scores 2 points.

```
  I N I T E
  . . . . . .
T I E   I N
  . . . . . .
```

She soon got her revenge with STOITS and TSOTSI! (STOIT being a Scottish verb to stumble and TSOTSI is a young South African hooligan.)

(The reason for the peculiar name of this game should be fairly obvious to those who enjoy this particular type of word play.)

The Consequence Series

Two games, either for adults or children. As their senses of humour will differ, so it is better to have all children playing or all adults rather than a mixture of the two.

1. CONSEQUENCES

An old favourite with a charm of its own. Many will know how to play it but, for those who do not, have freely available a boldly written list marked as follows:

1. adjective
2. girl's name
3. MET adjective
4. man's name
5. AT location
6. time and/or date
7. HE SAID TO HER whatever he said
8. SHE SAID TO HIM whatever she said
9. what he did
10. what she did
11. AND THE CONSEQUENCE WAS whatever it happened to be
12. AND THE WORLD SAID whatever it might choose to say

Each person now has his or her own long sheet of paper. Each writes any adjective suitable for describing a girl (WITTY, PRETTY, STUPID, SEXY, LUDICROUS or whatever) and folds the paper to conceal what has been written and passes this to the player on the left. If you have five players then five pieces of paper will be passed on simultaneously.

Each person now writes the name of a girl, folds and passes the paper.

At the third stage, the word MET is written followed by a suitable adjective for a man.

So it continues with each person writing something, folding the paper and passing it on.

When all twelve stages have been completed each person now reads out the story which has been created.

No winners, no losers, just a giggle for however many participate in the game.

2. PICTURE CONSEQUENCES

Great fun especially as few people would call themselves artists.

As with Consequences, everyone has a piece of paper. This time it is a very long narrow strip. About two inches wide is about right.

On the top of the strip, using as little of it as possible, everyone draws any picture he or she wishes. It is not folded yet.

This picture is passed to the person on the left without comment. No apologetic statement on the lines of, 'It's supposed to be a cow eating grass' or any other such words may be uttered.

Each player now writes a description of what he or she honestly thinks has been drawn, if the 'cow eating grass' looks like a dog sniffing a worm so that is what is written.

The original drawing is now folded so that only the description can be seen by the next player.

Obviously, everyone now illustrates what has been written. So the sequence continues until all the strips have been filled. Those filled first are put on one side until all are complete, but the final item has to be a description.

The fun arises in the comparison of the original drawing with the final statement. You will be amazed at the eventual description of the 'cow eating grass'.

The Cross Play Series

A series in which players take turns in calling out (if played on two or more sheets of paper) or writing down (if all players use the same sheet) letters or words of their own choice. It contains some of the greatest pencil and paper games. Expert players are particularly recommended to consider 5. **Words** and 14. **The War Game**. All, however, are worthy of consideration.

None are specifically children's games, but the brighter youngster should have no difficulties with 7, 8, 10, 16, 20 and 25.

1. FRENCH CROSSWORDS

A two person game each playing on his or her own 5×5 grid. Neither knows what the other is doing but both are attempting to make the higher score.

Players take turns to call out letters putting them anywhere they wish on their own grids. For example, the first player calls out Z. This Z could be put into squares as varied as:

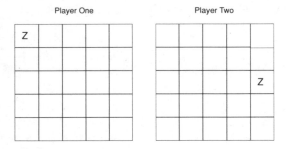

Player One   Player Two

The second player now calls out (say) D. These might be distributed in this fashion:

Player One   Player Two

As the object of the game is to make words in both a horizontal and vertical direction and score points for them, so it is obvious that Player One is attempting to make two words beginning with Z whilst Player Two has a totally different plan.

Play could eventually finish as shown below. The numbers indicating the points scored. Only the longest word in a line counts. Thus, one cannot have (say) both BRA and ZEBRA scoring in the same line. The achievement of a 5-letter word is rewarded with a bonus point. A 5-letter word scores, therefore, six points. A 4-letter word, four points. A 3-letter, 3 points and a 2-letter, two points.

Player One

Z	E	B	R	A	6
I	Y	O	O	L	2
L	L	M	A	P	3
C	A	B	D	U	3
H	U	T	S	S	4

6 2 4 6 3

Total 39

Player Two

C	H	I	L	D	6
O	P	L	S	A	2
B	A	L	M	Z	4
R	Y	O	U	E	3
A	B	U	T	S	6

6 3 3 4 6

Total 43

For the 2-letter words used in the above grids, see following game.

2. CHINESE CROSSWORDS

Both the French and the Chinese have similar small crosswords, hence the name of both this and its parent game, French Crosswords.

The Chinese, however, love to gamble and, effectively this game is Poker played with completed French Crossword grids.

For three or more people to play the basic French Crosswords game is less a game of skill and more a game of luck. With (say) four people taking turns to call out letters, one has almost no control whatsoever on the outcome. But, by gambling on the results – for points, for pennies or whatever – an interesting and stimulating challenge can be rescued from the frustration.

The four players, therefore, complete their five by five grids as described in French Crosswords. They compute their scores, but do *not* reveal them.

The top horizontal line is now considered. Each player has a limited number of (say) matchsticks. If he or she thinks that his or her top line is a good one it may well be worth staking a few matchsticks on. If not, they need not participate in the gambling.

Those who do participate, now wager on the outcome.

The person with the highest scoring word wins the matchsticks but, if two tie for the top scoring word, they share the total number of matchsticks having been wagered. For an alternative see the tie-breaker table opposite.

There is no fixed stake. This is set by the person making the first bid. High or low. The stake can be a bluff. Everyone, whether he or she intends to gamble or not, must put at least one matchstick forward at the start of this play. The first player (decided in advance by rota) now sets the stakes. Whoever participates must match the stake. The wagering continues until two players remain. They compare scores.

However, they must first state their scoring word and then reveal the contents of that top line. It is up to the other players to adjudicate on any disputed words and also, if they wish, to record what their opponents have written. These two players have now revealed parts of their future words, the less ambitious have not.

The second wager is on the extreme left-hand vertical line. The new first player will set the stakes for this.

So play continues, horizontal line then vertical line. The ambitious revealing more and more of his hand, the cautious still giving nothing away.

The winner being the one with the greatest number of matchsticks at the end.

Note. Both this and its parent game can be played with larger sized grids. The bonus scores for words of maximum length in the other versions are 7 (6×6), 9 (7×7), 10 (8×8), 12 (9×9). 9×9 is known as Arepo.

3. CROSSWORD

The world's first crossword puzzle was devised by Arthur Wynne, a journalist who emigrated to New York from Liverpool. His creation, which he called a word-cross, appeared in a Sunday newspaper, the *New York World* on 21st December, 1913.

Since that time, crossword puzzles have spread not only around

CHINESE CROSSWORDS TIE-BREAKER TABLE

The values ascribed to each individual letter in the anagram card game of Pelham are as follows:

10 points	J, Q, X, Z
5 points	K, V
3 points	B, C, F, H, M, P, W, Y
1 point	all other letters

In the event of a tie in Chinese Crosswords apply the Pelham values. Thus, in a Chinese Crossword contest using the previously mentioned completed French Crosswords grids in which Player Two beat Player One by 43 points to 39 points the difference in the tied lines are given below the grids.

Player One

Z	E	B	R	A
I	Y	O	O	L
L	L	M	A	P
C	A	B	D	U
H	U	T	S	S

Player Two

C	H	I	L	D
O	P	L	S	A
B	A	L	M	Z
R	Y	O	U	E
A	B	U	T	S

HORIZONTAL LINES

ZEBRA versus CHILD   ZEBRA (16) beats CHILD (9)

YO versus OP   remains tied at 4 points each

   (MAP versus BALM   BALM wins outright)

CAB versus YOU   CAB (7) beats YOU (5)

   (HUTS versus ABUTS   ABUTS wins outright)

VERTICAL LINES

ZILCH versus COBRA   ZILCH (18) beats COBRA (9)

   (LA versus PAY)

   (BOMB versus ILL)   all outright wins for the larger word

   (ROADS versus SMUT)

   (ALP versus DATES)

Note that in the only line still tied, YO versus OP, Player One might have chosen OO instead of YO. Had Player One done so then Player Two would have won on a basis of 2 Pelham points to 4 Pelham points. But, more especially, note that whilst Player Two won the French Crosswords game, Player One has the better Chinese Crosswords lines if the Pelham points tie-breaker is used.

the world but have been used as the basis of many word games of which Scrabble® is the peer. Most of these games are commercial but there are also some excellent pencil and paper games of which Crossword is one of the most demanding.

A 9×9 grid is drawn and any 9-letter word is placed anywhere on the grid either horizontally or vertically.

Assume that the word, CROSSWORD, has been chosen and placed as follows:

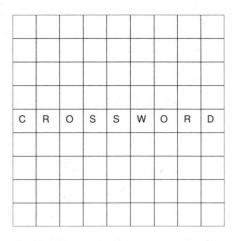

Players now take turns in adding any letter they wish providing that each letter they play creates a valid word. Each word they create scores points equal to the number of letters used.

Two examples of play will follow. One having a couple of average players, Bill and Ben, the other a pair of experienced rivals, Jack and Jill.

(a) BILL versus BEN: Bill goes first. He scores 2 points for adding an O below an S to create the word SO.

Ben has three options of which two are obvious. Either score 2 points for a different 2-letter word (say) DO or score 3 points for converting SO into a 3-letter word. The third option will be discussed in the Jack and Jill game. Ben scores 3 points for SON.

Bill scores 4 points for SONG
Ben scores 5 points for SONGS
Their score at this point is Bill 6 points and Ben 8 points.
The remainder of their game will be equally basic.

(b) JACK versus JILL: Jack goes first, he scores 2 points for SO. Jill immediately takes the third option and scores 4 points. She ceates two simultaneous 2-letter words in this fashion:

C R O S S W O R D
OO

The Scottish word OO scores her 2 points and WO provides the other 2 points.

Jack now scores 5 points from the following:

C R O S S W O R D
T OO

2 points for ST (see Appendix) plus 3 points for TOO.

Jill now scores 6 points from the following:

C R O S S W O R D
T OO N

2 points from ON plus 4 points for TOON (see Appendix).

Ignoring the fact that STOON is an obsolete form of the word STONE which would give Jack 7 points, we can reasonably assume that Jill has forced him to move elsewhere. The most he can now score is 3 points.

Jack studies the board. Ideally he would like to have TOONS but, as yet, that is impossible as no such word as 'RS' is valid. Therefore, what he must achieve is a word ending in R which he can pluralize. To do this he converts ON into TON so that whoever plays such as TE/ER for 4 points will immediately give him 8 points for ERS/TOONS as shown below:

T E
C R O S S W O R D
T O O N S

This is the game played at its most tactical and it follows that an awareness of 2-letter words is utterly essential.

The same is equally true throughout the whole of the game, as the following section of the board will illustrate. Many of the words shown could not have been played without a knowledge of some of the strangest 2-letter words.

ACROSS

	S	W	A	B
	1		2	3
	E		X	I
			4	
W	A	G	E	R
5		6		
A		L		D
S	W	O	R	D
7			8	
		W	O	O
		9		
		E	L	M
		10		
H	I	D	E	
11				

1 SWAB needed AB, the W then inserted between S and AB

4 XI (see Appendix)

5 WAGER could have arisen in various ways such as W blank G thence WAG, WAGE, WAGER. But, the existence of such words as WA, AG or GE give far greater opportunities for it.

7 This is part of the base word, CROSSWORD

9 WOO arises from either WO or OO as well as W blank O

10 ELM from EL apart from E blank M

11 HIDE from ID or DE thence IDE or HID.

DOWN

1 SEA from EA

2 AXE can only have arisen from a very complex route which depended upon building up from the R of WAGER. R had to become IR, thence BIR. The B had to become AB, the X was then inserted between the A and the E to create, simultaneously, AXE/XI. Thus, not even AXE was possible unless XI was also valid.

3 The nonce word, BIRDDOM, meaning the world of birds collectively depended upon both the creation of BIR (see 2 above) and D becoming DO then DOM. Finally, the D was inserted between BIR and DOM.

The remaining words were all created in similar, complex, 2-letter word based fashion.

The commentary opposite details two different lists of 2-letter words. The first is that used in the UK Scrabble Championship, the second is the negative mnemonic for the far greater number available not only for Crossword but any word game – including Scrabble.

The important thing is to play to words which you can prove exist should your opponent challenge you. It is up to you whether or not you are a Bill or a Jill when playing Crossword.

2-LETTER WORDS

Few people appreciate just how vital to word game play are the 2-letter words. Obviously the games of Crossword and Little Dominoes are completely dependent upon them and they make a contribution to such as French Crosswords, Chinese Crosswords, Getaway and Literary Battleships amongst others in this book.

However, they are just as indispensable for any of the commercial crossword-type games in a way that escapes the attention of all but the best players. It is not for themselves or the little score they produce that these 2-letter words matter, but the fact that they provide a link between the word that you wish to play and a word which is already in play that makes them so valuable.

No better illustration of this can be given than that of a game of Scrabble® between two of the leading players in the country which resulted in one of them, Russell Byers, creating a new world record for the highest total score ever achieved in a genuine game.

First, contrast their game with a typical family contest between two people with a good command of the English language. The winner will probably score in the range of 230 to 250 points and probably not utilize a single 2-letter word.

The *loser* in this world record game scored 434 points. He played 19 words, of which 6 were 2-letter words. Russell Byers also played 19 words and almost half of them – 9 to be exact – were 2-letter words. His score was a brilliant 892 points!

This game was played under strict national championship rules in 1988 to the then maximum availability of 92 2-letter words. It did *not* include the contentious word, CH, shown bracketed in the list below.

Since that game was played, the official reference dictionary for the UK Scrabble Championship has increased its number of 2-letter words so that the following 106 utterly invaluable little 'linking words' are now available:

AA, AD, AE, AH, AI, AM, AN, AR, AS, AT, AW, AX, AY
BA, BE, BO, BY
(CH)
DA, DI, DO
EA, EE, EF, EH, EL, EM, EN, ER, ES, EX
FA, FY
GI, GO, GU
HA, HE, HI, HO
ID, IF, IN, IO, IS, IT
JO
KA, KO, KY

Now for some boring rules to settle disputes.

1. Every word played must be capable of being confirmed in an agreed reference work or works.
2. An erroneous word has to be removed from the grid either with a rubber or typewriter correction fluid. The playing of an erroneous word results in a double forfeit. 10 points are deducted from that player's score and he or she has to forego the particular turn in question.
3. The game ends when both players agree that no further move is possible.
4. A player may not pass for strategic advantage. If a player claims that he cannot see a possible move he or she does not merely miss a single turn but *two* turns. (i.e. The opponent makes three moves in succession.)
5. All *sensible* words capable of being written in lower case are acceptable.
6. This means that plurals, slang, obscenities, obsolete words and goodness knows what else that feature in your agreed reference work(s) are perfectly acceptable. Two word compounds or hyphenated words are invalid. With hyphenated words it should be noted that where the use of a hyphen is either optional or a whim of a particular dictionary then the non-hyphenated form is acceptable. The modern tendency being the single form rather than the hyphenated. (These same word rules are equally applicable to Sumwords – Crossword on page 204 and 90.)

4. GETAWAY

Two players each select a geographical location of an agreed number of letters. For example, if one player has chosen a country it could be such as ENGLAND or DENMARK whilst the opponent might prefer a city like BELFAST or GLASGOW. All four of these contain seven letters. Whilst the opponents know what type of location the other has chosen they have no idea which. The object of the game being its discovery.

A large scale grid is drawn (say) 12×12 and players take turns in writing down any words they wish of any length. The only stipulation is that a 3-letter word *must* contain one of the letters of the chosen location – and it must be in the correct order.

LA, LI, LO
MA, ME, MI, MO, MU, MY
NA, NE, NO, NU, NY
OB, OD, OE, OF, OH, OI, OM, ON, OO, OP, OR, OS, OU, OW, OX, OY
PA, PI, PO
RE
SH, SI, SO, ST
TA, TE, TI, TO
UG, UM, UN, UP, UR, US, UT
WE, WO
XI
YE, YO, YU
ZO

Some of these words are defined in the Appendix as they occur within the explanations of various games. But, all of the above, together with more than double that number are to be found, with full definitions, in *Pears Advanced Word-Puzzler's Dictionary*. It provides no fewer than 247 2-letter words and rejects, for reasons fully explained in the Appendix, the nonsensical 'word' CH.

If you are wondering how on earth Russell could possibly have amassed such a huge score when nine of the words were so amazingly small that most people would not even bother with them, then compare his attitude to yours.

Many people consider that to play five to six tiles in one turn is some form of achievement. Russell and other top players regard this as childish. In this game he did play one 4-letter word, MAWK, not so much for the 39 points it gave him but simply to get rid of awkward letters! The rest of the time it was playing the odd tile in a strategic position or else a 2-letter word for a similar purpose. But, the 7-letter word, DENTURE, provided 68 points including the 50 bonus points for using all seven tiles. Everything else was 8-letter words utilizing strategically placed letters. VITIATED, 76 points followed by two in the 'triple/triple' outer line, SPITTERS for 140 points and RELIQUES for 284 points!

With a further fourteen 2-letter words now available, that world record was shattered in June 1989 by Phil Appleby of Kineton, Warwickshire, with a mind-boggling 1049 points. Once again, the 2-letter words were a vital factor of success and Phil could not have made his highest single move without utilizing the existing word ER. ER was on an outermost line and he used his seven available tiles (O, X, I, D, I, Z and S) around ER to produce OXIDIZERS for 374 points. A similar move on another outermost line gave him an additional 221

Suppose that Jack chooses DENMARK, Jill chooses BELFAST and they agree to 'getaway' from the Manchester prison of STRANGEWAYS. This word is now written in the centre of the grid and they build up a crossword from that base.

Jack is to go first and he decides to be cautious and constructs the word GOOD descending from the horizontally written STRANGEWAYS. His reason for this is that he now has complete control of where his letter D (of DENMARK) is to be sited. It might be the first letter of such as DIP, the second letter of such as ADO or the third letter of such as AND.

Jill decides to do two things. First complicate things for Jack if he is trying any tactic as outlined above and, at the same time, do exactly the same thing herself. She plays the word BOMBING in this fashion:

```
S T R A N G E  W A Y S
         O
         B O M B  I NG
         D
```

The tactics are many and varied and the game can end in a variety of ways.

(1) An opponent having discerned (say) DENM from the 3-letter words played, wins by saying DENMARK.

(2) One player has made a complete getaway.

(3) A player cannot possibly complete the word due to lack of space. For example, DENMAR is already on the grid but K cannot be contrived into a 3-letter word with a particularly cramped construction of words. He must now reveal that K to his opponent if she is equally frustrated. The winner being the first of the two to identify the location.

Note that as more and more 3-letter words are added it becomes increasingly more diffcult to remember in which order they were played. Therefore, players who wish to play a strictly adult game, are not permitted to keep notes as to the order in which opponents played words.

The word rules are the same as those of Crossword (see page 90).

5. WORDS

The classic pencil and paper word game, so great that pale imitations appear on television and you can even buy it as a boxed points in a game played to strict championship rules. It is gratifying to note that this game did *not* contain the offensive CH and all words played were legitimate.

However, the Pears Word Game Society (see page 216) accepts 229 of the 247 2-letter words of *Pears Advanced Word-Puzzler's Dictionary* and these words may be summarized as follows:

GROUP 1 Every possible combination which comprises a **CONSONANT** followed by a **VOWEL** or the letter **Y** is valid *except* for

JI JU JY   QA QE QO QY   VE   XE XO XY   YY   ZU ZY

GROUP 2 Every possible combination consisting of a **VOWEL** followed by **ANY LETTER** is valid *except* for

A	AG	AJ	AP AQ	AV	AZ
E		EJ	EQ	EV	EZ
I IB		II IJ	IQ IU		IY IZ
O	OG	OJ	OQ		OZ
U UB UC UD UE UF	UI UJ UK UL		UQ	UW UX UY	

GROUP 3 The following **DOUBLE CONSONANT** words are *valid*

dw hm hv hw nw sh st vg vp vs wp wr ws yd yf yk yl yn yr ys yt yw

The choice is yours!

game. It has long been a favourite pastime of word lovers everywhere and devotees even form their own informal clubs with leagues and knockout tournaments to play this truly addictive game.

You do not have to be an expert to play, but *don't* attempt to introduce it to someone who is baffled by the rudiments of Hangman and fails to obtain the simplest of words. Such a person would never appreciate the elimination skills so essential for success. It is a game for two players, both of whom hide their workings from each other. In the following example of play, Jack will use the **Words Word Table** detailed shortly and attempt to discover a particularly obscure word chosen by Jill and, for the sake of contrast, Jill will play a totally random game in an attempt to discover an ordinary everyday word chosen by Jack. In reality, two players normally start off by selecting ordinary words and progress to the obscure as expertise develops. They have no such visual aid as the **Words Word Table** – this represents Jack's experience with the game. Jill has never played it before, but she is nobody's fool.

Jack chooses the word, BREAD. Jill chooses the word, XENON. Neither tells the other what the 5-letter word is. The object of the game being the discovery of the other's unknown word first. The winner will always emerge within twenty guesses at the opponent's word. The Jack and Jill example is rooted in normal play, it has *not* been specially contrived.

First, however, a word or two of caution.

Players will make mistakes not in guessing but in replying. Such mistakes will be genuine and, for this reason apart from any other, it is vital that you follow the basic instructions. Mistakes of this sort are very frustrating and misleading and, once discovered, the game is normally abandoned and a fresh pair of words chosen. All words for all games are 5-letter words. Neither Jack nor Jill will make any mistakes.

When playing the game, you will not need to write down anything other than shown below in block capitals. Some books on word games show 'working alphabets' in their instructions. The writers of those books have either never played the game or else used inferior logic. You will only *ever* need to write down the words which you say to your opponent and the words which your opponent says to you. The net result is that you will have two vertical tables of 5-letter words. One containing guesses at your word, the other containing guesses at your opponent's word.

You base all your strategy on the developing table of guesses at your opponent's word. The table which develops under your own word will assist discussion over a possible 'mistake' − such discussion is quite frequent but usually groundless. It normally arises when a player has made a wrong assumption. This would occur if (say) Jill guessing at BREAD said 'TROOP' and was told that she had one of the letters correct but not *which* letter (the R) and, for her next guess, said 'BLOCK' and was also told she had a letter correct. As the O is common to both words she could easily assume, as many people do, that Jack's word has an O as the middle letter. Whereas what he *has* answered is that his word has a B for the first letter and an R for the second letter. *Two* letters *not* one

Rules
1. You always say how many letters correspond directly in *position* with the *original* word. For example, a guess at BREAD with BEARD should produce a reply of 'Two'. Only the B and the D share a *common position*.

2. You *never* give clues, you only ever state a number. You *never* impose limits on choice of word. You *may* have a tacit understanding to restrict play to 'normal' words, but that is for beginners only.
3. All guessing words (as BEARD for BREAD) *must* be real words. If, as with Jack, he has already discovered .ENON but does not yet know the first letter (X for XENON) he may *not* make up 'funny words' such as 'AENON', 'BENON', CENON' etc. in order to discover it. He already *knows* .ENON so, in order to eliminate A, B or C, he must say such as APPLE, BEAKS, CHASM or whatever. Only when he gets a reply of 'One' to such as XIPHS may he say XENON (assuming that he has never heard of the word). A reply of 'Nil' to APPLE tells him that it cannot be 'AENON' and a reply of 'one' to BEAKS tells him it cannot be 'BENON' as he already knows that E is the second letter, so the 'One'*has* to be that E.
4. Whoever has the first guess *must* allow his or her opponent one last guess to tie the match if that first player should prove successful.

Jack and Jill are now ready to play and both mark the tops of their pieces of paper as follows:

Jack head his columns ME and SHE and underneath ME he writes the word she is attempting to discover. Underneath SHE he writes five dots to represent the unknown letters. These are sufficiently widely spaced for him to pencil in the letters as they are discovered.

Jill heads her columns ME and HE (or whatever other description suits her mood) and writes XENON under ME and five dots under HE.

Jack is to guess first. We will follow his progress knowing that experience will have him following the pattern shown by the **Words Word Table**. Jill's sound tactics, albeit random, can be discerned. The 'funny' words Jack uses will be defined in the Appendix. We begin at the point where Jack has made his first guess. He is attempting to discover vowels, beginning with the most common of all, hence the 'funny' word SEEER.

ME	SHE
BREAD	. . . . .
	S E E E R 1

Immediately Jill has to say 'One'. So he puts a 1 beside SEEER. He does not know which of the five letters it is, so he will begin a process of logical elimination.

The next example is four guesses later when he has established that the second letter is E. Meanwhile he has recorded Jill's guesses under the appropriate column. He also records the numbers appropriate to both him and her. X denotes nil.

```
ME                SHE
BREAD             . E . . .
EAGLE    X        SEEER    1
ASPIC    X        SEVER    1
LOOPY    X        LEVER    1
CHART    X        LOVER    X
```

As the only difference between LEVER and LOVER is the second letter and LEVER scored one but LOVER scored nil so E *has* to be one of the letters in her word. Her word almost certainly has another vowel, so he will continue to find it.

We next study Jack's sheet at the point where he has *accidently* hit upon the consonant N in his logical pursuit of the second vowel. Once again we are at the point when he knows for certain what it is.

```
ME                SHE
BREAD             . E . . N
EAGLE    X        SEEER    1
ASPIC    X        SEVER    1
LOOPY    X        LEVER    1
CHART    X        LOVER    X
PETER    X        EXINE    X
SINUS    X        ARABA    X
QUEEN    1        BANAL    1
QUEAN    2        CANAL    1
QUART    X        CABAL    X
```

Whilst Jack knows *both* his letters, Jill is certain of only one, the A. However, she knows that the other is either E or N. She will soon catch Jack up. She did *not* guess wildly with QUART but very sensibly, looked back through her guesses and combined the barren CHART with the fruitful QUEAN. Also notice how she very cleverly switched her vowels and consonants around in her first ever 'fishing expedition' for a starting letter. Jack is already beginning to suspect that the next word he chooses for her for their next game will have to be a 'swine' – a CRWTH or a LLAMA or something equally horrendous.

THE WORDS WORD TABLE

In order to establish the 'shape' of an unknown word the quickest way is to find its vowels. True, there are some peculiar words such as OOMPH which prove exceptions to the normal rule but a table such as this will lead you directly to at least one vowel within seconds. Even OOMPH will have its second letter revealed in just nine guesses at the most.

SEEER	EXINE	ARABA	BANAL	VIVID	BOOBY	IGLOO	OUUEN	XYLYL
sever	exile	Arabs	canal	livid	booty		outen	
lever	axile	crabs	cabal	lived	booth		outer	
lover	anile	cribs	cabel	lives	broth		cuter	
loves	anils	crits	caber	gives				

You begin by saying SEEER. If the response is nil move directly to EXINE. Thus all five possible positions for an E, the most commonly used letter of the alphabet, have now been covered. A similar, but imperfect, treatment is accorded to the other vowels. A direct horizontal run of SEEER, EXINE, ARABA, BANAL, VIVID and BOOBY has covered, from the standpoint of normal vowel usage, in excess of 90% of the 5-letter words in the English language. This means that, nine times out of ten, you are going to get a positive response in just six guesses at the unknown word.

If the answer for SEEER is one or more then you progress *down* the SEEER list until you receive the answer, 'Nil'. At whichever word you receive the answer of nil then the letter you are seeking is the one you have just changed in the word *directly above*. Thus, if you are told 'One' for SEEER but 'Nil' for SEVER then the letter you have discovered is the middle E. If it is 'One' for SEEER, 'One' for SEVER but 'Nil' for LEVER then you have *accidentally* discovered a consonant, the S. This is a bonus and you should still continue the hunt for vowels. If you are told 'Two' for SEEER, 'Two' for SEVER, 'One' for LEVER (this is the S, of course), 'One' for LOVER and 'Nil' for LOVES the word you are seeking begins with an S and ends with an R. As you have eliminated all possibility of an E being part of that word so it *has* to be something like SOLAR or SONAR (you will not be facing 'clever' words like SKIRR at the beginner level of play) and so you are still really hunting for vowels to establish the 'shape'.

If you receive a reply of 'Nil' to SEEER move directly to EXINE for your second guess – to explore the SEEER list under these circumstances is a sheer waste of time and effort. Therefore, you travel along the top line until you obtain a positive response and, as previously stated, by the time you have guessed with SEEER, EXINE, ARABA, BANAL, VIVID and BOOBY you are virtually certain to gain a positive response.

But a negative response is still possible (and by negative this means

Jack has yet to find that second vowel. True, it could be a word such as WENCH but the odds still favour a second vowel. We next see him lighting upon it but accidentally hitting and confirming a second consonant *before* he is certain of the vowel.

ME		SHE	
BREAD		E N . N .	
EAGLE	X	SEEER	1
ASPIC	X	SEVER	1
LOOPY	X	LEVER	1
CHART	X	LOVER	X
PETER	X	EXINE	X
SINUS	X	ARABA	X
QUEEN	1	BANAL	1
QUEAN	2	CANAL	1
QUART	X	CABAL	X
ASPEN	X	VIVID	X
WREAK	3	SENOR	3
BREAK	4	TENOR	3
BREAM	4	TENON	4

To hell with it! Jill is *definitely* going to get a snorter next time! Jack is under pressure. He knows that Jill has B R E A . but he is facing either T E N . N or . E N O N.

The word he is attempting to find *cannot* be 'TENEN' (if such exists) as he has already eliminated E as a fourth letter (with LOVER). Equally it cannot be 'TENAN' or 'TENIN' and TENON is only worth 4. Could it be 'TENUN' or 'TENYN'? Doubtful. That leaves 'DENON' (he has already eliminated the possibilities of the first letter being A, B, C as well as E, L, S, T and V) but 'FENON', 'GENON', etc? It is a race, and he can only tie at best. Jill is *bound* to say BREAD next time and she still has a move in hand.

'HENON'? 'IENON'? 'JENON'? 'KENON'? 'MENON'? 'NENON'? 'OENON'? 'PENON'? Surely never 'QENON' – but she *does* know an awful lot of those peculiar Q words without a U, look how many times she used them in Hangman! 'RENON'?

The result is immaterial, the game is great. I thoroughly recommend it. If you like word games, you will love this one.

(*Note that Jack missed out BOOBY in the Words Word Table. He already knew the second and third letters, so BOOBY was a complete waste of 'vowel hunting' time.*)

no vowels – consonants are a bonus) and you *know* that the word is going to be a 'funny' one. It could be such as IGLOO, so try it. A nil response now eliminates three of the few remaining vowels. A positive response is a problem. How can you change IGLOO letter-by-letter in order to identify the relevant letter? You may be able to but you would need to know some very peculiar words to achieve this. The better policy is to try the most likely (such as the O in the fourth position) and guess with such as STROP which can be changed to STRAP for confirmation.

If nothing happens with IGLOO try the short OUUEN list. It will *not* turn out to be a QU- word as QU- is *always* followed by one of the vowels which you have already eliminated. It will, if the answer is positive, be a word like THUMB.

If it is *still* nil then it is going to be one of the following non-vowel words – and XYLYL followed by CRYPT is as good a pair to start with as any.

crwth	crypt	cysts	dryly	fyrds	ghyll	gymps	gyppy	gypsy	hwyls
hymns	lymph	lynch	myrrh	mysts	nymph	pygmy	pytch	rynds	rynts
rythm	shyly	shynd	skynd	skynk	slyly	styth	sylph	synch	syncs
synds	thymy	tryst	tymps	wryly	wynds	wynns	wytch	xylyl	xysts

(Of the above only CRWTH and XYLYL are defined in the Appendix but all are extant words. However, restrict play to those which you can prove to exist by consulting your own dictionary.)

Finally, if you are wondering why the I and the U for the fifth positions have not been covered try constructing a word like COYPU or RADII for which you have *not* already had a previous positive response. The same is equally true for the U in the fourth position as even a 'clever' word such as GYRUS has had its Y revealed by XYLYL. True, your opponent *might* know a word such as THRUM but if you play at a level which has words of this type then you are already an expert and will know how to cope wth it anyway. Thus you would also know words such as UMPTY or YCLAD to complete a personal Words word table which has all of the vowels and the Y in every possible position.

6. SUPERWORDS

The author's own variation on **Words** for three or more players. Only those already familiar with the skills of **Words** should attempt it.

When playing with three players, each person has two words for the others to find. The winner being the one who finds *both* unknown words, one from each opponent.

For example, Tom, Dick and Harriet are to play a three-way contest.

Tom chooses IGLOO for Dick and MYRRH for Harriet. Dick chooses QWATE for Tom and YCLAD for Harriet. Harriet chooses ZYGAL for Tom and FLUFF for Dick. They play a mean game!

Each player now compiles four lists. From Tom's standpoint it will look like this:—

DICK   HARRIET
he   me   she   me
. . . . .   I G L O O   . . . . .   M Y R R H

Each player now questions *both* of the others in turn. Tom will guess at Dick's word and write down the result. He will then guess at Harriet's word and write down the result.

Dick will then have his two guesses, followed by Harriet with her two guesses. Play continues in this fashion. Even if Dick and Harriet have both guessed Tom's words for them, he is still in the hunt until someone obtains both the hunted words. All that happens in this situation is that Dick and Harriet now ignore Tom and battle with each other whilst Tom (assuming he has not scored yet) still makes 'conversation' with them.

The author enjoys Superwords and, though he has never tried it with four or more, sees no reason why it cannot be attempted. Those who do will need wide paper.

7. JOTTO

Jotto should *not* be confused with the classic game, **Words**. Jotto is logical deduction for the hard of thinking. This time, instead of being told that one has found two of the letters in the mystery word, BREAD, by guessing with BEARD one is told that all five have been found.

Obviously one is seeking an anagram of BEARD.

8. JOTTO VARIATIONS

There are two. For the first one you make it even easier for the person guessing at BREAD with BEARD by saying,'Two in the correct position and three in the incorrect position.'

The second, devised by Don Laycock, is more subtle. This time, any guess you make at your opponent's word must be accompanied by a statement as to how many of these letters also occur in your own word.

Not as childish as it may seem, and Laycock's Jotto is the only one of the three forms of Jotto worthy of adult attention.

9. LITTLE DOMINOES

Two players write down – but keep secret from each other – six valid 2-letter words. Thus:–

JACK   AT, IN, ON, NO, TO, SO
JILL   BO, OB, GO, OO, TO, AT

Ignore the fact that BO, OB and OO are unusual words (they are defined in the Appendix) but note that the players have the words AT and TO in common. This is significant as no word may be repeated in play. How this is resolved will be explained later.

Jill is to play first and, on the mutual playing sheet, she writes the word OO in a little box. For fun she has it domino-style and writes it vertically. This is not necessary – all of the play is restricted to a horizontal plane – but makes for easier illustration in this example. Jill crosses OO off her secret list.

Jack now writes the word TO in a little box. This is in the accepted horizontal plane and has to be to the left of OO so that the letters in common are conjoined. Jack crosses TO off his list.

Jill plays AT. The position is thus:-

and now both of the words in common have been played. This was not contrived, but logical play in the circumstances.

Jack plays ON. Jill cannot make a move.
Jack plays NO. Jill plays OB.

Jack's remaining words are AT, IN, SO. Though none fit as they stand he does have the letter A available for a link if he can contrive a valid 2-letter word from any combination of his six letters. Therefore, he plays the word TA.

Jill plays BO.
Jack has IN and SO remaining. How can he use the O? He cannot

contrive ON, this has already been played. He does not wish to play the exclamation OI as this will leave him an utterly unplayable combination of N and S. He chooses the word OS.

Jill cannot make a move.

Jack cannot make a move.

Jack wins on the letter count. He has only two letters (the word IN) whereas Jill has four letters (the words GO and TO). The final appearance of the game is:-

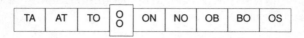

TA	AT	TO	O O	ON	NO	OB	BO	OS

What 2-letter words may one play? Essentially those which are given in your particular dictionary. However, the whole subject is discussed at greater length in the special article, **2-Letter Words** on page 95.

10. CLEWLOW'S DOMINOES

Two players agree upon a subject (say) ANIMALS. The object of the game is to force the opponent to surrender. No word may be repeated and no hyphenated compounds or two word descriptions (such as MUSK OX) may be used.

Unlike Little Dominoes, play is in both horizontal and vertical planes. But, like Little Dominoes, there are only two ends open for play. Thus, only the T and R of TIGER may be used, but these may be either the first or last letters of any valid word. Therefore, if TIGER is the first word played, one has four options. Once (say) the R of TIGER has been used it cannot be used again. At all times there are two ends and four options. The skill lies in creating 'dead' ends. A fairly quick game might end thus:—

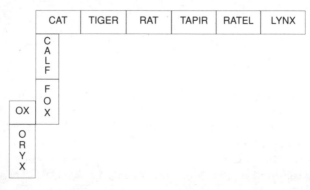

	CAT	TIGER	RAT	TAPIR	RATEL	LYNX

Whoever played the last 'X word' has won and if he knows that such as ASPALAX, HYRAX or ADDAX are still available keeps quiet about it. He wishes to force a surrender.

(The first of two games devised by Charles Clewlow.)

11. CLEWLOW'S SUPER DOMINOES

A strictly adult version of Clewlow's Dominoes with the playing format exactly as before.

However, this time both players write down the complete alphabet and the object of the game is to be the first to utilize every letter of the alphabet.

The letters may occur in any part of the domino played. Thus, if a player begins a game based on ANIMALS with the word QUAGGA then he or she deletes the letters Q, U, A and G from the personal alphabet.

If an impasse should arise with both players agreeing that no further play is possible or fruitful then the one with the greater number of letters utilized is the winner.

For word rules see page 114.

(The second of two games devised by Charles Clewlow.)

12. SIMON DOE

Simon Doe is one of the many anagrams of the word DOMINOES. There are dozens.

This is a domino game in which the winner is the first to play an anagram of an agreed word or short phrase. The only stipulation is that the anagram must be a minimum of two words.

A neutral word is agreed as the opening domino. Thus, if DOMINOES is the word, then ANAGRAM would make a perfect starting point as neither its first nor its last letters provide a link for any possible anagram. Finally, a subject is agreed (say) BIRDS. The words played must be either birds or else those which form part of one's anagram.

Only genuine words may be played and there is no objection to any of the three standard English single-letter words A, I or O. This means that such as SO DEMON I or O MISDONE are perfectly acceptable.

The skills lie not only in playing out the dominoes but in retaining the flexible combinations of letters till later. It would be silly, therefore, to play MISDONE and retain the single-letter word O. Far better to play O and save the flexibility of MISDONE. An even better play would be either OD or DO and retaining letters capable of becoming EONISM, MONIES or SIMEON.

The layout and rules are otherwise identical to Clewlow's Dominoes or else those of Chesterfield. The Clewlow formula tends towards 'wide open spaces' whilst the Chesterfield formula can lend itself to tactical play by restricting the opponent's freedom of access to essential space.

13. CHESTERFIELD

Probably the most dramatically different and demanding of all the games in this book is **The War Game**. Chesterfield is but Stage One of that six stage epic of word play for the truly competitive. However, the opening stage stands as a pleasant little game in its own right and the non-military title simply commemorates the fact that it was first played in that Derbyshire town.

Graph paper is ideal, but not essential, for this 2-person, twin subject challenge of the domino genre. Unlike any of the preceding domino games, words are not in individual boxes and 'end letters' are written once only.

First of all, players agree on a pair of subjects acceptable to both, (say) CAPITALS and COUNTRIES. One player then writes a 'secret list' of six capitals whilst the other writes a similar list of six countries. In the course of play other capitals and countries will need to be used, but players are restricted to their individual subjects. The object of the game being the first to play all of his or her six chosen words. Henceforth, these will be referred to as dominoes. All other words used in play will simply be called words.

The full word rules will be given in due course, but the essential rules are that only subject words may be used in play and no word may be repeated. Finally, a pin is stuck in a book or newspaper and the nearest 3-letter word to the pin is written in the centre of the graph paper. For convenience, this is called the 'pinword' and it provides the two end letters from which play will begin.

Two examples of play will be given. The first illustrates the basic action. The second illustrates other aspects.

EXAMPLE NUMBER ONE
Player A selected CAPITALS. His dominoes were LONDON, BERLIN, AMSTERDAM, MADRID, ROME and VIENNA.

Player B selected COUNTRIES. His dominoes were ALBANIA, FINLAND, SPAIN, DENMARK, THAILAND and AFGHANISTAN. The pinword was THE.

A spin of the coin had B going first. He played his domino, THAILAND, descending vertically from the T of the pinword:–

```
THE        His opponent then added MADRID as shown          THE
H          on the right:–                                    H
A                                                            A
I                                                            I
L                                                            L
A                                                            A
N                                                            N
D                                                       MADRID
```

The full game ended in this fashion:–

```
                                    V
                                    I
                                    E
                                    N
                                    N
                    R U M A N I A           L
                        O                   O
                        M                   N
                    T H E                   D
                    H                       O
                    A           A F G H A N I S T A N
                    I           M
                    L           S
                    A           T
                    N           E
        M A D R I D             R
        A                       D
        U                       A
        R       B E L G I U M
        I       E
        T       R
        I       L
        U       I
        S P A I N
```

EXAMPLE NUMBER TWO Anonymity of players is respected. One made a very significant error and the other failed to spot it. They are described as A and B.

A chose the following dominoes: TIGER, LION, HORSE, DZO, ELEPHANT and SNAKE.

B had MERLIN, EAGLE, FALCON, OSPREY, WINDHOVER and 'KITTYHAWK'.

The pinword was AND.

DZO was known to both and was no problem. WINDHOVER, which was never played, might have caused difficulties according to whichever reference work one may have resorted to in the event of a dispute. *Chambers* dictionary has it hyphenated as 'wind-hover'. But, who can argue with the *Oxford English* dictionary, which clearly shows it as a single word?!!

'KITTYHAWK' is where the trouble lies. It is not to be found in any dictionary or ornithological work. KITTY HAWK does appear, however, in the *Encyclopaedia Britannica*. It is the *place* where the Wright Brothers first flew an aeroplane! As both are respected Scrabble players at the highest competitive level, then B should have known this and A should have challenged.

What is significant is that the players both had opportunities to utilize the N of MARTIN for their dominoes.

LION had to be rejected as this would have clashed with the A of YELLOWHAMMER and produced a nonsensical 'ALION'. FALCON could have gone through YELLOWHAMMER in this form:–

```
      O          A
      W          T
      H          I
F  A  L  C  O  N
      M
```

but again had to be rejected as words cannot be interlinked.

Chesterfield has an intriguing twist. Unlike Clewlow's Dominoes, players may ask each other for help if they are stuck. Of course you help them – to a word which helps you!

The completed game is shown on the opposite page.

Either as Stage One of The War Game or as an independent game, Chesterfield requires its contestants to choose naturally related pairs of subjects. Ideally, these should be ones for which you possess some reference work or works which can be consulted in

```
                              D Z O
                              R   S
                              A   P
                              K   R
                      S N A K E   E
                      K           Y A K
                      U               I
                      A N D           T
                        U             T
                        C             Y
                        K I N E       H
                          A           A
                          G           W
                          L       K U D U
                      H O R S E         N
                      A                 I
G N U                 W                 C
E                     K                 O
E   A S S             Y                 R
S   U   H             E         M E R L I N
E L K   A             L         A
      G O O S E       L         R
            L         O         T
            E         W         I
            P         H         N U M B A T
            H         A               E
            A         M               R
            N         M           L I O N
            T I G E R
```

113

the event of a dispute. But, any subjects can be grist to your Chesterfield mill such as:

BOYS & GIRLS	(forenames)
LEFT & RIGHT	(political surnames)
TIME & MOTION	(months, zodiac signs/modes of transport)
WORK & PLAY	(occupation/games)
HERE & THERE	(home country cities/foreign cities)
WET & DRY	(geographical locations or creatures)
SOAP & WATER	(soap opera characters/fishes)
NUTS & BOLTS	(objectionable politicians/athletes)
FAST & FURIOUS	(athletes/boxers)

or any other combinations which have mutual appeal. Both players must agree *both* subjects as part of the skill lies in second guessing what dominoes the opponent is likely to have.

Word Rules for Chesterfield, Clewlow's Dominoes/Super Dominoes and Simon Doe

1. All words used in play must be capable of being confirmed in an agreed reference work such as an atlas or a dictionary in the event of a challenge.
2. All words must be within the category specified. For example. If the subject is CITIES, both EDINBURGH and GLASGOW are acceptable. But, if the subject is CAPITALS only EDINBURGH may be played.
3. An erroneous word must be removed and replaced with a valid word. If, however, it cannot be removed by virtue of having been utilized in a subsequent play it is deemed to be 'acceptable'.
4. If an erroneous word is also a domino an alternative domino must be added to the player's 'secret list'. First, however, the offending word (say) 'KITTYHAWK' must be replaced by (say) KITTIWAKE then the new domino chosen with letters incapable of being used at either end of the chain. Thus, if the two ends have KITTIWAKE and (say) TIGER with the T available, the new word may not either begin or end with the letters T or E.
5. Hyphenated compounds or two word descriptions are not permitted. Thus, only SPARROW is acceptable not HOUSE SPARROW and/or TREE SPARROW.
6. All words must be correctly spelt.
7. Standard plurals using an S are not permitted. The reason is that no contest could possibly ensue if one player's dominoes

were such as SWANS, SWALLOWS, SPARROWS, SKUAS, SHRIKES and SNIPES and his or her opponent had SHREWS, SNAKES, SERPENTS, SCORPIONS, SLUGS and SKINKS. Equally, if only one had plurals then he or she could pluralize every non-domino played (EAGLES, FALCONS etc.) and so create a totally unfair game. There is no objection to such as OXEN or GEESE. These can be fairly construed as being different words to OX or GOOSE. To argue that SHEEP in one play is singular and in another play is plural will not be accepted. GEESE, GOOSE and GANDER are all acceptable as are EWE, LAMB, RAM, TUP and SHEEP.

8. No incidental words *even if within the acceptable category* may be simultaneously created by the playing of any word. Apart from the natural connection, all words in play must be a minimum of one letter space distant from any other word already written down.

9. It is the responsibility of the opponent to challenge any word used in play.

For Simon Doe and the two Clewlow games these exceptions apply.

(a) There is no objection to plurals

(b) When an invalid word is played it must be removed and the opponent now has the option of either insisting upon a replacement word or else taking that opportunity to make a play for himself or herself.

14. THE WAR GAME

A saga for two wordsmiths with stamina.

The game will be played in stages but, first, the battlefield will need to be drawn, ideally on stiff card. This is a 4 × 3 grid, divided as shown, and on a scale large enough to accommodate whatever (such as coins or buttons) you will use as playing pieces.

North

1	3	6
2	5	6
4	5	3
4	2	1

South

You will require two sets of six pieces which are easily distinguished. For example, six 2 pence coins and six 10 pence coins.

STAGE ONE Play a game of Chesterfield (page 110) in order to acquire the cannon fodder for the subsequent battle. This will consist of the dominoes you are able to play. For each domino played so you gain a playing piece and the strength of these pieces will depend upon the total stock of individual letters contained within the played dominoes. No word, however, may consist of more than fifteen letters.

The winner of the Chesterfield stage will have six pieces but the loser must have at least one piece or else the contest is over at this point. The loser, however, will normally have three, four or five pieces.

Bearing in mind what you will need in the battle stage, described below, so you should select dominoes not only capable of winning that stage but of the greatest value for the battle.

STAGE TWO As the battlefield is divided into territories of North and South, so the example will use these same terms for the combatants.

Assume that North won the Chesterfield stage with the following dominoes:–
ALBATROSS, EAGLE, YELLOWHAMMER, TEAL, PENGUIN and SPARROW

South managed to play the following:– STICKLEBACK, CANDLEFISH, STINGAREE AND STEELHEAD

First of all, North will cover all of his home territory with (say) the 10 pence pieces and South having only four words will cover his tracts of territory numbered 1 to 4 with 2 pence pieces. South is now vulnerable to attack on tracts 5 or 6.

Players assign numbers to each domino, writing these down and leaving them on open display.

North has
1 TEAL
2 EAGLE
3 PENGUIN
4 SPARROW
5 YELLOWHAMMER
6 ALBATROSS

Additionally, North must arrange his troops in battle formation which consists of splitting each domino into 'regiments' of 4-letter words with 'reserve units' of a single letter. This is written down, but kept secret.

```
1 TEAL
2 GALE      E
3 PINE      N,  G,  U
4 SPAR      R,  O,  W
5 ROME, YELL, WHAM
6 BATS, ORAL       S
```

Three is the maximum permitted for both regiments and reserves for any individual number. Thus, the longest possible domino consists of 15 letters. A player who miscounts at Stage One and has (say) a 16-letter domino which is successful, loses it completely at this point.

If (using the example of 5, YELLOWHAMMER) a player either decides to, or can only, construct a number of regiments which produces a remainder of four letters (ROME, ELLA plus W, H, M, Y) then all four remaining letters have to be discarded. Only the two regiments are available for play. This means that words of 4, 8 or 12 letters must be divided into an exact number of regiments.

It follows that neither a 2-letter nor a 3-letter word can possibly form a regiment. Therefore, such words may *not* be selected as dominoes for stage one. There is no objection, of course, to 2- and 3-letter words being used in normal Stage One play. A player who, for whatever reason, selects (say) a 3-letter word as a domino is deemed to have transgressed rule 4 of Chesterfield and action is taken under that rule.

South, not having six dominoes, must assign two numbers to two of the words. Thus (say) 3 is also 5 and 4 is also 6. This information is made known to the opponent on the open display sheet. South's strategic data is as follows

```
1      DEAL, CHIN      F,S,       (from CANDLEFISH)
2      KICK, SEAL      B, C, T    (from STICKLEBACK)
3/5    EAST, HEED      L          (from STEELHEAD)
4/6    TEAR, GINS      E          (from STINGAREE)
```

South's counters are placed on squares 1, 2, 3 and 4.

The stage is now set for North to invade with any adjacent army. 6 SOUTH can be occupied either from 6 NORTH or 5 NORTH, 5 SOUTH can be occupied from either 5 NORTH or 4 NORTH. North *must* invade. The 'silver' army is on the march.

STAGE THREE Have to hand your dictionary, your atlas, your book of children's names and anything else you can think of. You will be disputing words left, right and centre. This is war.

The numbers assigned to each word relate to the square occupied by a counter. Thus, at the start of this example of play, North has three counters capable of occupying either of South's two vacant squares. Each counter is an army and its effectiveness depends upon the terrain where it operates. The three armies capable of invasion are located at 4 NORTH, 5 NORTH and 6 NORTH.

4 NORTH's army, if it remains where it is, has the power assigned to 4. In this example, SPARROW. But, the moment it occupies 5 SOUTH, its power changes and is that of YELLOW-HAMMER.

5 NORTH's army is that of 5, YELLOWHAMMER. If it invades 5 SOUTH it remains as YELLOWHAMMER. But, if it invades 6 SOUTH it becomes ALBATROSS.

6 NORTH's army invading 6 SOUTH begins and remains as ALBATROSS.

Moves are made only in a horizontal or vertical direction and battles are fought against an opponent located horizontally or vertically.

The initiative rests entirely with the attacker who, on moving an army, announces which enemy he intends to attack.

By attacking 3 SOUTH, North is facing the power of STEELHEAD.

By attacking 2 SOUTH, North is facing the power of STICKLEBACK.

The object of the game is to destroy the enemy letter by letter, word by word until he is either completely annihilated or else forced to attend a peace conference where he will lose the diplomatic arguments.

It is a vicious battle of literary attrition.

All battles must be decisive. This means that one side must lose a minimum of a complete regiment before a change of tactics is permitted. Reserves may be used in a battle or else held back for subsequent warfare. As casualties occur (the loss of a letter) these are recorded on the open display sheets by the deletion of that letter. Players are advised, but this is not mandatory, to mark their own secret lists accordingly.

In the following example of a battle fought between North and South, the first engagement will be between a Northern army located at 6 SOUTH and a Southern army located at 3 SOUTH.

Square 6 will give North the power of ALBATROSS which he has divided into two regiments. One is codenamed BATS, the other is codenamed ORAL. There is only one reserve, the letter S.

Square 3 will give South the power of the regiments EAST and HEED together with the solitary reserve, L.

All battles are decided by your ability to construct anagrams. Each anagram you produce must be matched by your enemy or else he will lose a letter (providing that he has a reserve to take its place) or else the complete 4-letter word from which he was constructing those anagrams.

Obviously, the anagrams are made from the codename of a regiment. Equally obvious is the fact that it is not the potential of the regiment which matters but your own ability to utilize that potential.

Everything hinges upon your personal word power. But, the game is not a simple test of anagramming ability it has as much to do with genuine game play tactics as any you will ever encounter. If you enjoy both words and games you will love this one.

North decides to invade 6 SOUTH from 6 NORTH. It is now Force ALBATROSS versus Force STEELHEAD. Neither yet knows which regiment will attack nor which will defend. The attacker opens the engagement by announcing the codename of a regiment (say) BATS and the defender now replies with the codename of a regiment (say) EAST. A strict time limit is enforced (say) 10 seconds for each salvo. Failure results in the loss of a complete regiment.

North:	BATS	(Opening with the regimental codename)
South:	EAST	(Replying with the regimental codename)
North:	TABS	(First anagram of codename)
South:	SEAT	(First anagram of codename)
North:	STAB	(Second anagram of codename)
South:	TEAS	(etc.)
North:	BAST	
South:	SATE	
North:	TABS	
South:	Repetition! Choose another word.	
North:	S is dead. (He deletes S from the display sheet) I am	

bringing in a reserve, a second S. I am now attacking with TABS.

South: EATS
North: BATS
South: ASTE
North: Challenge! No such word.

The dictionary is consulted and no such word discovered. South must now forfeit the complete regiment. This is deleted from the display sheet. The battle was decisive. As the winner, North has all the options.

1. He may continue with the same attack. Even though TABS and BATS have already been used in the reinforced regiment, they are still available for the next battle. This same attack may stem from either BATS or ORAL.
2. He may withdraw the depleted ALBATROSS and see what South decides to do.

If North withdraws, South may now move one of his own counters. This effectively changes his defences. These are his options and the results.

(a) Advance the counter from 3 SOUTH to 6 SOUTH. This counter no longer represents the depleted STEELHEAD but now, if defending, is STINGAREE
(b) Move from 3 SOUTH to 5 SOUTH and it will remain as STEELHEAD if attacked
(c) Move from 2 SOUTH to 5 SOUTH and convert a strong defensive STICKLEBACK into a weakened STEELHEAD
(d) Waive the option of the move.

North withdraws.
South remains in position.
North advances from 5 NORTH to 5 SOUTH. He announces that he is attacking 3 SOUTH (now only HEED, L) with YELLOW-HAMMER.

NORTH: ROME
SOUTH: HEED
NORTH: MORE
SOUTH: D is dead (D is deleted from his display sheet) and L is coming from the reserves.
HEEL

NORTH: The regiment is completely wiped out (E, M, O, R deleted) but I am bringing in a fresh regiment.
　　　　YELL
SOUTH: Surrender.

The whole of STEELHEAD has been destroyed. STEELHEAD is both 3 and 5, either North or South. South has now been seriously weakened. Any of his counters on any 3 or 5 is powerless. A counter may be moved to one of these but it will be instantly annihilated if attacked. This effectively reduces South to defending his bottom line of 4, 2 and 1. North can move his armies around at will. South needs to remain where he is.

North retains a counter on 4 NORTH. He does not wish South to have access to his territory other than by risking his forces crossing the deathtrap of the L-shaped 3/5 line. He has counters on 5 SOUTH and 3 SOUTH poised to attack. South does nothing. An attack is only made immediately following a move. South is prepared to wait.

North considers the situation. His 5 is weak. He attacks with 3. It is, therefore, PENGUIN versus CANDLEFISH.

NORTH: PINE
SOUTH: DEAL
NORTH: NIPE
SOUTH: Challenge! No such word.

The dictionary is consulted and NIPE turns out to be an obsolete noun and verb meaning nip. There being no objection to obsolete words, South must now reply.
SOUTH: LEAD
NORTH: N is dead. (It is deleted) A fresh N from the reserves
　　　　PINE
SOUTH: DALE
NORTH: NIPE
SOUTH: LADE
NORTH: E is dead. G from the reserves.
　　　　PING
SOUTH: LEDA
NORTH: Challenge: No such word.

An encyclopaedia is consulted and LEDA is proved to be the wife of a Spartan king seduced by Zeus in the form of a swan. North must now reply.
NORTH: GNIP
SOUTH: Challenge! No such word.

The dictionary gives it as an obsolete Scottish verb of a horse, to champ on its bit.

SOUTH: L is dead. F from the reserves.

LEAF

North surrenders. He runs out of time attempting to utilize his remaining reserve. The whole of PENGUIN is wiped out and the initiative is with South. South may now attack. He attacks 5 SOUTH from 2 SOUTH (North has only YELL and WHAM remaining from YELLOWHAMMER. South has STICKLEBACK)

SOUTH: SEAL

NORTH: YELL

SOUTH: SALE

NORTH: The regiment has been wiped out. A fresh regiment is taking its place.

WHAM

SOUTH: LEAS

North has been shattered. He still has four armies to South's three but now the 3/5 L shape is dangerous to both. South, however, still has the initiative.

What South does depends upon the position of North's counters. But, however they are placed, the only attacking and defending positions involve a border skirmish.

4 v 4 is a certain skirmish. 6 v 6 is only possible if North does not occupy the safe haven of 6 SOUTH, thus preventing South from venturing onto dangerous ground.

To attack a heavily defended frontier involves a sacrifice. Whoever mounts such an attack must first surrender a reserve or a regiment. South compares the potential of the two 4's. He considers STINGAREE to be far stronger than SPARROW. If North is of the same opinion then he will not attack. But, if South is to begin the skirmish he must sacrifice that valuable E. Unless, of course, he rearranges his forces (North has no idea of what he has) and rid himself of something else. What are his options? These include:—

(a) Keep TEAR, GINS and dispose of E.

(b) Create TEAS, keep E and dispose of GRIN.

(c) Create TEAS, GRIN and dispose of E.

Sensibly, he waits to see if North will attack — surrendering his right of the next move by saying, 'I stick'. North also passes, but South does not wish to attend the peace conference yet. If both players pass twice each in succession, then it is the peace conference and that is not until Stage Six!

South sacrifices GRIN. The attack ends in a tie after twelve sorties.

South plays TEAS, SEAT, EAST, SATE, ETAS and EATS twice by virtue of the E. ETAS is challenged but accepted (see Appendix). North plays SPAR, RAPS, RASP and PARS twice by virtue of the R. Then WRAP, WARP and PRAW. PRAW is challenged and discovered to be a Malayan boat. Finally, he plays PROW.

The battle has been fought to a standstill. No further fighting is possible.

(Note that in the above, final, exchange South could have played such as AETS and TAES (see Appendix) and continued the warfare. For the purpose of illustration, however, unusual words have been kept to a minimum.)

STAGE FIVE North has 21 letters remaining. These consist of TEAL, EAGLE, PROW and 'ALBATROSS'.

South has 25 letters remaining. These consist of CANDLEFISH, STICKLEBACK and TEAS.

They must now prepare to negotiate from strength and the advantage has finally swung in favour of South. As he has the greater number of letters so his total is divided by 6 to determine the number of 'rounds' of negotiations which will be undertaken. Thus, four rounds (6 x 4 = 24) will be the ultimate decider of the whole of this epic.

As the first stage was worthy of a separate name (Chesterfield – it is a game in its own right) so this final stage is equally capable of standing alone in circumstances where players are not handicapped as North now finds himself. It will, therefore, be shown as Conference and found on page 000. The rules of Conference being slightly different to those given below.

Negotiations take place on battlefield-shaped grids. To accommodate four rounds, so each player draws four 3 x 4 grids side by side and keeps them secret.

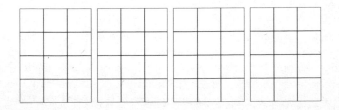

The stage is now set for the conference. However, as with all previous stages, one player can always resign if he considers the odds to be hopeless. But, North has not lost yet.

STAGE SIX Players take turns to call out any of their remaining letters, placing them wherever they wish on whichever grid they wish. Neither player knows where the other is placing his letter.

However, as each letter is called out so it is deleted from the open display sheet and this is a guide to your tactics.

Eventually, North runs out of letters but South may now add his remaining letters to any of the grids that he wishes.

Players tot up their scores. Only 3-letter words in the horizontal plane may be counted and only 4-letter words in the vertical plane may be counted. These score 3 points and 4 points respectively.

The winner of this epic word game is the one with the higher total.

Before attempting the complete War Game, you may well prefer to acquaint yourself with the essential skills of stages one and six. Stage One, Chesterfield, precedes this description and Stage Six, Conference, is the next game described in this book.

Finally, it should be noted that the warfare stage could result in just two 4-letter remnants of armies (say) PROW versus TEAS. A conference is still held with each player drawing his own solitary 3 x 4 grid. This could result in an honourable draw with neither player scoring a point or else various scores of up to a maximum of 8 points could be produced.

The rule for conference rounds is as follows. Divide the higher total by six and ignore any remainder. A minimum of one round is always undertaken if combatants have failed to settle the issue at any earlier stage.

15. CONFERENCE

The origin of this game lies in being the sixth and final stage of **The War Game**, the epic battle of word power and tactical skill for the true wordsmith.

However, played in the context of that very demanding contest it is normally an unequal struggle as players have fought through the preceding stages to gain the advantage at the conference table. As an independent game, Conference is not only a competition between equals but more than two may play. This basic description has a simple Jack versus Jill example with the rules for three or more players given subsequently.

Both players draw two 3 x 4 grids side by side on their personal playing sheets. These are kept secret. They now choose any two 6-letter words which they write down on separate sheets and display quite openly. Jack has (say) DAMAGE and QUEENS. Jill has (say) EXTRAS and SEEING.

Players now take turns in calling out letters from their chosen 6-letter words.

Jack calls out (say) G. He puts this anywhere he wishes on either of his grids. He crosses out the G in DAMAGE. Jill also writes G anywhere she wishes on either of her grids.

Jill now calls out (say) I. The procedure is exactly the same.

As play progresses so players gradually formulate the final patterns knowing what to expect. But, with this subtle difference, *not all of the letters will be called*. Both players will leave out two of their letters! Thus, Conference has some of the villainy of its origin – The War Game. In The War Game all letters are used but unequal numbers are available and similarly incomplete grids pertain.

DAMAGE, QUEENS, EXTRAS and SEEING were genuinely chosen at random. Jack chose QUEENS to make it difficult for Jill (he controls the Q and the U), Jill chose EXTRAS for a tricky X in a combination of highly flexible letters.

However, if we now presume that Jill says the letter T in addition to the I which she has already stated, then Jack is in a position to display gamesmanship at its most devilish. At no time will Jack say the letter U. But, his final letter will be the Q! The reason for this will be obvious when their final grids are compared and scored.

The object of the game is to score points. 3 points are awarded for every 3-letter word in a horizontal line, 4 points for every 4-letter word read from top to bottom in a vertical line. No other words count. The skill lies in maximising the two-way potential of each letter.

First, we will score Jill's grid and see that she had to dump that frustrating Q where it gave her the least trouble:–

S	A	G	3		T	E	A	3
I		E			A		X	
N		N			R	Q	E	Nil
E	M	E	3		E		D	
4		4			4		4	

125

Jill scored 25 points (see Appendix for EME). If Jack had said U instead of Q she could have scored an extra 3 points for either NUN or RUE. She merely stuck the Q in an available square.

Jack played a very different game and won with a score of 31 points. His masterstroke was the production of the unusual Q without a U words, QADI and QAT (see Appendix). ISM is also defined in the Appendix.

Q	A	T	3
A	X	E	3
D	E	A	Nil
I	S	M	3
4	4	4	

G	E	N	3
E			
N			
E	R	E	3
4			

For three players, draw three similar grids. Still select two 6-letter words each and, again, each holds back two letters.

For four players, four grids, two 6-letter words each but, this time, hold back only one letter. Beyond four it will cease to be enjoyable.

Two players, especially those in training for The War Game, may care to try a three grid version in which both select three 6-letter words. Only, this time, both hold back three letters.

16. SECRET SNAKES AND LADDERS

Great fun for all the family as the acknowledged expert can lose just as easily as anybody else – and doesn't that make a delightful change! True, there is a little more skill to it than throwing dice but the game is essentially the same as traditional Snakes and Ladders.

Draw a large scale grid (say) 8 x 8, or larger if you prefer, and number these squares in the traditional Snakes and Ladders format:–

A	64	63	62	61	60	59	58	57
B	49	50	51	52	53	54	55	56
C	48	47	46	45	44	43	42	41
D	33	34	35	36	37	38	39	40
E	32	31	30	29	28	27	26	25
F	17	18	19	20	21	22	23	24
G	16	15	14	13	12	11	10	9
H	1	2	3	4	5	6	7	8

Now add the letters as shown.

Assume two players for the moment, the rules for more will be given subsequently. Jack will play Jill.

They agree in advance how many snakes and how many ladders both will *secretly* arrange for the other. Naturally, both will want a nasty big boa constrictor running from the top row to the bottom, but neither will want the other to know from where to where. So, a boa constrictor is agreed from A to H. The players now mark their own playing sheets with the chosen squares. Only square 64 may *not* be utilized. Hence:-

	Jack	Jill
BOA CONSTRICTOR	61 to 1	60 to 1

Next they decide to have (say) a king cobra. This may have a descent of (say) only five lines. Therefore, it may have a drop from A to E, B to F, C to G or D to H. They mark their sheets accordingly. Other snakes and then the ladders are recorded. Their playing sheets now look something like this, after having agreed that no one line may feature more than two heads of snakes.

	JACK	JILL
BOA CONSTRICTOR	61 to 1	60 to 1
KING COBRA	62 to 25	40 to 2
RATTLESNAKE	32 to 2	58 to 33
SIDEWINDER	52 to 26	29 to 3
PUFF ADDER	46 to 17	53 to 25
VIPER	20 to 3	24 to 4
BANDY-BANDY	21 to 4	31 to 9
ASP	16 to 3	18 to 10
LADDER (5 rungs)	2 to 33	17 to 49
LADDER (4 rungs)	31 to 49	2 to 31
LADDER (3 rungs)	47 to 62	34 to 49
LADDER (2 rungs)	8 to 9	7 to 10

Notice that both players have ladders that finish up on a snake. Jack's 3 rung ladder leads to his king cobra. Jill's 4 rung ladder leads to her bandy-bandy. It is entirely up to you to have your own design rules! Also notice that both players have ladders starting on square 2 – gambling on opponent's greed, so missing it.

The rules are as serious as one wishes them to be but the essential rules are:–

(a) Words are limited to an agreed subject such as (say) ANIMALS

(b) No word may exceed six letters
(c) The only bar to repetition is if (say) the first player chooses DONKEY, the second player may not repeat it immediately.

Jack goes first and chooses DONKEY. He moves his counter to square 6.

Jill must now choose a word beginning with any of the letters of DONKEY. What should she choose? A crafty word such as DZOBO perhaps? But, a little word such as KA, KY, OX or ZO might have its advantages. She chooses OX and giggles. Jack not only has to reveal that she has climbed a ladder, but he has missed a similar ladder himself.

Faced with OX, Jack chooses OTTERS (plurals are perfectly acceptable) and moves his counter to square 12, far behind Jill on square 33.

Jill's RABBIT puts her safely on square 39 but Jack's RHINOS has him on square 18 to be greeted by Jill's nasty little asp and back he goes to square 10!

So play continues, up ladders and down snakes.

The top line is the one to consider. One must land exactly on square 64 to win. Obviously, if you can, you have a 2-letter word from square 62, a 3-letter word from square 61 and so on. But this may not always be possible. You might, for example, be forced to land on square 63. Either a tactically placed ladder or a word taken from a difficult combination of letters might do this. Under these circumstances, any chosen word (say) DONKEY has one counting both forwards then back again. Thus, one would go from square 63 back to square 59 by travelling forward one square to 64 then five squares back.

The other significant point about the top line is that if one descends the boa constrictor quite a few of the significant squares are now known, not least the boa constrictor. So, once a player descends a boa constrictor his or her opponent may now change as many or as few of the snakes and ladders as desired. Obviously, they must still conform to the agreed arrangement.

With three players, the game is exactly the same except that Jack would play to Jill's arrangement, Jill would play to (say) her mother's arrangement and Mother would play to Jack's arrangement.

Add another player and simply organize any logical pattern. Possibly the best, if the players are seated on each side of a square table, is to play to the arrangement of the person opposite.

No matter how many players there are, one always plays from

the last spoken word whatever the pattern of playing arrangements.

Finally, when drawing the Snakes and Ladders board, stiff card is far better than paper. The squares should be big enough for the chosen counters and boldly drawn.

17. LITERARY BATTLESHIPS

If you enjoyed Battleships when you were young then this tactical, adult, version should prove quite a challenge.

As with Battleships, draw a grid to personal taste and designate the horizontal and vertical lines with whatever system you once used. However, only one grid is drawn and, this time, you record your positions on your personal, secret, working sheet.

Agree a fleet with your opponent. As a child, the author played to the following navy:–
– One aircraft carrier (designated by the letter A and placed anywhere on the then personal grid)
– Two battleships (B, B and placed in a formation, horizontal, vertical or diagonal anywhere on that grid)
– Three cruisers (C, C, C in formation)
– Four destroyers (D, D, D, D in formation)
– Four submarines (S, S, S, S in formation)

A childhood fleet might well have been dispersed in this fashion:–

	1	2	3	4	5	6	7	8	9	etc.
1							D			
2		B						D		
3		B							D	
4							C			
5							C			
6							C			
7	A									
etc.										

Now, on the personal sheet, you record your positions by reference numbers and it might well take a form like this:-

AIRCRAFT CARRIER	1–7			
BATTLESHIPS	2–3	3–2		
CRUISERS	7–4	7–5	7–6	
DESTROYERS	7–1	8–2	9–3	10–4
SUBMARINES	12–1	13–1	14–1	15–1

The aircraft carrier, in this example, being located at square 1 across and 7 down. The battleships at 2 across and 3 down and at 3 across and 2 down etc.

Alternatively, you may prefer to draw a grid on your working sheet, placing your fleet in position for easier visualization.

The object of the game is to produce a legitimate crossword-type construction on the playing grid which sinks as many of your opponent's ships as possible whilst leaving yours unscathed.

The winner is the one with the larger fleet still afloat when both players cannot contrive any further legitimate words on the playing grid.

The first word played is always GO. This must be placed somewhere in the middle. If (say) your opponent selects square 7–6 for the G and square 8–6 for the O you now announce that he or she has sunk a cruiser. (See above example.)

Your literary problem is twofold. How do you defend the other two cruisers and simultaneously attack the enemy?

You are allowed a free choice of any word but it must link to either the G or O or even both in some way.

Obviously, a word such as STING is stupid – you will sink your two remaining cruisers if you do that.

What do you do? Would ZOO protect, if written like this:–

```
      Z
    G O
      O
```

It might. On the other hand, would it not give the position away?

Suppose you turn GO into FOREGONE. Is not that an equal giveaway and is not that, at the same time, bringing play danger-ously close to your aircraft carrier?

It is more than Battleships, it is more than constructing a crossword. It is a true battle of wits using words.

You cannot expect the childish satisfaction of destroying a complete navy but, as in real life naval battles, the remainder of the losing fleet steams away once it knows that it has lost.

The word rules are whatever you decide. But, words must be

correctly spelt and you may not have nonsense constructions such as 'ZQUEEN' whereby a Z is part of some other word.

If, in this example, QUEEN is a defensive ploy the opponent must use a perfectly legitimate means of attacking the horizontal square immediately to the left of that Q.

The recommended word rules are the same as those given for Crossword (see page 90).

18. JACK

Crown green bowling played with words. Three people are involved, but one of them stands down each particular game. Paper and pencil are used for writing down whatever information might prove of value. Reasonable time limits are imposed. The following example has Tom standing down whilst Dick plays Harriet to see who is the first to score 21 points.

Tom's task is to set the jack for the others to bowl at. He does this by choosing any 7 letter word he wishes (say) ENGLAND and announcing only one of its letters (say) G.

The others have four 'bowls' each. These are 4-letter words of their own choice. It is not essential that their 'bowls' contain the letter G, but they can only score with words which have at least one letter in common with ENGLAND. Both choose to incorporate the G.

Dick bowls at the jack. He chooses the word SWIG. Tom says nothing – yet.

Harriet bowls at the jack. She chooses the word GOAT. Tom now announces that Harriet is nearer to the jack than Dick. (Only the G in Dick's SWIG is common, whereas Harriet's GOAT has both A and G.)

Both Dick and Harriet have a problem. Tom has not announced a 'toucher' – a word containing four of the jack's letters – so, what do they do next?

It is Dick's second bowl. He cannot say GOAT (Harriet has already used that word) but there is nothing wrong with TOGA and he is certain to tie with Harriet. He chooses TOGA.

Harriet cannot use either GOAT or TOGA. What can she do? She knows that this combination must contain either two or three of the jack's letters. Two if Dick's SWIG only has the G but three if Dick's word contains two letters. She gambles on Dick's word only having one letter and decides to change one letter of the GOAT/TOGA combination. She says GATE.

Tom announces that Harriet has one bowl nearer the jack.

Dick cannot think of an anagram for GATE. What can he do for his third bowl? Tom has not announced a 'toucher' so GATE must have three letters in common, and G and E must be two of them. Harriet must also have had two in GOAT. The A or the T? He fancies the T, so combines, G, E and T with another letter. He says GENT.

Harriet also fancies that T. She says GERT.

Tom announces that it is a 'measure'. This means that neither has the nearer bowl overall.

Dick considers the situation. GATE and GENT must both contain three of the jack's letters, but could GERT have three as well? If it does then G, E and T are common to all three. What 4-letter word can he think of? GETS? No. SWIG eliminated the S. This is his final bowl. He says GELT.

Harriet does not wish to say GETS (or its anagram, GEST) but she cannot think of another G, E and T combination which has not been used. Does she say GETS or try the other possibility G, A and E? GAME? GALE? GAPE? AGED?

The following are the results of the game based upon three logical choices faced by Harriet.

GETS   The end is tied. The nearest bowl had 3 letters. It is a 'measure' so the results are compared. Harriet had GATE and GERT, both with 3 letters. Dick had GENT and GELT, both with 3 letters. The other words are immaterial.

The score, therefore, in the match between Harriet and Dick is 0 : 0

GAME   It is a 'measure'. Though Harriet had three words with 3 letters, and Dick had two, it is still tied.

The score is Harriet 0 Dick 0.

GALE   Harriet wins, but by what margin? She has the only word with 4 letters, GALE the 'toucher'. It is now a 'measure' for the second bowl. As both had two words with 3 letters so that means the second position is tied. No further score is possible for Harriet.

The score is Harriet 1 Dick 0

It is now entirely up to the players which option they wish to exercise. Dick and Harriet could continue until one of them is the first to 21 points. Alternatively, one of them could drop out (say)

Dick so Tom and Harriet play. On this basis, three matches are played simultaneously:–
Dick v Harriet, Tom v Harriet, Dick v Tom.

The only outstanding question is what would have happened had either player used the letter N. As there are two N's in England, would N score twice in (say) GENT?

The answer is No! It is just rather unfortunate that Tom's jack used the same letter twice. To limit jacks to 7-letter words containing seven different letters is imposing something of an unnecessary task, but care should be taken to minimise difficulties.

Obviously, luck is an ingredient in this game – but so it is in crown green bowling. The skill lies in capitalizing on the luck. Scores of 1 : 0 and 2 : 0 should be obtained with a fair regularity but a 3 : 0 win is less likely when both players are equally skilful. 4 : 0 is still possible between skillful players as can be seen from the following scorecard kept by Tom:–

jack	DICK		HARRIET	
ENGLAND	SWIG	1	GOAT	2
	GOBY	1	TOGA	2
	GOTH	1	GLUT	2
	TUGS	1	LAGS	3

In this game all four of Harriet's bowls were nearer to the jack than any of Dick's. His comments after

SWIG/GOAT	'Harriet 1'
GOBY/TOGA	'Harriet 2'
GOTH/GLUT	'Harriet 3'
TUGS/LAGS	'Harriet wins 4 : 0'

The scoring system and the terminology is the same as that used in bowling.

19. JILL

Target practice with words using a similar format to that of Jack. The example is the same, Tom sets the 7-letter word target, Dick and Harriet fire the 4-letter word arrows.

This time the task is to discover the 7-letter word. Tom chooses the word, ENGLAND, and announces its 'bull' – the middle letter, L. The letters A and G will, subsequently, be described as 'inners'. By a delightfully confusing coincidence, the two N's are the 'magpies'. E and D are 'outers'. Dick and Harriet now mark their papers with such as ... L ... and attempt to discover the missing letters.

Dick thinks that the word could be something like TELLING so he fires off with GENT.

Tom says nothing until Harriet has fired off her quiver of four arrows. She sees possibilities in PRELATE so says RATE.

Tom tells Dick that his scores, in order of closeness to the bull, are inner, magpie and outer. He does not say which are which.

Tom tells Harriet that she has an inner and an outer.

Players now have the option of firing off a quiver or guessing at the word. They may not do both. Play continues until one player correctly identifies the word.

The 7-letter word is never spoken by a person guessing. He or she writes the guess down on paper and passes it across to the umpire. Comment is reserved until all (more than two may participate in the action) have completed a round of firing. Thus, if Dick guesses he has to wait until Harriet has either also guessed or fired arrows.

Tom will only tell Dick if he is right or wrong. He makes no comment as to accuracy.

Tom's own target looks like this:–

so that he can make quick comments. Dick and Harriet write on their own paper whatever they wish.

20. FORE SCORE

The proverb, TOO MANY COOKS SPOIL THE BROTH, makes an ideal basis for a game of pencil and paper golf.

Two players, Jack and Nicholas, begin by writing the numbers 1 to 18 on their respective pieces of paper. These are written vertically down the left-hand side. Next, they design the 'course' with 'holes' that are par 3, par 4 and par 5 so that both have identical targets including a 'short par 3'. Finally, they write beside each agreed par 3 hole either the word TOO or the word THE; each par 4 hole either MANY or COOK; and each par 5 hole either SPOIL or BROTH. (Played at a more complex level, discussed subsequently, the par 5 choice is COOKS, SPOIL or BROTH.) Neither knows the words chosen by the other and their cards could look like this:—

				JACK	NICHOLAS
	1	par	4	MANY	COOK
	2		3	TOO	TOO
	3		5	SPOIL	BROTH
	4		4	MANY	MANY
	5		4	MANY	COOK
	6		3	TOO	THE
	7		5	SPOIL	SPOIL
	8		4	MANY	COOK
	9		3	THE	TOO
	10		5	BROTH	BROTH
	11		4	COOK	MANY
	12		4	COOK	COOK
short	13		3	THE	THE
	14		5	SPOIL	SPOIL
	15		4	MANY	MANY
	16		4	MANY	COOK
	17		3	THE	TOO
	18		5	SPOIL	BROTH

total 72

The object is to guess at the opponent's choices of words in a manner which produces logical golfing scores.

Guessing is by constituent word. For example, the word MANY comprises the single-letter word A, such 2-letter words as AM, AN or MY or such 3-letter words as MAN or MAY. The bigger the word, the greater the gamble. Thus, the more letters at risk, the more one will go either above or below par.

Consider hole number one. Assume that both players begin cautiously. Jack guesses with the single-letter word, A. He is wrong. Nicholas's COOK does not contain the letter A. Naturally, Jack knows that the word *must* be COOK but must wait until Nicholas has had his tee shot. (This particular convention is only essential at the complex level which reflects, more truly, the game of golf.)

Nicholas guesses with the single-letter word A and is correct.

Jack now says the word COOK and is one over par. Par for that first hole being 4 so his score is 5 and he writes this down beside hole number one on his sheet of paper.

Nicholas now says the word MANY and has made par. Par being 4, he scores 4. Nicholas is now leading by one stroke after the first hole.

By contrast, had Jack guessed with a 2-letter word (say) AN he would have been two over par and scored 6 (par + 2). But, had he guessed with the Scottish word OO he would have been *one* under par and scored 3. Similarly, a guess with a 3-letter word (say) MAN would have put him three over par for a score of 7 or else (say) COO and that would have put him *two* under par for a very remarkable score of 2 for the first hole. He may *not* have a 'tee shot' of a full word, that is only permitted at the short 13 hole.

The three single-letter words are A, I and O. But, it is important to note that O is common to both SPOIL and BROTH on the par 5 holes and it may *not* be used when guessing is being undertaken at these holes. Thus, on a par 5 hole, one is only permitted to say either the single-letter word, I, or else any larger word. Equally significant is the fact that the word, THE, does not contain a standard English single-letter word so the choice is between the caution of the exclamation, O, or else a larger word.

A sample list of guessing words is as follows:-

TOO	O:	TO	
MANY	A:	MY:	MAN
COOK	O:	OO:	COO
SPOIL	I:	IS:	OIL: SOIL
THE		HE	
BROTH		OR:	ROT: BOTH

The possible scores for the basic game are thus:-

par 3	3 or 4:	2 or 5		
short par 3	3 or 4:	2 or 5:	1 or 6	
par 4	4 or 5:	3 or 6:	2 or 7	
par 5	5 or 6:	4 or 7:	3 or 8:	2 or 9

Therefore, one can play with relative safety by sticking to single-letter words or else swing a mighty club and take the consequences.

On the basic game, par for the course is a reasonably easily obtained 72.

A more difficult game can be played by having the word, COOKS, as a third option for the par 5 holes. Under these circumstances both O and SO are disallowed for guessing purposes as the scoring already takes on an added complexity without coping with the ambiguities presented by these two words.

If, however, one is correct with a first guess (the tee shot) the rules are exactly the same as before. But, it is the fact that it can now take two guesses to be certain of the word which causes the need to amend the approach to scoring on the par 5 holes. Finally, one even has to state the correct word when making the final 'putting' shot as it is not impossible that one has made a wrong deduction. The penalty points are shown by type of word:—

SINGLE-LETTER WORD An error carries a penalty of one stroke. Write +1 on your scorecard. For each incorrect guess utilizing a single-letter word continue adding +1's until correct. The score for the hole will be par 5 plus accumulated penalties.

2-LETTER WORD An error carries a penalty of +2 on the scorecard. When correct it is 5 plus penalties.

3-LETTER WORD The penalty is +3. When correct, 5 plus penalties.

4-LETTER WORD The penalty is +4. When correct, 5 plus penalties.

Now try getting an albatross if you dare!

Finally, one can have a true championship golf course by naming the two cooks who spoil the broth. MAY and LOIS. MAY from MANY, LOIS from SPOIL. MAY is now a third option for the par 3 holes and LOIS is the third option for the par 4 holes. Penalty scoring exactly as given above, except for the differences in par.

The par 3 words being   TOO, THE or MAY

The par 4 words being   MANY, COOK or LOIS

The par 5 words being   COOKS, SPOIL or BROTH

A revised sample guessing table being:-

TOO	O:	OO	
THE		HE	
MAY	A:	AM	
MANY	A:	MY:	MAN
COOK		OO:	COO
LOIS	I:	IS:	OIL
COOKS		OO:	COO:	COOK
SPOIL	I:	IS:	OIL:	SOIL
BROTH		OR:	ROT:	BOTH

Your proverbial golf course is now truly realistic and the 'Cook's Tour' of the rough will make par 72 a real achievement.

In effect you have a choice of three games. One on the *Putting Green*, one on a *Pitch and Putt Course* and, finally, one on a *Championship Golf Course*.

21. BASE WORDS

A game for two, three or four players, but the more who play the more difficult it becomes to score and the more frustrating the whole exercise. A swear box fills very rapidly with more than two players.

The game is best played on lined paper turned so that the lines are vertical. Each player conceals his or her workings from the others but is honour bound not to cheat.

All write the identical word, BASE, in the following form:–

The top and bottom letters, B and E, constitute the extremities of available height, but the width is as wide as time permits. Play being for an agreed period of time.

Each player now adds two horizontal links from any two letters in either direction. For example:-

Tom   Dick   Harriet

B-   B   B-
-A   A-   A
S   S-   S
E   E   -E

A subject is chosen (say) ANIMALS and players are attempting to produce the greatest number of animals they can.

Players take turns in calling out one of two things, either any letter of their own choice or else say the word 'Link'.

If a letter is called this *must* be placed in a 'bubble' from an *existing* link. At this point Tom may use only B or A; Dick A or S; Harriet B or E. If, as will happen, no link is available a player has to miss the opportunity of using that letter and wait until either he or she or somebody else says 'Link'. The letter may *not* be added later.

If 'Link' is called, this may be drawn from any letter in either direction and may be horizontal, diagonal or vertical. No links may cross each other.

As words occur in the constructions these should be written down at the side of the paper for subsequent scoring. There is no objection to the same letter featuring in more than one word, nor to the same word being repeated and a word such as FOX which is both OX and FOX may be counted twice. However, one may not have both FOX and FOXES from the same basic FOX.

A word may be read in any direction and twist and turn however it may but no letter may be used more than once in the *same* word. For example, if the subject was FOOD & DRINK and a player wished to score with TARAMASALATA he or she would have to have six individual A's in order to do this.

Now, back to Tom, Dick and Harriet's game.

Tom, seeing the possibility of constructing the word BAT, chooses the letter T. Dick also realises that he can have BAT so makes a similar construction. Harriet rejects the combination BT as being unsuitable for any likely future word, but can see possibilities for TE. Hence:–

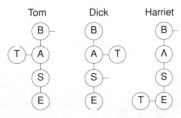

139

Dick, seeing the potential for CAT, now says 'Link' ready for his next turn. Tom decides to put that link to the S, without any particular creature in mind, but Harriet – seeing the chance for making STEER – links the S and T diagonally.

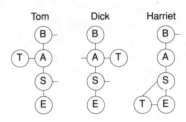

It is now Harriet's turn and she says 'Link' in order to pursue her opportunity for STEER. A player in a similar situation to Harriet might very well jump the gun and say 'E'. If so he must accept his misfortune (the other players may well have already written it down) and must *not* both write a link and follow this with an E in a bubble nor even write the E in advance, planning to join it up later. He must use the only existing link, the B. Whilst he may swear, he is on his honour to suffer the consequences.

When the time expired, this was how the players ended up.

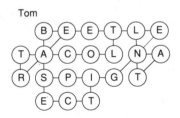

He swore a few times, being forced to waste good links on letters he did not wish to use but only once found himself unable to play a letter. An L in Dick's POLECAT. He scored 34 points for the 34 letters of BAT, CAT, BEAR, BEE, RAT, BEETLE, NEAT, GNAT and COLT. He was aiming for TIGER when the time ran out. He failed to spot the word PIG so lost the score for that word.

Dick

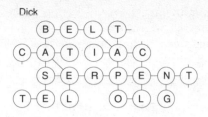

He also swore a few times but played a more open game so was never prevented from using a letter. He scored 29 points from BAT, CAT, APE, SERPENT, PEN, POLECAT and CAT. He was heading for a third CAT when time expired.

HARRIET

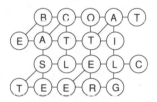

She played the tightest game of all and, in consequence, was forced to forgo the opportunities of using P, N and L. These were called when she had no available links. She scored 33 points for STEER, BAT, CAT, BEAST, COATI and, simultaneously in two different directions, EELS and EEL. This was the final call of the game and it was she who called the link. Thus she finished one point behind Tom but four points ahead of Dick.

However, had the game lasted for one further move she would have won. Tom would have been forced to call for a link, he has nowhere to fit a letter. No matter what he or Dick do with their links, they would lose. Harriet could immediately obtain 5 points for OTTER or 6 points for CATTLE or 8 points for a second and third EELS simultaneously produced:–

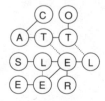

(Note that CATS would give only one point, CAT has already been scored.)
The tactical permutations of Base Words are a joy – but don't forget the swear box!

22. DOUBLE BASE

The two-person, single-sheet version of Base Words. Graph paper is ideal for this game as people's writing styles are so varied that its background of horizontal and vertical lines will assist visualisation.

The game is not played to a time limit but a size limit. This is agreed in advance on a basis of the numbers of vertical lines either side of the base word. Thus, if players agree to 'Three either side' this will give seven vertical lines with the original word in the centre. Whoever is the *second* to play chooses the original 5-letter word, which is written in the centre of the paper with full horizontal links either side.

An example of play follows. Jack is playing Jill, he is to go first and the word of her choice is BREAD. They agreed ANIMALS as the subject.

A player may make *either* a link or else write a letter in a bubble. Jack studies the base word. He sees the possibilities of ZEBRA by a circuitous route and Z is a safe enough letter to play at this stage. He puts a Z to the left of the R.

Jill makes a mistake that neither notice. She puts an R to the left of the A.

Jack, with his thoughts on ZEBRA, also makes a mistake. Jill will not only capitalize on this but realises her error of the R and use both to her advantage. Jack writes A to the right of the R of BREAD.

This is the picture he leaves his opponent:—

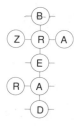

Jill pounces immediately. She writes B to the left of E and scores 4 points for BEAR.

By making a score, she is entitled to another turn. She writes a second B to the right of that E and scores 4 points for a second BEAR. Total 8 points.

Having scored again, this entitles her to yet another turn. She now makes a diagonal link from the E upwards and to the right, to the A pencilled in by Jack. This gives her two simultaneous scores, a third and fourth BEAR for 8 points. Total 16 points.

Jill now realises another aspect of her mistake which Jack (too concerned with a possible ZEBRA) also missed. RAT or RAM should have been taken by Jack. Jill makes it RAT for 3 points. Total 19 points.

The addition of the T now opens the way for yet another scoring move. Jill links B to A for BAT and 3 points.

Jill has now scored 22 points in just one turn. BABE is possible and the fish, DAB, has been accidently created but neither word really falls into the category as both understand it. She cannot see anything else, so what now?

Does she block with a spoiling letter, such as a Q? Does she play a safe but useful letter? She decides to add a safe link from the T.

It is now Jack's turn and this is what the sheet looks like:-

What does he do?
If he links Z to E, Jill can then link B to R for ZEBRA

If he writes E to the left of the original B, Jill will link Z to E for a different ZEBRA

Then he spots it. One that Jill missed and could have obtained very easily. BARB, a swift kind of horse. He links the second B pencilled in by Jill vertically upwards to an A for 4 points.

Now he spots another she could have got, BAT. 3 points for a link. Total 7 points.

Jill's 'safe' link from the T is no longer safe. Jack now uses it for an S which complicates scoring. This simultaneously produces BATS, BATS and RATS.

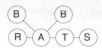

Irrespective of who scored the original BAT, BAT and RAT it is Jack who made the clever plural. *Unlike Base Words*, everything is scored again in full. 12 points for Jack. Total 19 points.

Jack cannot see anything else so he puts a U to the right of the original B to provide a potential ZEBU/ZEBRA simultaneous combination if and when the chance arises. This is what Jill now faces:–

Bearing in mind no lines may cross and that the same letter may not be used twice in the same word (the TARAMASALATA rule given in Base Words) what should Jill do next?

At least 17 points are available, using the names of animals already mentioned. If you can spot them, then Double Base is the game for you. You must, however, stick strictly to the rules and the answers are not published. This is a game, not a puzzle book.

When playing you may well need to add certain rules of your own to combat 'spoilers'. Taken to a logical defensive conclusion both of you could produce an utterly silly opening picture which looks like this:–

Under these circumstances you would have to impose limitations on the number of times any particular letter may be used in a non-scoring situation or else insist that, from the base word, a vowel must be written adjacent to a consonant and vice versa. Such limitations, however, being limited to a non-scoring play.

Do stick to categories, if you allow *any* words it will cease to be fun. No matter what the reasonably popular category you select, you will soon discover that you know more (say) animals than you could name off the top of your head. Finally, impose time limits for a move. As with all games of this nature, play with someone of equivalent mental agility. There is nothing so frustrating for a quick thinker as a contest with a deadbeat. Admittedly both Jack and Jill are quick thinkers and make mistakes, but they do *enjoy* the contests.

23. SQUARE BASHING

A stimulating, two-person, challenge rather like the simple pencil and paper of Boxes – but, far more subtle.

Graph paper is ideal (though not essential) for a basic grid visualized as five squares by three squares or any other agreed layout.

Players take turns to add any word to a word already in play. Thus, if CLIMB is the first word written down on the imaginary grid in (say) a horizontal plane, the opponent may now use either the C or the B to begin or end any other 5-letter word. The immediate object of the game being the completion of a square of 5-letter words and thereby claiming it. Thus:–

```
C L I M B
H
E
E
R A N D Y
```

would be claimed very easily with a host of words such as BADDY, BAGGY, BALKY, BALLY etc. by the player who made that particular completion. He or she would then have the bonus of another opportunity of writing a linked word.

Obviously, one does not give away squares easily and, in the above example, the player facing the construction of CLIMB/ CHEER would not have written RANDY as his or her move. Instead, that first player would have utilized any of the three available letters in a far more sensible fashion such as:–

```
        T                                                S
        H                                                O
        U                                                N
        M                                                I
CLIMB              CLIMB        TUNICLIMB        CLIMB
H                  H                       H                H
E                  E                       E                E
E                  E                       E                E
R           LOVER                          R                R
```

Once a box has been completed, the successful player claims it by writing within that box his or her personal identification. Below, this will be shown by the numbers 1 and 2.

The skills lie in creating difficulties for one's opponent and the following example of a genuine game shows how both players deliberately used such inflexible letters as the Q in order to force their rivals to give them 'easy' boxes. At least three squares are still available to be scored with fairly 'normal' words – can you spot them?

```
       SNIPSTEPS          ZEBUSTIFF
          K    T              T
          I  ②  O             O
          N    O              U
       QUINSHEEPHAS EMBERHOMB
       U     P          X    E       O
       I  ①  A          T  ①  C  ①  U
       N     C          R    A       N
       THINE        QUOTAHEAPLAID
       H            U     B     L     I
       I            A ① A ① U ② Z
       N            F     F     M     Z
       K        QUIFFIRSTHUMBUSTY
```

The rules are that no word may be repeated and each word played must be capable of being validated, if challenged, in a dictionary.

If a player cannot think of a suitable word he or she has to surrender that turn to the opponent. If neither can produce a word the game ends at that stage. This was true of the above genuine game. Player number one was leading by 5 squares to 2 squares and it was his move. He could not see a possible move and offered his opponent the chance.

In theory, he was handing victory on a plate. The final eight squares are ready to be taken in one fell swoop. A typical sequence would be the top left-hand box, S to Q, followed by the top right-hand box, F to B, then the top pair of boxes in the order Z to E, S to Z. Finally, the bottom four boxes in the order P to Q, E to Q on the horizontal, E to Q on the vertical and, last of all, K to Q. Such a run of moves being possible due to the bonus granted on completion of a box. There being no limit to bonuses.

Player number two also surrendered and so missed a chance of a face-saving 5-5 draw.

The final moves? There are no fewer than seven different words available in a standard dictionary to make the Z to E move. Of these the most common is defined as, 'An American interjection expressing surprise and pleasure.' For the F to B move and the S to Z move make logical guesses and confirm the solutions in the Appendix at FL- and SP- respectively.

(*Square Bashing was devised by Tom Wright.*)

24. TWINSET

Two players select an agreed number of versatile 3-letter words, ideally those which can feature either side of other equally valid 3-letter words to form a genuine 6-letter word. For example, PET. This can be prefixed by such as CAR to form CARPET or suffixed by such as TED to become PETTED. Each 3-letter word secretly chosen by an individual player must be different.

The object of the game is to be the first to play all of his or her 3-letter words, either as part of a 6-letter word or, less effectively, as a single 3-letter word. As neither player knows the other's words, so the basic ploy is to lead with a word which one can readily convert into the 'twinset' hoping that the other is incapable of so doing. In this event one gains the advantage, as the person who completes the 'twinset' leads off with the next 3-letter word. Sometimes, neither player can complete a 'twinset' and the advantage is lost.

In the following genuine game between two wordsmiths the players are described by their differing gender.

He chose ARC, ARM, ASS, BEL, CAP, DOG, ERS, GED, HER, LET, LOW, MAN, ORT, PAS, PET, RED, ROT, TED, TEN, TOR.

She chose BAR, BED, BOB, CAN, CAP, CAR, DID, DON, ERS, FAG, FOR, GET, GOT, HAM, LET, PAR, PER, RED, SON, TED.

Both players had twenty words with CAP, ERS, RED and TED in common. A spin of the coin had the lady going first and she wrote

down the word, RED. He converted this
into MANRED (see Appendix) and so
began the next potential 'twinset' with
ROT.

    The game ended when he had used
all of his 3-letter words and she still
had CAR and HAM unused. The full
play is given alongside, with the original 3-letter word featuring as the central unbroken column. His final word
was PET and the only other unconver-
ted 3-letter words (DOG and GOT) had
to have both players passing before a
new 3-letter word could be written
down.

```
M A N R E D
    R O T T E D
    B O B B E D
C A N D I D
    F A G G E D
    P A S T O R
B A R R E D
    C A P E R S
    A S S O R T
    A R C H E R
    B E L L O W
    T E N D O N
A R M L E T
    D O G
    P A R T E D
    C A P E R S
P E R S O N
F O R G E T
    G O T
    P E T
```

(Twinset was devised by Juliet Titchener)

25. FOXO

Noughts and Crosses played with the word FOX. One player is X,
the other is O. Both players must, however, write the word FOX
each time they play.

    A 5 x 5 grid is drawn and suppose that O is to go first and writes
FOX in a descending diagonal line which puts O in the centre
square:–

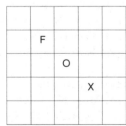

It is now the turn of X to play. He has two options:–

(a) Write the complete word FOX anywhere he chooses.
(b) Utilize any existing letter as part of his own need to produce
     the word FOX.

Once three O's or three X's are produced in a horizontal, vertical or diagonal sequence these are drawn through and credited to that player. In this respect Foxo is identical to Noughts and Crosses but, unlike Noughts and Crosses, the following scoring is permitted:–

(a) The game is not ended with the first person to make such a credit.

(b) The same symbol may be utilized as many times as the player can create different combinations which contain that symbol. For example, a line of 5 O's has the central O occurring in three different combinations, each of which is counted for the score.

Scoring opportunities occur very quickly. If the above with FOX written diagonally by O is continued for just two further moves thus:–

Move number 2. X utilizes the O by writing F and X either side of it.

Move number 3. O blocks an upper line of X's and simultaneously creates a threat of a diagonal line of O's.

It is now the turn of X to play. He has three opportunities for his credit of a run of three X's. Notice that on one of them he gives, simultaneously, a credit of three O's to his opponent. This is by writing the complete word FOX in the fashion shown alongside. However, if he utilized the existing FO of the central vertical column he would achieve the same effect without helping his opponent. The opponent could still score these same three O's but at the cost of a move. If X chose the vertical X's of the fourth column he has still failed to provide a defence against O scoring on the diagonal. What should he do?

That's Foxo.

26. NASTIER FUN

The word, NASTIER, is far and away the most flexible of all 7-letter words. It has 30 perfect anagrams, of which a short selection will follow. It has an amazing 126 andagrams, of which an even shorter selection will follow. (An andagram is an anagram of a word with the addition of another letter, as NASTIER + D becomes RANDIEST.)

The object of the game is to see who is the first to play NASTIER or one of its anagrams or andagrams on (say) a 15 x 15 grid. Wordsmiths can take the game a stage further and see who, of two players, can produce the greater number of NASTIER words on the grid.

It is a two stage game and both parts are stimulating and fun.

STAGE 1. A subject is agreed and a written form of the game of Wimbledon is undertaken. You record both your own and your opponent's words. The purpose is twofold. You are creating your own basic material for use on the grid and, at the same time, taking note of your opponent's material to frustrate his or her success in the second stage. Finally, stick a pin in a book or newspaper and the nearest 3-letter word opens the Wimbledon-type rally.

The following example has Jack versus Jill, the subject is COUNTRIES, the pinword is AND, Jack is to play first.

Jack now has to choose a country beginning with D, the last letter of the pinword, AND. He selects DENMARK. This gives him four of the NASTIER letters (A, E, N and R). Both he and Jill write DENMARK on their playing sheets.

Jill now has to select a country beginning with the letter K (the last letter of DENMARK). Her choice is KENYA and this gives her three of the NASTIER letters (A, E and N). Jack must now choose a country beginning with the letter A.

Play continues in this fashion until both players have upwards of fifty letters each. There is no need to be exact, but one can quite easily call a halt to the proceedings when both players each have about a dozen words. If a player is stuck at this stage and asks for help, give it freely. Especially if you think of one of little or no value to your opponent.

The Wimbledon stage might well end with the following lists:-

JACK	JILL
DENMARK	KENYA
AUSTRALIA	AUSTRIA
ALGERIA	ARGENTINA
AFGHANISTAN	NEPAL
LIECHTENSTEIN	NIGER
REUNION	NORWAY
YUGOSLAVIA	ANTIGUA
ANDORRA	ALBANIA
ANGOLA	

having exhausted the names of countries beginning with the letter A as no words may be repeated in this stage.

Note that Jack not only has more letters than Jill (77 to 51) but also a greater NASTIER arsenal. With only one S, Jill has direct control of only one NASTIER, whereas Jack has the potential command of four NASTIER's. This will not matter for the basic game and even at wordsmith level she can still win.

STAGE 2. No more than seven letters may be played on the crossword grid at any one time. The scoring rule is that if you can utilize all seven currently available letters in the construction of any valid word which contains the letters A, E, I, N, R, S and T you have either won or been credited with a point at wordsmith level.

This means that the playing of such a word as NASTIER or RANDIEST, providing that you supply *any* seven of the letters, is a winning move. But (say) merely to convert an existing TIE on the grid to NASTIER by adding, N, A, S and R is of no consequence whatsoever.

Players are limited to the consideration of seven letters taken in strict sequence as produced during the Wimbledon stage. As one or more is deleted by being used on the grid, so the next in sequence forms the replacement or replacements. Thus, Jack's first set of available letters is the 7-letter word DENMARK and however many of these he uses on the grid will be replaced by the constituent letters of AUSTRALIA in strict order. Jill's first set is KENYA together with the A and U of AUSTRIA.

The one with the greater number of letters goes first. In this example, Jack. He must construct a word from DENMARK and place it anywhere in the centre of the grid. Ideally, of course, he would like to dispose of D, M and K. This is impossible, so he must utilize one of his three vowels. The sensible choice is the letter A, as this is going to be replaced immediately by the first letter of AUSTRALIA.

Jack plays the word, MAD. He deletes these letters from DENMARK (so does Jill on her sheet) and now has the replacements of A, U and S. From a NASTIER point of view he has five of the vital letters (A, E, N, R and S) and is close to the remaining I and T.

Jill is equally strongly placed. In fact she needs to dispose of fewer letters before she has NASTIER. She makes her first crossword-style move in this fashion:-

M A D
Y A K

AY and DA are perfectly valid words as Jack well knows, so he raises no objection whatsoever.

It is now Jack's turn to play and he must build on this existing construction from his stock of A, E, K, N, R, S and U. Jill's playing stock consists of A, E, N, R, S, T and U, and I is the next letter available for her. She has only to dispose of the U and it is hers. Jack is well aware of this. He must now choose a word which not only helps him but also prevents Jill from merely disposing the U in some legitimate fashion.

That is Nastier Fun!

A short selection of NASTIER anagrams

ANESTRI, ANTSIER, ASTERIN, EARNITS, ERANIST, NASTIER, NERITAS, RANITES, RATINES, RESIANT, RESTAIN, RETAINS, RETINAS, TERSINA, STAINER, STEARIN, TANIERS, TIRANES.

The more obscure of these words are defined in the Appendix but others are instantly available in *Pears Advanced Word-Puzzler's Dictionary*.

An even shorter selection of NASTIER andagrams

+A, ARTESIAN: +B, BANISTER: +C, CANISTER: +D, STRAINED:
+E, RESINATE: +F, FAINTERS: +G, ANGRIEST: +H, HAIRNETS:

+I, RAINIEST: +K, KERATINS: +L, ENTRAILS: +M, RAIMENTS:
+N, ENTRAINS: +O, ARSONITE: +P, PINASTER: +R, RESTRAIN:
+S, SNARIEST: +T, STRAITEN: +U, URINATES: +W, TINWARES

To play an 8-letter scoring word one does not need to have NASTIER in one's personal stock. Suppose that the personal stock consists of any of the following together with the 'remaining' letter exposed on the grid:–

(a) AASTIER   in stock with N on the grid
(b) NAATIER   ,,   ,,   ,,   S ,, ,, ,,
(c) NAASIER   ,,   ,,   ,,   T ,, ,, ,,
(d) NAASTER   ,,   ,,   ,,   I ,, ,, ,,
(e) NAASTIR   ,,   ,,   ,,   E ,, ,, ,,
(f) NAASTIE   ,,   ,,   ,,   R ,, ,, ,,

One can now play not only ARTESIAN but any other valid lower case andagram of NASTIER + A such as ANTISERA, ARTISANE, RATANIES, RESINATA or SEATRAIN. Upper case words such as Asterina, Erastian and Raetians being invalid.

If a player cannot go by virtue of (say) having no vowels, he or she must pass if the opponent cannot enforce a move from that player's stock. A player who passes is at the mercy of the opponent's decision. He or she having the option of making any move of his or her choice for that player or else having a second move of his or her own.

In the wordsmith version, play ends when no further scoring moves are possible.

All words must be capable of being proven to exist in an English dictionary. They must be lower case and unhyphenated. The fact that one dictionary may well hyphenate a word, contrary to modern practice, can be sensibly ignored if that same word can be clearly shown to exist in an unhyphenated form elsewhere.

The classic example of this is one particular dictionary which will have a word such as BLADDERWRACK given a main entry heading of 'BLADDER-WRACK' but refer to it elsewhere in at least two other places as BLADDERWRACK! It has literally hundreds of these unique hyphens and, of course, dozens are given on other of its pages in a non-hyphenated form.

Basically, let common sense prevail.

If an invalid word is played, this must be erased and the offender forfeits that turn. However, as this could be done for strategic purposes, the opponent has the option of enforcing a move of his or her choice from the opponent's letters.

27. SEVEN UP

The same game, rules and playing format as Nastier Fun but with two vital differences:–

1. You do not know for certain what letters your opponent possesses. This time, during the Wimbledon stage, you do not reveal (say) the country of choice merely its last letter.
2. Any word for which you provide seven letters scores points on a scale reflecting difficulty of achievement. Scoring is as follows:–
    (a) A basic 7-letter word scores 10 points with an additional 10 points for each of the following letters which you are able to utilize, J, Q, X, Z. All letters other than A, E, I, N, R, S and T (NASTIER) score an additional point.
    (b) An additional 5 points for every letter in excess of seven in any one play that involves your playing seven letters. Thus, an 8-letter word scores a minimum 15 points, a 9-letter word a minimum 20 points etc.

For example, the word ZED is on the grid and you preface this with your seven letters Q, U, I, X, O, T and I to make QUIXOTIZED will score as follows:–

10 letter word	25 points
Q	10
X	10
Z	10
U	1
O	1
D	1
	58 points

The only other difference in the rules is that in the event of a player making an invalid move he or she must not only erase that error but reveal the 7 letters he or she had available for that move. The opponent now has the option of enforcing a valid word of his or her choice from that set of letters or else taking the opportunity of playing his or her own word instead.

The Polyominoes Concept

Solomon W. Golomb, a Californian mathematician, introduced the concept of squares linked together as a simple game of shapes. However, his 1954 discovery makes an admirable basis for such an enormous number of word games which can be played by any number of people at any level of linguistic ability that I have devised only the merest sample to illustrate the potential.

The sample is limited to the three games which would otherwise feature in the major pencil and paper series of Cross Play (in which two or more people challenge each other), Classroom (a large gathering concerned with an identical task) and Solitaire (individual amusement). The shapes suggested for each game are purely illustrative and there is no reason why these shapes should be rigidly adhered to.

For simplicity's sake all three games are shown as pentomino games (played with shapes created by five squares linked together in varying formations) but they could just as easily be hexomino games (six linked squares) or any other combination which appeals.

1. FIVES

A solitaire challenge to score the maximum points possible with a single word. The five shapes selected have the potential for scoring progressively more points providing that, in each case, you can create valid 2-letter and 3-letter words.

Let us assume that the word TEARS has been chosen. This is written crossword-fashion in the lowest-scoring shape:–

T	E	A	R	S

One word of five letters gives us 5 points.
For our second play we create from TEARS two 3-letter words to give us six points:–

The third play has a shape with the potential for scoring 7 points. It has two 2-letter word spaces and one 3-letter word space. How many points can you score from TEARS? All seven? Five? Four? Try it.

The shape for the fourth play can produce 8 points, if you can create four 2-letter words from TEARS.

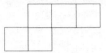

Finally, 9 points. Three 2-letter words and one 3-letter word.

The maximum score is 35 points. Did you make it? If not, could you have done so if any of the chosen shapes had been twisted around. For example, the fifth one. Is this a more acceptable arrangement:–

Or would either of these have been easier:–

Ignoring the factor of twisting a shape around (which is very significant in word play) one has a choice of twelve basic pentomino shapes. There is only one 5 points shape but there are five different 6 points shapes:–

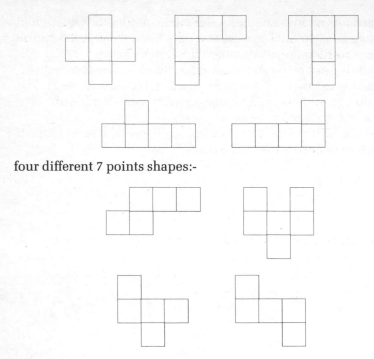

four different 7 points shapes:-

but only one 8 points shape and only one 9 points shape.

Your solitaire challenge with TEARS utilizing all twelve shapes (however you wish to twist them) brings the potential score to 80 points.

TEARS was chosen, incidentally, solely on the basis that it has the greatest number of anagrams of any 5-letter word. Despite what the *Guinness Book of Records* may tell you, it is *not* the word with the greatest number of anagrams of *any* word (ANGRIEST is the supreme anagram) and it may or may not have the potential for scoring the greatest number of points in any re-run which must utilize *different* words for each shape. For example:–

A	S	T	E	R

S	T	A	R	E

R	A	T	E	S

would each score 5 points in a second, third and fourth run at either the 35 points version of Fives or the 80 points version of Fives which, for convenience, may be termed Great Fives.

The rules for Fives are as follows:–

Five different-scoring basic shapes are chosen. Once 35 points has been achieved, a re-run utilizing any five different-scoring basic shapes may be selected in any attempt to achieve 70 points.

Thereafter, providing one has succeeded in obtaining the maximum points, additional re-runs may be undertaken until a failure ends the consideration of a particular 5-letter word.

All words must be genuine and abbreviations are not permitted. Note, however, that ST is a valid word in its own right (see Appendix) even though most people will regard it as an abbreviation for either street or saint.

In re-runs ST, for example, may be repeated in the same shape if the other word or words are different:–

but twisting the shape and having identical words is invalid:–

In Great Fives the rules are the same.

Which word has the potential for scoring the maximum possible in

(a) Fives?
(b) Great Fives?
(c) Fives and Great Fives?

The challenges for Sixes/Great Sixes, Sevens/Great Sevens etc. are equally possible, all you have to do is design the requisite polyominoes in advance of the task.

2. PANIC

Tom is going to play Harriet in a fast-moving game of pentomino decisions. They agree in advance a total number of moves (say) twelve. Dick is the taskmaster, timekeeper and referee.

Dick selects any 5-letter word he wishes and Tom and Harriet have one minute in which to record it in *any* pentomino shape they wish. There is no need to draw squares so long as it is clear which shape has been selected in the event of any subsequent dispute. Dick chooses the word, FIRST.

As they only have a minute in which to record their results which shapes will they choose?

Play safe and score 5 points for FIRST?

See the potential for 6 points with such as:–

```
    S T I R              F                  F R I T
      F        or      S I T      or          S
                         R
```

Or gamble that RIT is a genuine word (see Appendix) and try for 7 points with

```
                         S
                       R I T
                         F
```

Once Dick calls time, they tear their results off the top of their scrap pads and hand them to him.

At the end of the twelve similar moves, the papers are checked. Let us assume that RIT is challenged but not found in the pocket dictionary they have to hand. Despite the fact that both IF and ST are perfectly valid and worth 4 points, *no score whatsoever* is given for that particular play. If, however, a good dictionary was available then the word would have been accepted and the full 7 points scored.

Whoever, Tom or Harriet, had the higher score is the winner and is awarded 2 points. Had they tied it would have been a point each.

The points scored in play are ignored as the object of the exercise is to see which of the three of them over an agreed number of games is the winner and some words have a far greater potential than others.

Tom will now play Dick with Harriet in charge of proceedings then Dick will play Harriet with Tom in charge.

In order to ensure fair selection of words any book or newspaper is used as the base. One merely opens up at any page, selects a paragraph at random and calls out 5-letter words in the order of occurrence. If this means that a particular word is repeated, so be it.

Naturally, the options for using 6-letter words or 7-letter words are just as suitable for this fascinating contest.

3. GOLOMBOES

The twelve basic shapes originally described by Golomb are drawn on paper (see p. 156) Photostats are produced equal to the number of contestants.

The challenge is to fill all twelve shapes using as few different letters as possible.

However, unlike Fives or Great Fives, no individual word may be repeated in *any* of the pentominoes. Note, too, the fact that you have established the arrangement of these shapes and that they cannot be twisted to suit.

The ideal of utilizing only five letters will, for all practical purposes, prove impossible. But, how few letters will they employ?

As a letter is used this should be shown on the paper as a separate entry. Perhaps the easiest way of doing this is to have a complete alphabet typed in advance at the top of the page and, as each letter is utilized, so it is ringed.

Finally, note that the solitaire challenges (Fives and Great Fives) and the classroom contest (Golomboes) are mutually interchangeable. This will also prove true of some of the games described in the Classroom Series and Solitaire Series which follow. Essentially it is a question of the level at which you pitch the degree of attainment.

The Classroom Series

Whilst adults can, and do, enjoy these games they are ideal for enlivening an English class by encouraging the children to think in a sporting environment.

1. WORD LADDERS

Devised by Lewis Carroll, who called them Doublets, and first brought to the attention of the public in a letter of his published by *Vanity Fair* in 1879. The example he gave was turning HEAD into TAIL by changing one letter at a time. Carroll's solution was:—

```
               H E A D
               H E A L
               T E A L
               T A L L
               T A I L
```

Any logical pair of words can be changed in this fashion. CAT to DOG for example:-

```
        CAT  CAT  CAT  CAT  CAT  CAT
        COT  COT  CAG  CAG  DAT  DAT
        COG  DOT  COG  DAG  DOT  DAG
        DOG  DOG  DOG  DOG  DOG  DOG
```

The CAT/COT changes are obvious but the CAT/CAG changes are just as valid, a cag being a keg and dag has various meanings. The third possibility of CAT/DAT can be ignored as it involves an obsolete Scottish form.

Not that Scottish words can be dismissed, as any child north of the border could produce a perfect solution to Carroll's HEAD to TAIL by the use of HEID (head) and HEIL (heal) so making the change with the minimum number of steps. Another perfect solution is to utilize TEIL, the lime or linden tree, in this ladder:—

```
               H E A D
               H E A L
               T E A L
               T E I L
               T A I L
```

Perfect solutions are not always possible. Carroll's APE to MAN is particularly tricky as the vowels have to become consonants and the consonant a vowel. Carroll took six steps whereas the journal, *Scientific American*, has published several solutions shorter than Carroll's including the one shown to the right of the original:—

```
          A P E      A P E
          A R E      A P T
          E R E      O P T
          E R R      O A T
          E A R      M A T
          M A R      M A N
          M A N
```

In setting the company any test of this fashion have your own solution to hand. But, be prepared to arbitrate on some of the results obtained.

To illustrate this point, consider the following transformations first published in 1893. Both are imperfect and both can be bettered quite easily. The HAND to FOOT perfect alternative uses a Scottish past tense and the BLACK to WHITE imperfect alternative has a word no longer considered to be of polite usage:—

HAND	HAND	BLACK	BLACK
HARD	FAND	SLACK	BLICK
LARD	FOND	STACK	SLICK
LORD	FOOD	STALK	SLICE
FORD	FOOT	STALE	SLITE
FORT		SHALE	SHITE
FOOT		WHALE	WHITE
		WHILE	
		WHITE	

FAND is a Scottish past tense of the verb FIND.

BLICK is the iridescence appearing on gold or silver after the refining process.

SLITE is a rare verb to slit or split.

The impolite word, incidentally, is perfectly valid for the UK Scrabble Championship.

The name of Word Ladders was coined by the late Dmitri Borgmann, the modern American master of word play, and is far more apt ᴜs some of the following games will show.

2. BUILD UP

Word ladders as the basis of a very different contest. Play with 4-letter words and challenge the company to create a much larger word. To make it fun, set them a task such as to 'Build a battleship from a cart'.

First of all they write the word, BATTLESHIP, at the top of their individual sheets of paper. Now they write the word, CART, directly below it.

As the letters A and T are common to both words so they now delete the A of BATTLESHIP and one of the T's. The challenge is to see who can be the first to utilize each of the remaining letters with valid words. For example, six different contestants might begin as follows:—

1	2	3	4	5	6
CART	CART	CART	CART	CART	CART
CARS	CARE	HART	PART	TART	CARP

1   Deletes the S of BATTLESHIP
2   Deletes the E of BATTLESHIP
3   Deletes the H of BATTLESHIP but *not* the second T.
4   Deletes the P of BATTLESHIP but *not* the second T.
5   Deletes the second T of BATTLESHIP.
6   Deletes the P of BATTLESHIP.

As one of the contestants might begin by changing CART to BART this is pointed out in advance as being invalid as it is an abbrevation for BARONET.

It is entirely up to you as to what limitations you impose. Are you going to permit such as the names of countries (i.e. MALI in a sequence which runs CART, CARE, MARE, MALE, MALT, MALI) or common personal names?

If, in the classroom, the winner's solution is written on the blackboard might it not be easier to insist that every word used must be found in the dictionary? This way no one can dispute some of the weirder names that are sometimes inflicted upon children and any 'funny' words can be shown either to exist or not exist as the case may be.

Quick finishes to each of the above examples imposing the limitations of words found in the dictionary could be as follows:—

1	2	3	4	5	6
CART	CART	CART	CART	CART	CART
CARS	CARE	HART	PART	TART	CARP
BARS	HARE	HARP	TART	PART	HARP
BATS	TARE	HARE	HART	PARE	HART
BETS	BARE	HATE	HALT	HARE	HARE
BITS	PARE	HALE	SALT	HIRE	BARE
PITS	MARE	BALE	SILT	SIRE	BALE
HITS	MALE	SALE	MILT	SILE	SALE
HOTS	MILE	PALE	MILE	BILE	MALE
LOTS	MILK	PILE	BILE		MILE
	SILK				

Note that only numbert 5 has the absolute minimum run and this contained the dialect word, SILE, found only in larger dictionaries. However, it would be known to children in the Sheffield/

Chesterfield area where the word is in common usage. All of the other examples involve at least one 'non-deletion' move. These occurring at the ends of the different runs with only one letter requiring utilization. Perhaps you may care to find the perfect minimum run not only for building a battleship from a cart without resorting to dialect but for any construction you decide to use.

3. OTHER LADDER GAMES

It is possible to go through the complete alphabet using word ladders. When I conceived this notion my example for publication was as follows:—

JAZY, HAZY, HAZE, HACE, HATE, HATS, QATS, VATS, PATS, PANS, BANS, BINS, BIND, MIND, MINX, MING, MINK, RINK, OINK, WINK, LINK, LUNK and FUNK.

and I defined

JAZY, HACE, QATS, OINK and LUNK in the Appendix.

However, to my astonishment, the same idea occurred to a contributor of *Word Ways* (August 1988) who produced a far better example using much simpler words. Jeremy Morse's minimal run takes this form:—

FOXY, FOGY, BOGY, BONY, BONE, BANE, CANE, PANE, VANE, WANE, MANE, MARE, MARL, MAIL, HAIL, JAIL, SAIL, SAID, SKID, SKIT, SUIT, QUIT and QUIZ.

It is interesting to note that both of us chose to begin with words which dispose of as many of the problem letters as we could and both elected to use 4-letter words. This raises the question of other minimal runs utilizing such as 3-letter words or 5-letter words apart from the obviously easy 4-letter run.

An alternative challenge for a junior classroom is to set simple tests to see who can first find a particular letter. To provide a suitable starting word – cheat! Begin with the letter you wish them to find, then work backwards a couple of steps. You can now pose the task of who can find the X from ICED (ICED, ACED, AXED) or the Z from LIME (LIME, LAME, LAZE) or any other suitable apparently difficult letter.

A different ladder game has been devised by Kyle Corbin of Raleigh, North Carolina, USA and was first published in the May 1988 issue of the magazine, *Word Ways*. This he called **Minimal Word Ladders** as it consists of changing one letter at a time to produce a totally different word which ends at the point where every letter is completely different. A 3-letter word, therefore, undergoes three changes and a 4-letter word four changes to qualify as minimal.

Kyle has discovered that up to 7-letter ladders can be produced quite easily without resorting to unusual words. These are some of his examples:–

ANY	SOAP	ELATE	BRAVER	CANNONS
AND	SWAP	PLATE	BEAVER	CANTONS
AID	SWAY	PLACE	BEATER	CANTORS
KID	AWAY	PEACE	BETTER	CANTERS
	AWRY	PEACH	SETTER	CASTERS
		PERCH	SETTEE	MASTERS
			SETTLE	MASTERY
				MYSTERY

Others include ACORNS to SOAKED and PICKED to BALLOT which you may care to try for yourself.

But, the most delightfully frustrating of the other ladder games is equally enjoyable as a solitaire amusement. It is called **Q-Dye**.

Q-Dye is a Japanese University at which the second chapter of the Pears Word Games Society (see page 000) is based. In order to provide the chapter with an original contest I devised this little challenge – see who can get to PARADISE with the minimum difficulty.

The word, PARADISE, can be divided into any number of two 4-letter words – such as PEAR and SAID. PARADISE constructed from *any* pair of 4-letter words is the target. The first step of the ladder is the word, QUIZ, repeated as a pair. The contestant must now write QUIZ twice and begin two separate ladders which end *simultaneously* with (say) PEAR + SAID. Thus a typical pair of ladders might begin:–

QUIZ	QUIZ
QUIT	QUIN
SUIT	RUIN

at which point the first column has the S and I of PARADISE

whilst the second column has the R and I of PARADISE. Two moves later:–

QUIZ	QUIZ
QUIT	QUIN
SUIT	RUIN
SLIT	RAIN
SLAT	REIN

and, now, the first column has the S and A of PARADISE with the R, E and I in the second column. A rather nasty little rule needs to be mentioned – a word may *not* be repeated in the same column. This means that having achieved (say) SAID in one column too soon for combining with such as PEAR, PARE, REAP or RAPE one may not juggle the other column in this fashion:–

SAID	
SAIL	
SAID	
SAIL	
SAID	etc

but must now begin the change of SAID to such as DAIS or even abandon that particular split entirely.

PARADISE has many combinations of two 4-letter words. Can you get there?

Q-Dye can have any 8-letter word as its destination so long as such word is capable of being divided into two 4-letter words. For example, RICHMOND might prove easier to get to than PARADISE:–

QUIZ	QUIZ
QUID	QUIN
QAID	RUIN
RAID	ROIN
LAID	COIN
CAID	CORN
CHID	MORN

though the fairly obscure words such as QAID (an alternative spelling of CAID, an alcade or Spanish/Portuguese magistrate) and ROIN (an old verb to growl, found in Spenser's *Faerie Queene* with the spelling ROYNE) make the attainment of CHID + MORN (Richmond) relatively simple.

Not that one needs to restrict oneself to QUIZ + QUIZ as the opening but it is as challenging a pair to begin with as any.

4. GUGGENHEIM

There are two explanations for the name of this game of which the better known is that it was first played by the Guggenheim family. The other – first mooted by Frank Scully in his book, *Fun in Bed* (published in 1934) – has the game originally entitled Categories but changed to commemorate a malapropism. According to Scully, a category of PRINTERS was included in a session played by Jerome Kern, Howard Dietz and P. G. Wodehouse and Kern wrote down GUTENBERG. Apparently Wodehouse had never heard of Gutenberg nor believed Kern's assertion that Johann Gutenberg (circa 1400–1468) was the first printer. When, some months later, Dietz suggested another session of Categories, Wodehouse is supposed to have said: 'All right, but no more of your Guggenheims.'

To play, choose any word of any length but a 5-letter word is reasonable. This is written, as individual letters, across the top of the competitor's sheet of paper. A series of categories is chosen and players now have to write down examples of these beginning with each letter of the original word.

A session of Guggenheim based upon the word, SOLVE, with its first two categories being BIRDS and COUNTRIES might look like this:–

	S	O	L	V	E
Birds	swan	owl	lark	vulture	eagle
Countries	Sweden	Oman	Libya	Venezuela	Egypt

When played in the classroom, ensure that answers to all letters are feasible. For example, can you think of another country beginning with O or would the children have heard of a vireo?

The game is not as simple as it first appears.

5. WORDSWORTH

Any longish word is selected but the ideal ones are those which have a wide variety of any of the following letters:– A, E, I, L, M, N, P, R, S, T. The reason will shortly be self-evident.

Suppose you choose TERMINAL. The object of the company is to discover it from the clues which you give to the individual letters.

First of all, create a number of words from its constituent letters, such as MERIT, MENIAL, MINE, MENTAL etc. Now devise clues for each word – a simple dictionary definition is as good as any.

Announce to the competitors that they are attempting to discover an 8-letter word of which the third, seventh and first letters mean a large rodent (RAT). Continue giving clues of this nature until the word is discovered.

The author presented an adult version of this game on local radio with cryptic clues. It was a phone-in programme and the lines were busy even before he had covered every individual letter in any of the chosen words. With clues matched to your classroom's level, you should have an equally intelligent response.

6. HIDDEN WORDS

Compile a list of words each of which incorporates (say) the name of a creature. Examples include KNEEL, WRENCH, TAPED, BATH, BENEVOLENT, SEALED, CHART, BEHIND, SNAG, CROCK, TRAIL, KAYAK, COLLIER, ESCARPMENT, SHAKE, PLANTER, SHARED, GRASPING, BOAT and CLASP. Now add a twist. BULLION, SCOWL, CATCHFLY and FOXGLOVE.

This is read out to the company and, apart from being a spelling test, is the basis of a fun puzzle. Each person writes the words down and is then challenged to discover the hidden creatures. Twenty four words and, logically, there will be twenty four creatures.

However, study the twist!

7. CLASSROOM BACK TO FRONT

The Back to Front concept of verbal play can be adapted for written activity by a group.

Compile your own Back to Front journey ensuring that it consists entirely of two word phrases. The previously mentioned SCHOOL to COLLEGE example has but four simple stages:–

SCHOOL TIME
TIME LOST
LOST ART
ART COLLEGE

and these can be used as the basis of a Classroom challenge. Take each constituent word (SCHOOL, TIME, LOST, ART and COLLEGE) shuffle them around and dictate the result of that shuffle to the contestants. Now challenge them to reassemble in a logical order.

Obviously, a four stage journey is far too short for a competition. However, consider this one:–

SCHOOL-WORK-BACK-BREAKING-DOWN-TOWN-HOUSE-PARTY-
TIME-LOST-ART-COLLEGE

Note that this eleven stage journey also contains not only the basic simple four stage journey but two five stage journeys:–

SCHOOL-PARTY-TIME-LOST-ART-COLLEGE
SCHOOL-WORK-TIME-LOST-ART-COLLEGE

a six stage journey:–

SCHOOL-HOUSE-PARTY-TIME-LOST-ART-COLLEGE

as well as the potential for breaking down with such as:–

SCHOOL-TIME-LOST-ART-WORK-HOUSE-BREAKING-DOWN-
TOWN.

The concept has as much potential as your wit. The task is simply to get from SCHOOL to COLLEGE. The rules of the game are whatever you care to make them, within the time limits you care to set.

To keep the action going, you can award (say) 4 points for the bright spark who spots the four stage journey and tell him or her to win yet more points for other possible journeys whilst the others are still struggling to make a first logical word association. The wittier you are in the original compilation, the more fun and frustration for everyone else.

The Back to Front series of verbal games is discussed on pages 62 to 69.

8. SHELLING PEAS with GRAMPS

(a) Shelling Peas A game as easy as shelling peas – or is it?
The contestants write down a short list of ordinary words read out by the organizer. These will be such as:–

1.   IT

2.   AT

3.   TO

and they are told that the object of the game is to see who can add the greatest number of P's to these words in order to change them from one genuine word into another. They are given the example of the first word, IT. By converting this into PIT they score one point and, if they also have TIP as well as PIT, they will score two points. Most contestants will then score six points for the remaining two base words with APT, PAT, TAP and OPT, POT, TOP. A total of eight points.

However, if the list continues with:–

4.   ALE

5.   TOE

6.   DEAL

this is where the fun really begins!

ALE not only has ALPE, LEAP, LEPA, PALE, PEAL, PELA, PLEA but it also has the 'double P' words APPLE, PAPLE and the 'triple P' word PAPPLE: 14 points.

TOE not only has PETO, POET, POTE, TOPE but EPOPT and POPPET: 9 points.

DEAL not only has PADLE, PALED, PEDAL, PLEAD but APPLED, DAPPLE, LAPPED, PALPED and PLAPPED: 15 points.

and these scores ignore the wealth of material provided by the obsolete words! The Appendix will define ALPE, LEPA, PELA, PAPLE, PAPPLE, PETO, EPOPT, PADLE and the verbs PALP and PLAP together with any other obscure words subsequently quoted but the above examples are, by no means, exceptional.

Even a simple little word such as AS has PAPS apart from ASP, SAP, SPA, the obscure PAS and PSA and the dialect word APS. LA can score even more. It has ALP, LAP, PAL and LAPP, PALP, PLAP.

There is no need to work out all the answers in advance. Simply choose any word containing at least one P and, once the P or P's are removed, see if the remaining letters produce a valid word. For example, PEPPERPOT. Removing its four P's leaves a sterile set of five letters. However, as PEPPERPOTS (not every dictionary hyphenates it or treats it as two words) it has a base word of STEREO. Can STEREO plus any other combination of P's create a word? Essentially it does not matter as you have already provided a challenge worthy of standing alone. OPPRESS can be reduced to ROSES or SORES. As SORES the word SPORES is immediately obvious and, as ROSES, PROSES (prose as a verb) is equally apparent and POSERS follows that quite logically. If a contestant submits SOPPERS this can easily be confirmed as being valid. PIPER provides an excellent example of the valid and the invalid. As the base word IRE it has (apart from PIPER) PIER and RIPE together with the obscure word PIRE. But, what about 'PIPPER'? Logically it would describe one who or that which pips in any sense of the verb and a far more likely word than PIRE. But, not even the *Oxford English Dictionary* records such a seemingly sensible noun.

To avoid the tedium of constantly consulting the dictionary keep the contest within the bounds of knowledge – not guesswork – by making clear from the outset that any words which prove invalid result in a loss of points on a basis of one point per P. Thus 'PIPPER' would involve a penalty of a three points deduction and guesses based on STEREO plus fewer than four P's would be held in check.

In attempting to lull the unwary into assuming that only a single P is intended to be added to most (if not all) base words, consider SEA and EDITOR originally selected on a basis of transposable value involving a single P. SEA, designed to produce APES, APSE, PEAS with SPAE as the 'clever' word might well have a competitor providing the Scottish word for popes, PAPES. At the most advanced level of competition with EDITOR as the base for five 'clever' words – DIOPTER, DIOPTRE, PERIDOT, PROTEID and the obsolete (but valid at this level) TORPIDE – could well have a wordsmith supplying PTEROPID!

At the classroom and adult fun levels, a simple list of only eight little words is ample for a wide variety of scores. Knowing that IT, AT, TO, AS, LA, ALE, TOE and IRE have the potential for more than fifty points without resorting to the obsolete words (which may be deemed valid only at wordsmith level) a reasonable time limit can be imposed. Under these conditions the winner is much more likely to be the one who first appreciates the 'ordinary' words such as APPLE, PIPER and POPPET rather than one who has heard of obscure words such as LEPA or PETO. Even such obvious words as APT, OPT and PLEA will be overlooked by the cleverest of players who, having discovered the 'double P' and 'triple P' aspects, miss the points which others obtain.

Basically all you need for the competition is a single 'multi-P' word (say) POLYP. As LOY you can see that it can become PLOY.

If a competitor comes up with a lucky guess, the perfectly valid LOPPY, that is his good fortune but that same gambler is just as likely to fail with 'PLOPPY' and fail to spot your 'clever' word POLYP. Couple that with APPLE (as ALE) even if you only appreciated PALE as the obvious disguise and the remaining half dozen words can be of the IT, AT, TO type.

For an advanced level competition you would have the larger words such as DEAL, STEREO, EDITOR and, if you reduce APREST to (say) STARE, the expert can score at least 30 points from just that single base word! Not that you fail to give the serious-minded adults little words – AS is ideal for them – and, if you would care to indulge in a little bit of fun, test yourself with AY. It is perfect for any level of play and its 'P words' are given at AY in the Appendix. Deduct points for any wrong guesses you make.

(b) GRAMPS

Gramps is the two-person, face to face version of Shelling Peas in which any letter is added to any small word in ignorance of the potential. Essentially it is a Fan-Tan not a Classroom game but, for convenience, is given here.

One person writes a letter (say) P on a small piece of paper which is then placed face down in the centre of the table. The other player then states a small word (say) ALE and the game is on. Both players now attempt to make as many words as they can from ALE plus as many P's as they wish. Neither tells the other what he or she has written down and another letter and another small word are similarly chosen for the next round.

The 12 points attainable with ALE + P's has already been discussed but now consider an absurd example.

The small word is AA (it will be defined below) and the letter is K. These are the possibilities in an 'impossible' combination:–

AAK	an old spelling of OAK and still retained in dialect
AKA	any of several species of New Zealand woody vines
AKKA	the Egyptian piastre, a small coin which circulated in the Ottoman Empire. British servicemen's slang, it is sometimes spelt ACKER.
KAA	an alternative spelling of KA in its senses as a verb. Meanings include 'of a partridge, to utter its cry'. Now only dialect.
KAAK	a verb of a crow, to utter its cry. No longer extant.
KAKA	a New Zealand olive-brown coloured parrot
KAKKAK	a species of bittern on the island of Guam

13 points when K is added to

AA   a cooled cindery substance consisting of sand, earth, stones and melted lava

Basically, however, one player will suggest 'sensible' letters such as L, M, N, P, R, S or T whilst the other will provide highly flexible base words such as AT, IN or EAT. (If, for example, T is suggested for EAT then assume EA as the base word and score a point for each T including EAT.) Players take turns in the provision of words and letters with the person providing the letter in charge of the time allowed for that particular round.

Four rounds constitute a set and the whole game is played to an agreed number of sets. Once a set has been completed, players take fresh sheets of paper for the next set. This is necessary as there is no objection to a player adding words to an earlier round in the current set and, if too many combinations were available for play, it would cease to be a fun game of interaction and be more like a Shelling Peas contest. Therefore, a player may not return to the workings of a previous set.

At the end of the game players check their opponent's results not merely to confirm scores but, hopefully, to deduct points for invalid submissions.

(*Shelling Peas with Gramps was suggested by the stage, television and film actor, Maxwell Caulfield, as a tribute to his grandfather, Thomas Newby.*)

9. SQUARING UP

Essentially this is French Crosswords played *en masse* using the **Bingo Letter-Frequency Table**.

Each member of the company draws a simple grid, five by five is ideal, and the leader calls out letters which people are free to place in any square of their own choosing.

Scoring will not be as high as the 35 to 45 points average with French Crosswords, but a sufficiently wide range will be produced. French Crosswords is described on page 88 and the **Bingo Letter-Frequency Table** is on page 73.

10. STRIKE

Tenpin bowling played with words. The basic description fits the concept exactly, but the game can be scaled down to any desired level. First, a word about tenpin scoring.

Ten pins are bowled at. If (say) 6 are knocked down with a first bowl and (say) 3 are knocked down with a second bowl this produces a score of 9 for a frame. A total of 10 frames are played.

However, if (say) 6 are knocked down with a first bowl and 4 with the second bowl, this does *not* result in a score of ten. It results in a score of 10 *plus* whatever the next bowl knocks down. Thus, the first bowl of the *next* frame scores twice. If it is (say) 7, then the total for the *first* frame is 17 and the 7 will be counted again in the second frame. The standard term for such an achievement is a SPARE.

The best possible achievement is a STRIKE. This is all of the pins knocked down with one bowl. Under these circumstances, the next two bowls are added to the 10 and that total represents the score for the first frame. If one's first three frames are all strikes, then the score for the first frame is 30, for the second frame is 20 plus whatever the next bowl is and, for the third frame, 10 plus whatever the next two bowls bring.

In the event of a spare being recorded in the tenth and final frame, one final bowl is permitted. If a strike is recorded in the tenth frame this gives two extra bowls. The maximum possible score, therefore, is 300 produced from 12 strikes.

The tenpin word game has twelve combinations of ten letters written down in this form:–

```
 1 A A A I L N R S T U      6 A A D E I I M N N T     11 A C D E I I M N O T
 2 A A C D E G L O T U      7 A A G I L L M N R Y     12 A C E E N N O R T V
 3 A A C E I M N O R T      8 A A G I N N O S T T
 4 A A C H I M N O R S      9 A B D E E L N O R S
 5 A A D E E H M R S T     10 A C D E E I L N R T
```

Contestants now bowl at this collection. Number 1 represents frame number one.

If a player can produce a 10-letter word in a frame, this is a strike. If a player can produce two words which total ten letters, this is a spare.

A player who achieves a spare in frame number ten may now attempt to do the best he or she can with the letters of frame number eleven to produce one word only.

Frame number twelve may only be considered by a player making a strike in frame ten and a strike in frame eleven.

A player who fails to make a strike or a spare in frame ten may go no further.

In this example, each frame contains a minimum of two 10-letter words and three of them contain three 10-letter words. Those three being frames six, nine and ten.

The point is not the discovery of these anagrams but the finding of one 10-letter word per frame in order to gain a strike. Failing that, to do the best one can. When scoring a spare, the better of the two words obtained in the next frame is deemed to be the next bowl.

To scale down to an easier level, one has two choices. The first is to have 10-letter words all of which end with -ING or have some other equally recognizable element common to all. Any words suffixed -SHIP or prefixed OVER- would suit the purpose.

The other choice is to have smaller words and smaller maximum scores.

The game is yours to play at whatever level you wish. If you require the definitive list of strikes for the above or would like to have the anagram concept as a permanent feature you will find 35,000 words each with at least one perfect anagram in *Pears Advanced Word-Puzzler's Dictionary*. It also defines any of those words which are unusual.

The words in the tenpin example are all fairly well known.

11. SHOT PUTTING

Until 1988 no one had exceeded 23 metres in putting the shot though both men and women had exceeded 22 metres. This game with each individual *additional* letter considered as a metre, has a theoretical but, for all practical purposes, impossible maximum of 26 metres. The 'world record' can, however, be broken.

The game is based upon the concept of andagrams. (An anagram of a word plus an additional letter – see Appendix.)

The technique of word selection will be given shortly, but a basic, highly flexible, word is selected and this is considered to be the shot. The task is to throw the shot as far as one can. The method is to run through the alphabet adding a different letter each time and making just one andagram for each different additional letter. Each andagram with a *different* letter is a metre. How far can the competitors put the shot?

The game can be as easy or difficult as you wish to make it. Essentially, the smaller the shot the easier it is to throw.

Take a very simple example, the word TEA.

The letters B, D, F, G, H, K, L, M, N, P, R, S and T will give, respectively, such as BEAT, DATE, FATE, GATE, HEAT, TAKE, LATE, MEAT, NEAT, TAPE, TEAR, SEAT and TEAT. A '13 metre throw' almost anyone can produce within a very short space of time. The outright winner, therefore, will need to utilize letters such as C, V, X, Y and Z for CATE, TAVE, EXTA, YATE and ZETA, all of which are defined in the Appendix.

Even 18 metres is not a champion's throw for TEA. Anyone prepared to delve into the *Oxford English Dictionary* will bring E, J, O and W into play with such as ATEE, JEAT, OATE and WATE and, now, all that remains are the 'easy' letters A, I and U plus, of course, the Q. The *Oxford English Dictionary* may well have words to cope with these.

In the game of Nastier Fun (see page 151) a '20 metre throw' comprising reasonably well known words was given as an example of just some of the 126 andagrams of the word, NASTIER.

Neither TEA nor NASTIER are exceptional. Whilst, for example, the 6-letter word, SATINE, has slightly fewer andagrams (121) than NASTIER it is capable of being thrown the 'world record' distance of 23 metres. Only J, Q and Y failing to be utilized.

The supreme andagrammable word is ASTER. This has at least 270 andagrams. These range, alphabetically, from the archaic adverb, ASTARE, to ERSATZ. How many metres can it be thrown? That is up to your contestants.

To produce a highly flexible word select, without duplication, from the following letters:–

> *vowels*   A, E, I
> *consonants*   L, N, R, S, T

and combine in the required length of 2-letter, 3-letter, 4-letter or whatever 'weight' of shot is suitable for the company.

The contestants begin by writing the complete alphabet down the left-hand side of their pages. They tackle the letters in any sequence they wish but do *not* advise them to ignore such difficult letters as X and Q. With SEAT as the shot, they could easily discover TAXES and with SAT you never know but one bright little spark might well have heard of the perfectly legitimate QATS.

Have a very good dictionary handy!

(*If you require a mnemonic for those highly flexible letters, choose between ENTRAILS or LATRINES.*)

12. DENBY DALE PIE

The history of Denby Dale Pie began, in 1788, when this Yorkshire village celebrated the return to sanity of King George III with the biggest meat pie in the world.

From time to time the village has baked bigger but not always better pies. One 19th century pie, for example, had an additional ingredient of game which went off and the whole thing had to be buried in quicklime. On another occasion the pie was so big and heavy that it crashed through the floor. The latest pie was baked in 1988 and voted a huge success. Its ingredients included meat, onions and gravy.

This contest brings game back into the pie.

The company suggest suitable ingredients for the pie. When sufficient have been named, a halt is called and the challenge is to produce the biggest word one possibly can from the words which have been accepted.

For example, a 'recipe' of DRIED PEAS, SALT, ONION, MEAT and FAT is more than ample for such blockbuster words as DEPARTMENTALISED or even DEPARTMENTALISATION, so keep it fairly simple.

CLASSROOM NOTE
The Solitaire Series which follows also contains concepts ideal for scaling down to children's level.

The Solitaire Series

Some of the games mentioned elsewhere are quite suitable for a personal challenge. Two which are both stimulating and, at the same time, good practice for a subsequent contest are Crossword (see page 90) and the battle aspect of The War Game (see page 115). In the case of battle play, simply begin with sample dominoes and see just how many salvos you could create.

Equally entertaining are some of the Classroom games such as devising your own perfect solutions for a pair of Build Up words (see page 163), other solutions for the complete alphabet challenge discussed in Other Ladder Games (see page 165) and discovering the most ingenious baseword for Shelling Peas (see page 170).

Even the Back to Front series of spoken games can be adapted for solo pencil and paper activity and your results used as a basis for another's verbal task.

However, anagrams apart, this series is concerned with con-

cepts not covered elsewhere and it begins with one of the oldest
known examples of word play.

1. ANAGRAM WORD SQUARES

The most famous of all word squares is written in Latin and has
been found carved or scratched on stone at Roman sites as far
apart as Cirencester, Pompeii and Dura-Europos in Mesopotamia:

```
R  O  T  A  S
O  P  E  R  A
T  E  N  E  T
A  R  E  P  O
S  A  T  O  R
```

First of all, it reads the same in all directions. Secondly, if AREPO
is presumed to be a personal name, then the whole translates as
The sower, Arepo, controls the wheels with care.

But, the third and most fascinating thing of all is that it may
have an esoteric significance. Certainly it could prove to be a
secret sign of a Christian community because the whole thing is a
most remarkable anagram. Consider this construction:-

```
            A

            P
            A            Paternoster is the opening word
            T            of the Lord's prayer. A and O
            E            stand for Alpha and Omega, a
            R            synonym for God.
A  PATERNOSTER  O            Finally, this anagram can
            O            only be constructed in the
            S            shape of a cross.
            T                Other solutions have been
            E            suggested but none match this
            R            for ingenuity.

            O
```

To play with anagram word squares begin with a 3 x 3
construction. If you have never devised a word square previously
you will find that it is so pathetically simple to produce a 3 x 3
that it is not worth bothering with, unless it has some additional
challenge.

There are various anagram challenges worth trying. The first is to construct a single 3 x 3 square in which every word is an anagram of the other five words. The author's own solutions to this task are given below. But, can you devise better ones which do not necessitate the use of rather obscure words?

```
E A R     T E A     S P A
R E A     A T E     A S P
A R E     E A T     P A S
```

Obviously, any of the above can be shuffled around but each will still use the same six different words no matter how you arrange the particular square.

A different type of anagram word square is one which contains exactly the same letters and mirrors the same pattern of at least one other square. Consider the following eighteen squares. The author began with one very simple square which had the same words running both horizontally and vertically and then produced no fewer than seventeen anagrams of it. The unusual words are defined in the Appendix and ENA, of course, is the feminine Christian name.

```
T A N     T A N     R A N     N E T     N E T     T E N
A R E     E R A     A T E     E R A     E N A     E R A
N E T     N E T     N E T     T A N     T A R     N A T


T E N     T E A     T A E     R E T     R E N     R A T
E T A     E R N     A R N     E N A     E T A     A N E
N A R     A N T     E N T     T A N     N A T     T E N


N A T     N A T     E N T     E N T     A N T     A N T
A R E     A N E     N E A     N A E     N A E     N E A
T E N     T E R     T A R     T E R     T E R     T A R
```

A third type of anagram challenge is to take a 9-letter word and make a 3 x 3 square of it. For example, GALENGALE. This aromatic rootstock of certain plants of the ginger family is not only capable of providing the basis for a square but even that square has anagrams:-

```
N A G     L E G     L A G     L A G     G A L
A L E     E N A     A L E     A N E     A N E
G E L     G A L     G E N     G E L     L E G
```

In each case the pattern of the same words running both horizontally and vertically is maintained. Quite a few additional anagrams can be produced by utilizing the Christian name of LEN, the slang word GAN and the obsolete word NEG apart from any others which may well exist.

The challenges are to find better examples than these, apart from taking the whole concept a stage further by considering larger squares.

2. SUPERSQUARES

The construction of word squares up to 5 × 5 is such an easy task that it is not even worth attempting unless it has some degree of entertaining difficulty. However, if the anagram word square holds no appeal, try to create an ever increasing square which, at each progressive stage, consists entirely of genuine words.

Begin with a single letter which is a word in its own right – A, I or O are common English words but such geographical names as E, a Scottish river or Y, an American town, are equally valid. The task is to commence with a nominal 1 × 1 then convert it into a 2 × 2 , thence 3 × 3, 4 × 4 etc. The author's example, admittedly using the occasional obscure word given in the Appendix, builds up to 5 × 5.

```
                              R A T A S
                   R A T A    A F A R E
          F A R    A F A R    T A P E R
   P E    A P E    T A P E    A R E A R
A  E A    R E A    A R E A    S E R R Y
```

Can you produce an example without the use of obscure words or else create the world's first ever 6 × 6 progressive word square?

The above concept is original but the ultimate challenge is the classic palindrome square exemplified by the Latin ROTAS/ SATOR discussed in Anagram Word Squares. Two English examples of a palindrome square are given opposite. The only real difference between them is the G and the K in whichever diametrically opposed corners you wish to place them:–

```
S T A N K          G N A T S
T E N O N          N O N E T
A N A N A          A N A N A
N O N E T          T E N O N
K N A T S          S T A N G
```

and their unusual words are defined in the Appendix.

However, if you prefer to attempt squares larger than 5 × 5 without any restrictions, the superlative is the 10 × 10. Dmitri Borgmann is, as far as is known, the only person who has ever achieved this and his contained a mass of the most obscure words imaginable. Other experts, even with the aid of computers, have attempted to match his achievement but without success.

Borgman's 10 × 10 is a traditional square, having the same words running both horizontally and vertically. Specialist word play magazines carry pleas from computer buffs for assistance in the construction of a 10 × 10 double square (one having different words in both the horizontal and vertical planes) in their attempts to achieve a 10 × 10 'first'.

But, even Borgmann's 10 × 10 is imperfect as he was forced to repeat the words ANDOLANDOL, NGOTANGOTA and GALAN-GLAN in the same plane both horizontally and vertically. He admits that no fully satisfactory 9 × 9 square has ever been produced either, as the best of these required a dialect word in order to ensure completion.

The 8 × 8 traditional or double square may, therefore, be regarded as a supersquare and even the best of these will require an explanation of some of the words utilized.

The 7 × 7 is regarded as the first of the higher orders of squares and, like the 8 × 8, is really the province of the expert.

This leaves the 6 × 6. To construct one of these is a worthy accomplishment and, whilst it cannot be considered a super-square, nevertheless it is a challenge worthy of being undertaken. Of the two forms, the traditional is easier than the double.

3. WORD OBLONGS

An easier task than supersquares and one where you begin with a pair of logically related words and see how far you can take them as ever increasing acrostics.

For example, the words THE and END. As triple, quadruple, quintuple and sextuple acrostics one could have such as:-

```
T H E      T H E E      T H E R E      T R A I S E
H E N      H E R N      H E R O N      H E R D E N
E N D      E Y E D      E N D E D      E X T E N D
```

with the aid of an obscure word or two.

What is the best pair of words to consider and what is the ultimate acrostic which can be built up in this stage by stage fashion?

4. CRYPTARITHMETIC

There are two different approaches to the compilation of these little gems. Either begin with the mathematics and then find words to fit or, as the author has done below, begin with words which aptly express a statement then find numbers which agree.

The result is a mathematical puzzle in which each letter represents a different digit from 0 to 9 and one has to work out which letter is which numeral. For example:-

```
        P E A R  S
        W O R D +
        _____
        G A M E  S
        _____
```

This contains ten different letters (A, D, E, G, M, O, P, R, S and W) so that each one must represent each of the different numerals from 0 to 9. D *has* to be zero, no other possibility exists. Therefore, it is impossible to carry forward any remainder into the next column. Thus, R + R = E and one has only to consider 1 + 1 = 2, 2 + 2 = 4 etc. Whichever combination one considers (say) 1 + 1 = 2, so the digit 2 has to be written in the position occupied by the letter E. Thus:-

```
        .  2  .  1  .
        .  .  1  0 +
        _____
        .  .  .  2  .
        _____
```

If this fails to produce a satisfactory conclusion after considering the other letters in relation to this supposition, continue with combinations until you find one which will meet all conditions such as:–

$$72164$$
$$9360\ +$$
$$\overline{}$$
$$81524$$

Now attempt to solve the following. If you succeed, then you will have little difficulty in compiling your own.

The very best have only one possible answer and make a witty or apt statement.

```
W R O N G          F A C E T          N I N E
W R O N G +        F A C E T          N I N E
───────────        F A C E T +        N I N E +
R I G H T          ─────────          ─────────
───────────        W H O L E          H E L P
                   ─────────          ─────────
```

5. WORD SEARCH

In terms of numbers of people who attempt published word puzzles, the word search is by far the most popular. But, have you ever tried to compile one? Anyone is capable of scattering half a dozen words over a large enough grid and then filling in the remaining spaces with any old letters.

However, if you wish to provide an entertaining challenge for others to attempt, then go to one of two extremes.

(a) A masterpiece involving as many words relevant to the chosen subject as you can. If it is good enough then others might well care to solve it, either in the form of photocopies of your original construction or else in (say) the staff magazine.

(b) Take a single word, such as SINGLE. Write this word once only on the grid. Now fill the remaining spaces with S's, I's, N's, G's, L's and E's. When doing this you must take great care to ensure that you have only a single SINGLE. But, fill the remainder with infuriations such as 'SINGEL', 'SINNGLE', 'SIGNGLE', 'SLINGLE', 'SINGL' or whatever and you will have produced one far superior to some of the banal constructions which people are actually paid to devise. It will also be far more difficult to solve.

The searches created by Tom Wright, the inventor of Square Bashing, are even more superior. First you find the hidden words *then* you have to solve his puzzles.

To illustrate how popular such effort you undertake might prove, consider this example. A regional newspaper ran one of Tom's special word searches, a Scrabble puzzle of mine and a cryptic crossword all of which offered similar prizes. Whilst few competitors gave correct solutions to the word search or the Scrabble puzzle, the submissions were on a basis of ten word searches to every three Scrabble puzzles to every one crossword. This is not to say that this was the ratio of attempt, as people only submit entries which they believe to be correct. The reason for the higher Scrabble than crossword response is that one *knows* if one has solved the crossword but none knew if they had found the highest possible Scrabble score (it was full of red herring lower scoring opportunities) but the popularity of the word search cannot be denied.

Tom's special? Find the words then, from these, isolate the significant letters which will give you the solution. Readers were told that the answer was a newly-published book by the widow of the comedian Eric Morecambe. The overwhelming response was for 'Morecambe and Wise'. The actual title was a very apt *Morecambe and Wife*!

To construct a word search for publication, use graph paper for your working then submit a typewritten copy to the editor. Check it thoroughly first. Obscenities are easily introduced by accident.

6. DEFINITIVE FUN

A solitaire challenge to run through the alphabet producing witty definitions.

At its simplest, a punning alphabet which begins:-
A for ISM
B for PORK
C for THIGHLANDERS

But, at its best, a compilation after the style of the masters of the subject, Ambrose Gwinnet Bierce or Gordon Bowker. These are examples of their terse gems:-

ALONE In bad company. (*Bierce*)
BORE A person who talks when you wish him to listen. (*Bierce*)
GAY To be thoroughly bent on pleasure. (*Bowker*)

HOOKER A fisher of men. (*Bowker*)
LAWYER One skilled in the circumvention of the law. (*Bierce*)
MOONIE A lune with a view. (*Bowker*)
TOY PISTOL A gun-of-a-son. (*Bowker*)

The puns, of which Bowker produces the best, are much easier to devise than the satire of Bierce whose *Devil's Dictionary* was published at the turn of the century and is still in print.

For a 'directory of famous people' you might care to rephrase the following classics of graffiti:—

    ARCHDUKE FERDINAND FOUND ALIVE : FIRST WORLD WAR A
      MISTAKE
    LEDA LOVES SWANS
    YOU THINK OEDIPUS HAD A PROBLEM – ADAM WAS EVE'S
      MOTHER
    PINOCCHIO IS A SWINGER
    SOCRATES EATS HEMLOCK

and, in so doing, develop your own satirical or punning style.

Preserve your wittiest definitions for others to enjoy.

7. THINGS

Things are adult rebuses or, as *The Mail on Sunday* calls them, Dingbats. Rebus is the Latin for THINGS and became part of the English language several centuries ago.

Anyone can produce an adult rebus; a witty challenge for others to solve and confined entirely to letters, words, numerals and symbols. The following examples are all the author's Things, some of which have featured as fun clues in his cryptic cross-words.

To solve, study the construction.

$$\boxed{\text{Y O B}}$$

YOB is BOY written backwards. As a Thing it means, therefore, *backward boy*. To place a Thing within the confines of a box gives one the additional scope of position, as two of the following will show.

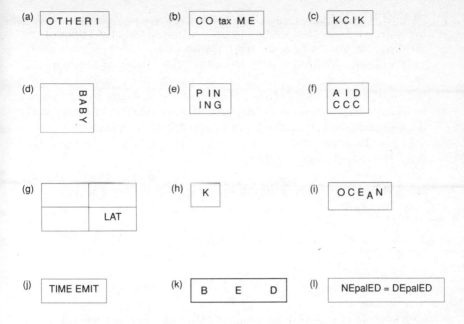

The answers are given below. But, time yourself before attempting to make sense of this last one. The solution, ironically, is in the Appendix – somewhere!

th HOW did/it U 12feet is

8. ACRONYMS

The construction of an apt description of a word or short phrase by using its constituent letters in the correct order. Thus, SNAKE could be described as 'singularly nasty animal knavishly elongated'.

The *New Statesman* runs competitions on this concept and readers' gems on the subject of plays and films include:–
Just a white shark.
Endless vivacity in the Argentine.
This has everything: syrupy outbursts, uplifting nannies, dancing over flowery mountains, unctuous songs involving children.

Set yourself a theme and see what you can produce.

9. POETIC LICENCE

Limericks, clerihews and all manner of verse forms are worth emulating.

A classic limerick was once inserted in a newspaper by Monsignor Ronald Knox in a most un-limerick like form. It read:–

> Evangelical vicar in want of a portable secondhand font,
> would dispose of the same for a portrait (in frame) of the
> Bishop-elect of Vermont.

The clerihew is a four-line versified biography invented by Edmund Clerihew Bentley (1875–1956). His masterpieces include:–

> The digestion of Milton
> Was unequal to Stilton.
> He was only feeling so-so
> When he wrote *Il Penseroso*

Even shorter verse fun can be achieved by taking a well-known line of verse and adding a second line of your own. For example:–

> I wandered lonely as a cloud –
> I did look ghastly in a shroud.
> Or
> I wandered lonely as a cloud –
> Offensive smells were disallowed.

Channel 4's *Countdown* featured a sequence of tiny 'poems' which needed incredibly lengthy titles in order to make sense of the resultant rhyme. The smallest of all were created by the author and by John Meade, the producer of the programme. These, both wittily described, were:—

I   IO
Eye   IO

The 'world's shortest poem' is still waiting to be written, all it needs is a suitable title.

10. MAN'S LAUGHTER

If MAN'S LAUGHTER means nothing to you then FORGOT HIST AS KIN SO LIT AIR ESK ILL.

CAT CHIN THEMES, SAGE looks equally weird but, correctly punctuated, tells you that this has a CATCH IN THE MESSAGE!

This challenge is to produce a longer or wittier statement.

11. THE WORLD'S LONGEST WORD GAME

Begin with a letter which is also a word (say) A. Convert this into a 2-letter word (say) AT. Now continue with such as HAT or ATE and see what is the longest possible word you can create in this fashion.

Alternatively, try and build the tallest possible vertical column with overlapping words in the way that the top Scrabble players score their 7-letter words with consumate ease.

Faced with (say) LIMPETS already in play and having the bonus-scoring adverb AHEIGHT on his or her rack the top player will automatically consider what 2-letter word combination gives the best score. For example:-

(a)   A H E I G H T
                        L I M P E T S

(b)   L I M P E T S
                                    A H E I G H T

(c)   L I M P E T S
                            A H E I G H T

all utilize valid 2-letter words and the choice of the third option, other things being equal, would be made almost immediately.

For this solitaire challenge ignore the first option and see how you could build up (say) the second option. It might develop in this fashion:-

```
       L I MP E T S
                AHE I GHT
       V I NTAGE
                SW I MME R
```

assuming that you limited yourself to 7-letter words.

But, you may care to give yourself greater flexibility and build up at either end with words of any length and see just how tall a construction you can produce. With LIMPETS as the base, this particular run ended with two 5-letter words, GALAS and SITES, one 6-letter word, STANKS, and one 7-letter word, DUNITES. Apart from a result of a 7-letter word, one could view the personal attainment as being (say) 23 points by combining the total number of letters in all four words so constructed.

```
              D I D
              G U N
         MAN       A S
         L I M P E T S
         C AT       A I M
         S E R V A N T
              SO    KE L P
              C L A S S
```

This technique of simultaneous horizontal and vertical word scoring is one of the ways in which top Scrabble players differ from the parlour player no matter how adept at words he or she may be.

Even the average player aware of the basic attitudes can devastate the masterminds when facing each other in competition. For example, the Scrabble enthusiasts' magazine, *Onwords*, reported a contest between a team of quite ordinary members of a Scrabble club and MENSA. No Scrabble player was surprised at the result – MENSA was sunk without trace.

If Channel 4 ever brings *Television Scrabble* back again watch how a celebrity such as Sylvia Syms makes mincemeat of her opposite number. She uses this double scoring ploy quite naturally apart from, as she demonstrates on *Countdown*, being pretty good with words anyway.

12. TRIPLETS

Three different challenges to take trips with words using the technique of logical addition and subtraction of individual letters. Each change must be to a genuine word and no word may be repeated.

(a) **MINIMAL PAIRING** Change any pair of logically associated words such as TO to FROM, AS to WHEN, NO to YES, BOY to MAN, HORSE to CART, using as few words as possible:–

TO	AS	NO	BOY	HORSE
O	A	NOY	BO	HOSE
FO	AE	OY	O	HOE
FRO	WAE	OYE	AO	HO
FROM	WE	OYES	A	O
	WEN	YES	AN	AO
	WHEN		MAN	A
				AT
				CAT
				CART

(b) **ONE TO ONE** Build up from a single-letter word to the largest word possible and return to a different single-letter word:–

A
AN
RAN
RAIN
TRAIN
STRAIN
ESTRAIN
RESTRAIN
RESTRAINS
RESTAINS
RESTAIN
RETAIN
RETIN
REIN
RIN
IN
I

(c) **LENGTHY TRIPS** Begin a journey by starting from HOME and see where you can get to. For example, HOME to BRAZIL via KENT and SPAIN. Alternatively, incorporate a number of logically associated words such as PEARS WORD GAMES.

1	HOME	1	PEARS
	HOE		EARS
	OE		EAR
	O		EA
	ON		A
	EON		AO
	EN		O
	KEN		OR
2	KENT		WOR
	KET	2	WORD
	KETA		WORLD
	ETA		WOLD
	TA		OLD
	A		GOLD
	AN		GOD
	PAN		GOAD
	SPAN		GAD
3	SPAIN		GA
	PAIN		GAM
	AIN		GAME
	AI	3	GAMES
	AIL		
	RAIL		
	BRAIL		
4	BRAZIL		

The unusual words featuring in these challenges are defined in the Appendix, together with BAZIL for a continuation from BRAZIL to the flexible single-letter word, I.

In any form of tripping the most highly flexible and attractive-looking point is that where reduction has been made to a single-letter word, preferably A, I or O. Considering the category of famous people, for example, finds many forenames and titles easily reduced to this point. Even PRESIDENT, with the aid of a 17th century spelling of RESIANT, also falls prey to the tripper:–

PRESIDENT	POPE	PETER	MARY	JACK	JEAN	CHARLES
RESIDENT	POP	PETE	MAY	ACK	JAN	HARLES
RESIENT	OP	PET	MA	LACK	AN	HARLE
RESENT	O	PEAT	A	LAC	A	HARL
RESET		EAT		LA		HAL
REST	KING	EA	JOHN	A	DAVID	HA
RET	KIN	A	JON		AVID	A
RE	IN		JO	JILL	AID	
REA	I	PAUL	O	ILL	AI	DIANA
EA		PAL		MILL	A	DANA
A	TSAR	PA	IAN	MIL		DAN
	TAR	A	IN	MI	BOB	AN
	TA		I	I	OB	A
	A				O	

The name of Triplets is not so much a pun on the word, trip, as an alternative form of word play in the genre of Lewis Carroll's Doublets (see Word Ladders page 161). Carroll produced his own alternative, a highly complex and rule-bedevilled game which he called Syzygies. I considered including a description of Syzygies but, to be honest, found it not only difficult to understand but rather tedious. However, it should be mentioned in a review of word play and the reader who wishes to investigate that alternative to Doublets will find a full description in the Penguin paperback, *The Magic of Lewis Carroll*.

Triplets, therefore, is my own compensating invention to achieve Carroll's objective of turning such as COOK to DINNER. The Triplet and Syzygy step-by-step moves are contrasted but, to make sense of Carroll's reasoning, it will be necessary to read a full exposition of his methods as these involve non-words ('inne' is one of them) in a formula which makes every game in this book look as though it is intended for a mentally retarded child.

Triplet	Syzygy
COOK	COOK
COO	(remove the K to leave COO
OO	and add S and PING either
O	side of it)
OI	SCOOPING
I	(pin)
IN	PINNED
DIN	(inne)
DINE	DINNER
DINER	
DINNER	

Obviously, in tripping, an exception to the rule of repetition needs to be made when going to and from the same pair of words. Thus,

TO and FROM	THIS and THAT		
1 TO	1 THIS	THINS	HATS
TOM	HIS	TINS	HATE
OM	IS	TIN	ATE
ROM	I	IN	TE
2 FROM	AI	AIN	THE
FROME	AIT	AN	THEN
ROME	AT	A	THEIN
ROE	HAT	EA	THEINE
OE	2 THAT	EAT	THINE
TOE	TAT	HEAT	THIN
1 TO	TAI	THEAT	THING
O	TI	2 THAT	THINGS
FO	TIS	THATS	THIGS
FRO	1 THIS	HATS	1 THIS
2 FROM			

These exceptions being strictly limited to the destinations, all other words must be different.

However, an even simpler concept than my Triplets or Carroll's Syzygies is Dmitri Borgmann's Synonym Chains (see page 000).

13. WORDSMITHERY

Antigrams, lipograms, palindromes, pangrams, pseudodromes and univocalics are amongst the other specialized forms of word play that appeal to the individual and the best examples of which please the many. Classics in each category are given as a spur to your own creativity.

(a) Antigrams
The best anagrams are those which are the most apt, the most ironic or the exact opposite in meaning. An antigram is the one which is the exact opposite, though this can sometimes depend upon your point of view. The following are all anagrams. Some are obvious antigrams, some are clever ironies and only become antigrams in personal opinion.

boardroom	*Broadmoor*
circumstantial evidence	*can ruin a selected victim*
considerate	*desecration*
diplomacy	*mad policy*
enormity	*more tiny*
evangelists	*evil's agents*
funeral	*real fun*
infection	*fine tonic*
legislation	*is it legal? no*
marriage	*a grim era*
misfortune	*its more fun*
mother-in-law	*woman Hitler*
protectionism	*nice to imports*
united	*untied*
violence	*nice love*

(b) Anagram Curiosities

Many words which are basically mutually related remain as anagrams no matter how they are reconsidered in the light of addition of prefixes and suffixes. CORK and ROCK, for example, are still anagrams when they become CORKS/ROCKS; CORKING/ROCKING; CORKLIKE/ROCKLIKE and UNCORKED/UNROCKED.

However, this is not true of all such pairs. ACT and CAT cease to be anagrams as present participles – ACTING/CATTING. By contrast, previously unrelated pairs become anagrams only with the addition of suffixes and prefixes and the letter E features in a considerable number of these.

CASH and CHASE only transpose as verbal inflections:–

CASHED/CHASED; CASHES/CHASES; CASHING/CHASING

but, consider how this letter can take CART to TRACE to CREATE:–

CARTED/TRACED
TRACEABLE/CREATABLE

Can you produce a similar or better chain of E factor anagrams or, indeed, bring any other aspect to bear in the study of these curious aspects of the language?

(c) Lipograms

Since classical Greek times a few writers have produced compositions which deliberately exclude a particular letter of the alphabet. For example, the great 16th century Spanish dramatist, Lope de Vega, wrote five novels each of which suppressed a different vowel in turn.

However, the most famous lipogram is Ernest Vincent Wright's 50,000 word novel, *Gadsby*, which was written, according to his introduction, 'with the *e* type-bar of the typewriter tied down.' It is one of the world's rare books and a copy complete with dust jacket was once sold for $1,000. What is so poignant about this is that Wright never received a penny for his efforts. He paid for the book to be produced and died on publication day, October 6th 1939.

It is fitting to record that one of the few people known to possess a copy is the editor of *Word Ways*, A. Ross Eckler, whose lipogram versions of Mary Had A Little Lamb are the most oft quoted examples of this art. Here are just two of them. The first omits the letter S and the second is minus the T.

> Mary had a little lamb
> With fleece a pale white hue
> And everywhere that Mary went
> The lamb kept her in view;
> To academe he went with her,
> Illegal, and quite rare;
> It made the children laugh and play
> To view a lamb in there.

> Mary had a pygmy lamb,
> His fleece was pale as snow,
> And every place where Mary walked
> Her lamb did also go;
> He came inside her classroom once,
> Which broke a rigid rule;
> How children all did laugh and play
> On seeing a lamb in school.

(Also see Qwaints (page 202) for a particularly apt lipogram.)

(d) Palindromes

A word, such as DEIFIED, is called a palindrome as it reads the same when read in either direction, so too is a phrase or statement such as these:

Madam, I'm Adam
Never odd or even
Dennis and Edna sinned
Nurse, I spy gypsies. Run!
A man, a plan, a canal – Panama
Satan, oscillate my metallic sonatas
Sums are not set as a test on Erasmus
Able was I ere I saw Elba (Attributed to Napoleon)
Egad! A base note denotes a bad age (Attributed to Henry
Purcell)

My own contribution to this genre is unique. It is based upon the
English word XI. XI describes the fourteenth letter of the Greek
alphabet. In upper case xi is written in Greek as Ξ and half a dozen
of these appear as:

Ξ Ξ Ξ Ξ Ξ Ξ

Described in English, aptly using capital letters, this becomes:

SIX XIS

and so, both in English and in Greek, the palindrome not only
reads the same forwards and backwards but also upside down!

(e) Pangrams
A sentence that contains each letter of the alphabet is a pangram.
Examples:

The quick brown fox jumps over a lazy dog	(Complete alphabet + 7 letters)
Pack my box with five dozen liquor jugs	(Complete alphabet + 6 letters)
Waltz, bad nymph, for quick jigs vex	(Complete alphabet + 2 letters)

The ideal pangram not only contains each letter only once but is
also easily understood. Unfortunately the best minimal pangrams
published to date have not only needed the majority of their
words defining but the resultant statement still needs an explanation even when the meanings have been given. These are three of
the very best:

Cwm fjord-bank glyphs vext quiz
(Carved figures (GLYPHS) on the bank of a fjord in a

rounded valley (CWM) vexed (VEXT is a 17th century
form) an eccentric person (QUIZ).)
Cwm kvutza qoph jynx fled brigs
(The wryneck bird (JYNX) from the communal farming
unit (KVUTZA) designated by the nineteenth letter of the
Hebrew alphabet (QOPH) and situated in a rounded
valley (CWM) fled from the prisons on a ship (BRIGS).)
Vext cwm fly zing jabs Kurd qoph
(A vexed (VEXT) fly in a rounded valley (CWM),
humming in a shrill fashion (ZING) jabs at the nineteenth
letter of the Hebrew alphabet (QOPH) drawn by one of a
Moslem people dwelling mainly in a region situated in
NW Iran, NE Iraq and SW Turkey (KURD).)

The difference between these three minimal pangrams and the
'Waltz bad nymph' construction is immense. Not only does the
latter require no words to be defined but its statement stands
complete. Is the ideal pangram possible? No words should be
defined and no explanation offered.

The use of the obsolete VEXT provides the key. A reasonable
person can both understand it and assume it to be an old spelling
of a word in current usage. Given that convention for this
particular form of word play do you understand this following
attempt of mine to achieve the first 'perfect' pangram? If you do
not, then I have failed and it is no better than any of the others.

Qwyk bitch vox jumps glaz'd fern

However, the truly fascinating aspect of these six words is that
they can be rearranged into a parody of the famous 'Quick brown
fox' pangram known to most typists. A detailed explanation is
required – though Devonians who still retain VOX in the adjective
VOXY, where others have FOXY, will be a step ahead of most.
GLAZ'D (this abbreviated form of GLAZED can be found in the
Oxford English Dictionary) is no longer considered in the above
sense of 'covered with frost' but, believe it or not, as a synonym for
BROWN! Amazingly, both GLAZED and BROWN once held
identical meanings as 'shining'. FERN is no longer the plant of the
above but its former adjectival sense of 'ancient' is revived for the
parody. True, ancient and lazy are hardly the same thing but an
ancient canine would certainly behave in a similar sluggish
manner to that of the famed lazy dog. Typists of the English-
speaking world, here is your revised fingering test. I hope you like
it.

Qwyk glaz'd vox jumps fern bitch

(All of the above words including QWYK can be found in the *Oxford English Dictionary*.)

(f) Pseudodromes

A type of palindrome in which the words of a sentence read the same when written in reverse order. Examples:–

> *Bores are people that say that people are bores*
> *You can cage a swallow, can't you, but you can't swallow*
> *a cage can you?*
> *Women understand men; few men understand women.*
> *Girl, bathing on Bikini, eyeing boy, finds boy eyeing*
> *bikini on bathing girl.*

(g) Univocalics

Writings which consist of a solitary vowel and tend to find their best expression in verse:–

> Idling, I sit in this twilight dim
> Whilst birds in wild, swift, vigils, circling skim,
> Light winds in sighing sink, till, rising bright,
> Night's Virgin Pilgrim swims in vivid light.
> (C.C. Bombaugh, 1890)

But, beyond the established word play which finds itself the basis of complete books on the subject, new literary amusements rise and get taken up by others. Six examples follow. The first of these is an extension of Lewis Carroll's portmanteau word creation, the second is further discoveries in letter-shifting pioneered by A. Ross Eckler and the remainder are, literally, self-descriptive.

(h) Sportmanteaux

Coining new words by combining the elements of two other words can produce some interesting effects. Vernon D. Maclaren of Augusta, Maine, has devised numerous portmanteau descriptions for citizens of various American towns and cities. Among his best are Antwerps (not silly Belgians but residents of a town in New York state), Baltimorons. Bermutants, Lebananas and Wood-stockings.

As few of these are likely to find acceptance, least of all locally, so the author suggests that some of them have greater appeal with a different meaning. Consequently he has redefined the following:

Belfasteroids	inter-community communications freely exchanged in Ulster's capital city in times of trouble
Buffellows	non-Masonic lodgers
Moscoundrels	Leonid Brehznev's in-laws
Spartisans	ancient Laconian freedom-fighters
Waterloonies	either commuters to London from the southern suburbs or those who willingly followed Napoleon on his last imperial venture

On this basis one has greater flexibility for wit and, by considering the world at large, it could be interesting to read a 'Devil's Sportmanteau Gazeteer' including Amsterdamp, Berlinguist, Chicagoing, Durhamburger, Elbanned, Falmouthed, Godalmingle, Harlechery, Industry (rivers not being excluded), Japanic, Kansasses, Londone, Madridden, Niagrian, Omaharm, Pakistandard, Quebeckon, Rangoonish, Sedantry, Tampacked, Uttoxeterm, Vichiest, Widnest, Xeater (the alternatives to this Devonian city are obscure places such as Xanthi in Greece which would need footnotes), Yorking and Zuricher with definitions after the style of the master, Ambrose Gwinnet Bierce.

Surprising as it may seem, words of this ilk do become established in the language. Connecticutie, describing a pretty girl of Connecticut, was first used in 1938 by the essayist Frank Sullivan about Mrs Heywood Brown then, in 1947, by a journalist for the Hon. Clare Boothe Luce. It reached *Playboy* in 1968. It is not simply a matter of coining a word but in coining an apt word capable of more than a nonce usage which determines the lifespan of a geographical portmanteau.

(i) Alphabet Soup

David Morice is an Iowan wordsmith who discovers pairs of numerically related words with the aid of an empty soup tin. He wraps individual strips of paper each containing a complete alphabet, round the tin and twists these strips until he locates a word. For example, he located INKS then noticed that, alhabetically, J, O, L and T immediately follow. STEER to TUFFS is another of his soup tin discoveries which is a single step in letter-shifting.

Letter-shift pairs are not restricted to those adjacent to each other alphabetically as the 7-letter shift from CHEER to JOLLY is regarded as the classic in this genre, the words being related in sense.

Morice, however, does not restrict himself to the discovery of mere pairs of words as his 'soup tinnery' has produced a 3 × 3 word square:—

```
L A P
A P E
P E T
```

(in which each letter is 15 steps away from the one to its right and the one below) and all manner of other word shapes such as triangles:—

```
L I V I N G
R O B O T
H E R E
D A N
I
```

which he describes as a pyramid.

He has discovered so many words of this nature that he has even written a ballad of letter-shifted words. If the music matches these lyrics . . .

Munch wolf muffs by bum. Oafs win
Satin curl, Sally. He has ugly cot.
Yak! Boa! Bulls punt gulls! Wits bin.
Sue, hug Harry. John, marry cozy, hot.

. . . and that's only the second verse – then watch out for soup opera!

(The letter-shifting in this 'verse' has the second line six steps from the first line (MUNCH/SATIN; WOLF/CURL; MUFFS/SALLY etc.) and the fourth line six steps from the third though I suspect he has some of his words on the wrong lines. Surely it should be:

Yak! hug etc.
Sue, boa etc.

But, it probably does not make sense if one is too pedantic!

(j) Self-referential English

The word **four** is unique. It is the only number which contains letters equal to its value. Therefore, its intrinsic quality of describing itself makes it an example of a self-referential word.

The words **nonhyphenated** and **polysyllabic** are equally self-referential but **uppercase** and **lix** only become self-referential when specially contrived. Written as UPPERCASE it qualifies but lix (a 17th century word for a Roman camp follower) would only be self-referential if it were used for a 59-year-old Roman camp follower!

The discovery of words such as these produces little more than personal satisfaction – unless one happens to be Douglas Hofstadter.

Hofstadter is the master of self-referential prose and his column in *Scientific American* sparkles with such as:

> This is not a complete. Sentence. This either. You have,
> of course, just begun reading this sentence which you
> have just finished reading.

For his book, *Beyond Language* (1967), the American writer, Dmitri Borgmann, devised a related form which requires no explanation of an individual self-referential word. These he termed suggestive words and are such as **war** with the letter A in the shape of a missile rising from a silo or the arm of the letter T taking the shape of a bow tie in **bow tie.**

However, Darryl Francis conceived yet another form of these words which has a greater potential than Borgmann's concept, as its absence of artwork renders it capable of being reproduced in every publication.

These first appeared in the February 1978 issue of *Word Ways* as aberrant forms of self-referential English and, with Darryl's permission, I reproduce them below under the apt description of Qwaints.

(k) Qwaints

Qwaint is more than being a Middle English spelling of the adjective, quaint. To the twentieth century reader it possesses the quality of *looking* quaint and, thereby the meaning of the word is reinforced. Furthermore, in the days when it was spelt qwaint, it had the additional meaning of 'ingeniously designed'.

Thus (bearing in mind that quaint has also served as a noun) we have the perfect word to describe what followers in the witty self-referential footsteps of Darryl Francis have termed 'unique varieties of self-descriptive word-like letter-sequences' for their own published examples. A Qwaint may, therefore, be defined as 'an ingeniously designed self-descriptive word-like letter-sequence possessing the quality of the word suggested'.

Darryl Francis's Qwaints:–
twogether, Decembrrr, HUMiLiTY, mispelling, neverendin, unsofisticated, millionaire$$, defectivə

Anthony Sebastian's, Renee Merriam's and Ivy Dixon-Baird's Qwaints:—

vwllss, exxxxcess, sur++++, underscored, SP O RAD I C, cndnsd, TEARDR$_O$P, close harmony.

Peter Newby's Qwaints:—

greeed, exc!amation, SP CE, Linda Lusaaaahdi, anoise, slowth, inelastick, judoh, jaIIIl, dynamight, dsylexia, ampers&, shorthnd, booob, mi££ionaire, INLeT, ffffreezing, metricat10n, caMel, ˙ʇɐq Rnst Vincnt Wright, psighchoanalysis, prufe reeder.

Finally, one which has appeared in literature ever since it was first coined in the sixteenth century, It has appeared in both the singular form:

lithp

and the plural:

lithpth

which reinforces the case for having an historical word to describe this delightful form of word play.

(l) Hectowords

Philip M. Cohen of Pennsylvania collects mathematically defined words which have a metric base. These are some of his best, all of which have been devised by readers of the American journal, *John Hopkins Magazine*:

1 mentality = 100 centimentality
2×10^6 pinpricks = 1 MHz
3 camp beds = 1 tricot
3 unicorns = 1 triceratops
1 magnum opus = 10 grand opera
2 tribes = 1 diatribe
10 glassfuls = 1 decanter
1½ dice = 1 trice

To which he has posed the question:

Should the amount of suspense in a mystery novel be measured in whod units?

(m) Synonym Chains

In his book *Beyond Language* (1967), Dmitri Borgmann presented two examples of brilliant word play which has since captured the imagination of others in just the same way as Carroll's Doublets (Word Ladders) seized the attention of his fellow wordsmiths some eighty-eight years previously.

Borgmann turned BLACK into WHITE and UGLY into BEAUTI-FUL simply by the use of synonyms:–

> BLACK-DARK-OBSCURE-HIDDEN-CONCEALED-SNUG-
> COMFORTABLE-EASY-SIMPLE-PURE-WHITE
>
> UGLY-OFFENSIVE-INSULTING-INSOLENT-PROUD-LORDLY-
> STATELY-GRAND-GORGEOUS-BEAUTIFUL

The potential for this form of solitaire amusement has been demonstrated by a research scientist in the USA who, with the aid of his computer, has constructed several thousand synonym chains based on *The New Collins Thesaurus*.

A. Ross Eckler has drawn attention to the fact that these chains are not necessarily reversible but that the opposite journey can still be achieved. His examples include TRUE into FALSE/FALSE into TRUE and LIGHT into DARK/DARK into LIGHT:–

> TRUE-JUST-FAIR-BEAUTFUL-PRETTY-ARTFUL-ARTIFICIAL-
> SHAM-FALSE
> FALSE-UNWISE-FOOLISH-SIMPLE-UNCONDITIONAL-
> ABSOLUTE-POSITIVE-REAL-GENUINE-TRUE
>
> LIGHT-BRIGHT-CLEVER-CUNNING-SLY-FURTIVE-SECRET-
> HIDDEN-OBSCURE-DARK
> DARK-OBSCURE-VAGUE-VACANT-EMPTY-FOOLISH-SIMPLE-
> EASY-LIGHT

Finally, I conclude this review of wordsmithery by turning play from WRITER to READER:–

> WRITER-SCRIBE-CLERK-SCHOLAR-ACADEMIC-LECTURER-
> READER

14. BYRON

An advanced form of the classroom game, Wordsworth. This time the object is to decipher a complete statement from as few clues as possible. The first clue has to be a single word which summarises the whole saying, thereafter individual clues to words are given as one sees fit. The net result is a puzzle to challenge other word-smiths. They are permitted to consult the dictionary (which, in the following example, is represented by the Appendix) only as a last resort.

This ten word saying comprises thirty-six letters distributed in this order:–

1   2 3 4 5   6 7   8 9 10   11 12 13 14 15   16 17 18 19

20 21 22 23 24   25 26 27 28 29   30 31   32 33 34 35 36

Clues
1. Gul
2. 26, 27, 28 comes from the 2, 3, 4, 5
3. 26, 27, 28 is 32, 33, 34, 35, 36
4. 2, 3, 4, 5, is a 16, 17, 18, 19
5. 26, 27, 28 is 13, 11, 9, 5, 7
6. 6, 7, 2, 3, 9 is the 16, 17, 18, 19 of the G, 17, 18, 19
7. 6, 7, 2, 3, 9 introduced the new 16, 17, 18, 19 for a 2, 3, 4, 5, to the English language
8. The following numbers all represent the same vowel: 5, 14, 19, 27, 34, 35
9. The following numbers all represent the same vowel: 1, 8, 17, 30
10. The following numbers all represent the same vowel: 3, 11, 21
11. 22 is a fourth vowel
12. There are no other vowels
13. I am not in this puzzle though you will find 18, 19 again in the eighth word
14. 10, 11, 22 are in this puzzle
15. Consult the dictionary for the meaning of mel
16. Consult the dictionary for the meaning of gul
17. Clue 15 will solve clues 2, 3 and 5
18. Clue 16 will make sense of the other cross-referring clues 4, 6 and 7.

15. SUMWORDS

On average, the letters B, G or V will occur once each in every hundred letters of standard English prose. By contrast, those same hundred letters will include 13 E's, 9 T's but K, Q, X, J and Z will, in all probability, be completely absent. Assigning individual letter values on this basis and including decimal points up to 0.5 (beyond that they become letters of higher value) we have the following table:

A	8.5	G	1.3	M	2.5	T	9
B	1.5	H	6	N	7.5	U	3.3
C	3.5	I	7.3	O	8	V	1
D	4	J	0.2	P	3.1	W	2.3
E	13	K	0.5	Q	0.4	X	0.3
F	3	L	4.5	R	7	Y	2
				S	6.5	Z	0.1

and the most fascinating study of words is now available.

Take a simple example, the 3-letter words. TEE (9+13+13) totals 35, whereas the Hebrew coin, the ZUZ (0.1+3.3+0.1) is, at a total of 3.5, a tenth of the 'value' of a golf peg. But, is there a 3-letter word to outscore TEE or one which can undervalue ZUZ? Equally, do either of these have a numerical 'anagram', a word possessing the same value?

If we assume TEE to be the ultimate high scoring 3-letter word, what is its superlative sumgram (sumgram being a numerical 'anagram')? When I posed this question to the chairman of the Nottingham chapter of Pears Word Games Society, a lecturer in Scrabble at the Basford Hall College of Further Education, she studied the problem for a short while and produced a magnificant answer, the 9-letter word QUIZZICAL. Can you find a better sumgram that Mrs Ivy Dixon-Baird's QUIZZICAL?

Perfect sumgrams have no letters in common with each other, otherwise all anagrams would be automatic sumgrams and this would reduce the personal contest to a pure word study which renders the mathematical aspect superfluous. However, if one tolerates a degree of imperfection then a broad approach to the quest is retained.

What are the superlatives in every sensible category of word length and what are their superlative sumgrams?

Questions of that ilk are for the pure wordsmith but the fun player can turn to irony and make all manner of discoveries. Scotland has a tiny river with the smallest known name. It is simply the river E. E is the highest value Sumwords letter. Contrast this mere freshwater trickle with the mighty river OB which runs for 2,600 miles through Siberia. We now have the ludicrous fact that OB (9.5) is 'smaller'' than E (13). What are the most delicious ironies one can discover?

For even greater fun we can turn to adjectives and discover such as the SEXIEST women in the world. Which women have names which total the same as SEXIEST (55.6)? How about the world's LARGEST (49.8) insects or UGLIEST (44.9) men?

What are the relative values of saints and sinners? Which saint and which sinner equate mathematically? Can we discern ideal partners? It is hardly surprising that ROMEO (38.5) and JULIET (37.3) are star crossed lovers – who would have been a better computer match for either?

Sumwords' letter values, however, have their greatest potential in all manner of different combative pencil and paper games. Consider a written form of Wimbledon in which Jack plays Jill with the subject Birds. They limit themselves to (say) six birds each and set about the task of making the *lower* of the two scores. Essentially, therefore, they are looking for words with lots of Q's and Z's in them and as few E's as possible. Jack is to go first and the pinword is THE, thus he is stuck with a high scoring letter E to commence the name of his first bird.

JACK:	EMU	
JILL:	URUBU	(a South American vulture)
JACK:	UMBRE	(the hammerkop, a storklike bird)
JILL:	EYAS	(an unfledged hawk)
JACK:	SKUA	
JILL:	AUK	
JACK:	KIWI	
JILL:	IBIS	
JACK:	SMEW	
JILL:	WREN	
JACK:	NIGHTJAR	
JILL:	ROC	

The result is a resounding victory for Jill with 131.6 to Jack's 153.4.

Had either failed to reply, a penalty of 100 points would have been added. Best of all, one could even play a crossword-type game which rewards the skilled use of the lowest value letters. Once again one is attempting to make the lower of the two scores.

Draw a grid of any reasonable size (say) 15×15 and insert the pinword in the centre. You now build from this with any word you choose.

Each player (on a grid of this size) has a limit of any 50 letters and the game ends as soon as one player has exhausted his or stock. The unused letters of the opponent are now deemed to be 7 points each and the resultant computation added to that player's score.

In a Jack versus Jill contest the pinword (the nearest 3-letter word found by sticking a pin in a book) is TWO and Jack is to go first. He plays the word DIZZY in this fashion:

D I Z Z Y

T W O

and records the fact of having *added* five letters to the grid. He scores 13.5 points for DIZZY and 12 points for DO. His opening total is 25.5.

By playing QUIZZICAL (35 points) through either Z of DIZZY, Jill has *added* eight letters to the grid and has only 42 letters remaining to Jack's 45. As Jack went first and it is only fair that Jill should have an equal number of turns so, should Jack be the first to finish, he must still allow Jill one last turn. Jack may have the lower score but Jill has the advantage in letters used. Whilst neither player is likely to convert QUIZZICAL to QUIZZICALLY at this stage of play, one or the other may be forced to do so at the end of the game in a desperate attempt to shed his or her last remaining letters.

No word may be repeated. Penalize on a basis of 7 points per *added* letter for an invalid word if you do not wish to make a mess of the grid, otherwise the offending word is removed and the turn forfeited.

16. SUBJECTIVE DISCOVERIES

A word is selected. The object of the game being the production of related words utilizing only the letters of that original word. Consider the example of the word HAMLET.

As a description of a geographical location its potential is zero but, as a personal forename, it can be transposed immediately into the anagram, THELMA. Personal forenames (Christian names, Biblical names, classic deities, acceptable short forms i.e. TEL for TERENCE etc.) is an especially fertile field and, therefore, the game will be illustrated with personal forenames as the subject.

HAMLET/THELMA is arranged in its alphabetical order as AEHLMT and this is termed the basic unit. Each time a basic unit is employed in full this will score a point so that HAMLET and THELMA have produced a score of 2 points. The Biblical HAM together with TEL also utilizes a basic unit and the score is now 3 points. For convenience, consider HAMLET and THELMA as 'individuals' the combination of HAM/TEL as 'twins' and now we have the third category the 'family' which is where the fun really begins.

ALMA could be produced from two basic units by the deletion of A, L, M from the first unit and A from the second unit. Thus we are left with the units EHT and EHLMT. No points are added. MEL (a short form of MELANIE) is taken into the family and our units are now HT and EHMT. To delete EHMT as 'THEM' is invalid – it is beyond the limits of the subject – and it may be that in order to delete the HT of the first unit we choose ALTHEA. The units are now as follows:–

First unit, exhausted. Second unit, HMT. Third unit, EHMT. Fourth unit, EHLMT. A point is now available (for that first unit) *only* if we can utilize *all* of the remaining letters of *all* the remaining units. We must now score not *one* point by beginning a family with ALMA but at least *four* points with a family which has ALMA, MEL and ALTHEA.

Finally, the most frustrating rule of all – no word may be repeated.

To illustrate the utter frustration of Subjective Discoveries the example of a base unit AADLNOR in the category of Personal forenames is given below:–

Individual (male) ARNOALD (1 point)
Individuals (female) ARNOLDA: ORLANDA: ROLANDA: RONALDA (4 points)
Twins ROD, ALAN: RON, ALDA (2 points)
Married couples DON, LARA: DAN, LORA: ROD, LANA: DAR, NOLA (4 points)
First family AARON, DANA, DOLL, ALAN, DORA, DONNA, DARRAL, ROALD, LORNA (6 points)
Second family ARNALD, ARNOLD, RONA, ALDA, DONAL, ROLAND, RANDAL, RONALD, OONA, RA, ADA, NORA, ALLARD, ORLANDO, DONALD, AARON, LARA (12 points)

29 points except that some of the names have been repeated so one has to edit accordingly.

ROD is both a twin and husband.
ALAN is both a twin and a member of the first family.
ALDA is both a twin and a member of the second family.
LARA is both a wife and a member of the second family.
AARON is in both families.

The twins can be deleted. DON and LARA can be divorced but

AARON is the blighter and, in the interests of greater points, the first family has to be torn asunder.

The score now stands at 20 points and one has DON, RON, DANA, DOLL, ALAN, DORA, DONNA, DARRAL, ROALD and LORNA not to mention ANN, ANNA, ALAN, AL, ALARD, AANNA and goodness knows who else desiring to belong to a family so increasing the score.

Can you do it?

Alternatively, suppose you break up the second family and have all their names available in a complete rearrangement of everyone. Would another divorce help? Only the five individuals are sacrosanct in any attempt to exceed this current score of 20 points.

Subjective Discoveries is frustration at its most sublime.

(Note: All of the curious names quoted have appeared in print. Some are early forms (for ARNOALD see ARNOLD in the *Oxford Dictionary of English Christian Names* as a typical example of these) whilst the others may well be personal or parental affections possibly limited to a single individual. I know of DAR only from the late Dar Robinson, the famed stuntman who performed the classic fall in the film *Highpoint*, whilst AANNA came to my attention after completing the above example. She was interviewed for an issue of *You* magazine dated 13th November 1988 and, as A was one the 'problem' letter in the construction of the two families noted above, so it may well be that AANNA is a particularly useful female in the absorption of the problematic A.)

The Postal Play Series

Two very different games, one makes a pleasant little postscript the other is the aristocrat of word play and can comprise the whole of the letter. Only the first is suitable for children.

1. CENTURION

The object of the game is *not* to have the last word. The correspondents are both aware of the rules and, as the game lasts for only a few moves, so a result is quickly obtained.

Each letter of the alphabet is assigned a number according to its position. Hence A = 1, B = 2 etc. culminating with Z = 26. Assume that the contest is between Uncle Sam, who lives in America, and his favourite niece, Jill, who lives in the UK. Jill is to go first and must begin with a 3-letter word totalling 10 or less on the scale. Hence she could chose such as ABA, a Syrian cloth of camel's hair, which would total 4 points, or BAA which would also total 4 points or any other low scoring combination such as BAD for 7 points or CAD for 8 points. Anything, so long as she stayed within the limits. She decides upon BAG for 10 points.

Uncle Sam must now reply with a 3-letter word beginning with the last letter of her word. Not that it will happen yet, but he must not exceed a total score of 99 points or else he loses. He chooses GUY for 53 points so bringing the total of the two words to 63 points.

Jill has a dilemma. Her word must begin with a Y. That will immediately bring the total to 88 points, leaving her only eleven points to play with. Obvious 'Y' words such as YAK, YAM. YES or YET will exceed the total. By contrast, YEA (an archaic word meaning yes) will put her in jeopardy. Uncle Sam has only got to reply with ABA (BAG + GUY + YEA + ABA = 98 points) and she has lost. Ideally she needs a word to bring the total to 96, 97, 98 or 99 points.

Jill consults her dictionary and is spoilt for choice. The Appendix will define the two extant words YAH and YED which could make the total 97 points and the obsolete word YEE which could make 98 points.

(Centurion was devised by David Parlett as a face-to-face game. Played as such, the dictionary may be consulted only in the event of a dispute.)

2. CODE BREAKING

Consider being told that the following list consists of 3-letter words written in code:

CGE
ELA
ALB
BQI
ILZ
ZLU

These words could be virtually anything. For example:

HIT	CAB	BUN	ZEL	WAS
TAP	BET	NIT	LOG	SUQ
PAY	TEN	TIP	GOT	QUA
YOB	NIL	PEA	TIC	ARM
BAN	LED	AIL	COB	MUD
NAG	DEW	LID	BOX	DUG

are just five out of the hundreds of possibilities if one assumes that the letter L represents a vowel. However, if these same words appear in a larger message written in that same code then any reasonably intelligent person could crack the code in the time he or she normally solves a crossword. The longer the message, the easier it is.

Code breaking clubs and societies exist worldwide and members challenge each other by post or else hundreds participate in the same postal contest which has them all concerned with the same message.

The game described below is ideal for two friends separated by distance but sharing a mutual interest in good word play. An example of a code will be given, from which you will be able to determine what

CGE
ELA
ALB
BQI
ILZ
ZLU

really stand for, should the aristocrat of word games appeal to your taste.

Two people agree to correspond with each other in code. Neither tells the other what the code will be, nor gives any clues whatsoever as to the content.

The easiest way of devising a code is to assign each letter of the alphabet to a different letter. Nothing so childish as that devised by Julius Caesar with A = E, B = F, C = G, D = H etc. Such a code is pathetically easy to crack and not worth the effort. Make it completely random but do ensure that if, for example, A = K and B = D that every time you write an encoded letter you are accurate. It is so simple to have A = K in one word but to slip up and have A = A in another word. Such errors, whilst under-standable, are very frustrating.

Having devised the code, then write a short message in that code. Providing that you use standard English for the message, even if it contains one or two very unusual words, the task will give great pleasure to the wordsmith recipient. No more than a paragraph need be written in order to make a solution possible. Use normal word spacings and punctuation.

The solver now scans the coded message for the inevitable 'giveaways'. The single letter is almost certainly either the word A or the word I. The 2-letter words. Does that same cluster appear in a 3-letter word or a 4-letter word? The double letter. Could it be a vowel? If so, it is almost certainly either EE or OO. The apos-trophe. Is it T, as in **couldn't**? Or is it S as in **Peter's**?

Any normal paragraph of standard English will have its individ-ual 'giveaways'.

Now to the example. No solution will be provided as the whole purpose of the exercise is for you to test yourself. If you can solve an easy crossword, you are quite capable of making complete sense of this. The spacing is extra wide to enable you to write the solution directly under the coded message. Once you are certain of a particular letter write it in the box provided on the left. For example, G is either A or I as G is a word. Once you have determined which it is then place G against either A or I in the box and put either A or I directly under every G in the message.

Discovering the first letter will be the hardest part of all, thereafter it will become progressively easier until the last dozen or so letters are virtually child's play.

You are assured that if any unusual words occur in the text, naturally these will be defined in the Appendix.

If you wish to rate your performance then note the time when you begin the task.

Under 15 minutes	EXPERT
Under 30 minutes	EXCELLENT
Under 45 minutes	VERY GOOD
Under 60 minutes	GOOD
Under 75 minutes	FAIR
Over 75 minutes	TOLERABLE FOR A BEGINNER

In private U.K. contests, players challenge each other on an honestly timed basis. In the worldwide challenges set in various languages and with codes beginning at this simple level but ascending to the standards used by the most sophisticated intelli-

Dearest Uncle Sam,

A
B
C
D
E
F
G
H
I
J
K
L
M
N
O
P
Q
R
S
T
U
V
W
X
Y
Z

ULNO'B   FDBZBNXGFZ   NDJBGBZB

DC   FLGXB   DC   KDXVB   GVMLS

CDX   NMJZQXGDJ.

G   WLRM   MJNDVMV   ZWM   KDXVB

'IQGE'   LJV   'ZLAG'   ZD

MJLTSM   PDQ   ZD   QJVMXBZLJV

ZWMH.

YDDV   SQNO.

Lots of love,
Jill

p.s.   CGE,   ELA,   ALB,   BQI,   ILZ,

ZLU

Best wishes,
Jack

gence agencies, the time is of no consequence. The solution is the object. The character of Uncle Sam is a tribute to the American Cryptogram Association which organizes these worldwide competitions.

A more popular form of secret correspondence has two people sharing the same easily remembered code. The simplest and best known method is to chose a keyword and base an alphabet upon it. As that keyword can be changed as often as one wishes so the system retains a high degree of confidentiality. But, once again, if sufficient facts are available the code can be broken by a cross-word addict. However, one needs to appreciate how the keyword-based system works before attempting a solution. Suppose that one's keyword is KEYWORD. First of all a standard alphabet is written and KEYWORD is written directly below it – not arbitrarily but commencing at the letter G. The reason being that KEYWORD has seven letters and G is the seventh letter of the alphabet:

A B C D E F G H I J K L M N O P Q R S T U V W X Y Z
            K E Y W O R D

The remainder of the coded alphabet is now written commencing with the N through the Z thence to F ensuring that one omits the letters D, E, K, O, R, W, Y as these have already been encoded. Hence:

A B C D E F G H I J K L M N O P Q R S T U V W X Y Z
s t u v x z K E Y W O R D a b c f g h i j l mn p q

Thus two people can decide what their keyword is and change it whenever they wish. However, they normally restrict themselves to keywords in a logical sequence.

Appreciating this technique imagine that you have intercepted all three messages from me to any fellow inventor of word games whose creation or creations are being published for the very first time and exclusively in this book. That is all the information you have and need. If you can make a reasoned judgement as to our three different keywords then you can make complete sense of all three messages:

1. President George Bush has the American Secret Service codename of M S F P K Q H D E.

2.   The First Lady, Mrs Barbara Bush, has the American Secret Service codename of N L X H K P B F B N U
3.   Queen Anne used to sign her letters to Sarah, Duchess of Marlborough, as Mrs F I L D G U.

Once you have solved these final cryptograms you, the inventor and I have, very aptly, concluded **Pears Word Games.**

Pears Word Games Society

The author and those fellow wordsmiths named in this book who reside within easy travelling distance of each other regularly play many of the adult games described on the various pages.

For fun we organized ourselves as the Pears Word Games Society and, for a while, held all the world championships in the many original games – other than mentioned below – appearing in print for the first time. However, others wished to follow suit so not only did we surrender our world championship titles but became a mere chapter of a society which is now an association of independent groupings of word game players. The Society has, at the time of going to press, three chapters of which two are in the United Kingdom and one is in Japan centred on the university of Q-Dye, Fukuoka. The original UK players now belong to the Scarsdale chapter of northeast Derbyshire and have friendly rivals in the nearby Nottingham chapter. The only games for which we did not determine a world champion are Maxwell Caulfield's Gramps (as he lives in Hollywood, USA, and we have yet to face the Gramps champ of his neighbourhood), Goal! and Q-Dye as these games were test-played in Japan.

It may be that other groups of word game players – be they based in a school, university, a tavern or wherever – might wish to form their own chapter of the Society not only to determine their own local champion in any game described in the book but to have away games against other chapters eventually, perhaps, leading to a revival of the world championship concept.

Any reader, therefore, who has succeeded in forming a chapter and wishes to be put in contact with similar groups of like-minded games players should write to

Mrs P.J. Smith,
Pears Word Games Society
26, Belvedere Avenue
Chesterfield
Derbyshire

detailing the name and address of the chapter's secretary or other member agreeing to act as the contact; the games (both original and traditional) which prove to be the most popular and the preferred dictionary or dictionaries. All three existing chapters tend to use the nearest dictionary to hand and supplement this with *Pears Advanced Word-Puzzler's Dictionary*.

The use of *Pears Advanced Word-Puzzler's Dictionary* is not mandatory though it is a unification factor which has established contacts between the Society and word lovers in the USA and New Zealand apart from Japan and the UK.

Any organization interested in any of the original games for commercial exploitation should, in the first instance, make approaches via the publisher

> Pelham Books
> 27, Wrights Lane
> London
> W8 5TZ

who holds the legal title to the trade name of Pears in all matters relating to the contents of this book and at whose pleasure the Society may use the name so long as it is strictly non-commercial and remains within the bounds of good conduct as the publisher so decrees.

Target Scores

Some of the pencil and paper games have the potential for recognition of a personal achievement and the reader may well care to measure his or her results against those of other players.

The following are the best results achieved by members of the Scarsdale Chapter of the Pears Word Games Society in some of the traditional and original games.

1 FRENCH CROSSWORDS (see page 88)

The maximum possible score is 60 points and the Chapter's record is held by Dawn Hawkins who also holds the record for the greatest margin of victory. She defeated her opponent 53 to 39 and their respective grids are as follows:

S	M	A	C	K	6
T	I	L	L	A	4 (till)
U	N	D	E	R	6
M	C	A	R	T	4 (cart)
P	E	R	K	S	6
6	6	3	6	6	

(ald)

T	R	A	M	P	6
R	E	D	C	L	3 (red)
T	A	S	L	U	3 (tas)
C	R	E	A	M	6
K	I	N	K	S	6
X	4	3	2	6	

(rear) (ads) (la)

(Dictionary: *The Concise Oxford* supplemented by *Pears Advanced Word-Puzzler's Dictionary*)

2 CLEWLOW'S SUPER DOMINOES (see page 108)

There are two versions of this game depending upon choice of format and members of the Chapter have played both.

(a) The Original Format

The ZEBRA PLAYER deletes Z, E, B, R, A
The ZEBU PLAYER deletes Z, E, B, U.

(b) The Chesterfield Format

```
Z E B R A
E
B
U
```

Assuming that the ZEBRA PLAYER went first he deletes Z, E, B, R, A. However, the ZEBU PLAYER merely deletes E, B, U *not* Z.

The differences in skilled play are quite remarkable as the original version has the player attempting to 'bury' the difficult letters within the body of the word – i.e. SQUIRREL has the Q in an untouchable position – whereas the Chesterfield version is more frustrating and tends to require the playing of more dominoes.

Theoretically, a single domino containing every letter of the alphabet can win either version in an optimum play but the most prolific word known to the Chapter is the scientific term, BLE-PHAROCONJUNCTIVITIS (a disease of the eyelid), which still leaves D, F, G, K, M, Q, W, X, Y, and Z unaccounted for. However, players tend to prefer 'popular' subjects such as ANI-MALS and the author utilized seven dominoes in a game played to the original format whilst Russell Byers needed fourteen dominoes to win a minimal game played Chesterfield style.

(Dictionary: *Webster's International*)

3 CROSSWORD (see page 90)

On a standard grid and using CROSSWORD as the basic word, the Chapter's record is held by Joan Smith with a superb 151/88 victory. Both she and her opponent gambled on the validity or otherwise of some of the strangest-looking words and readily accepted the obsolete.

The only word likely to prove contentious is EROSES (EROSE is perfectly acceptable) as it may not be capable of being pluralized – the dictionary's evidence for this possibility is based upon a quotation of 1793 which refers to 'an erose'. ABE is a typical gamble which paid off as it proved to be, when challenged, an obsolete form of the verb ABYE. By contrast, her opponent's 'cater/astoons' attempt to gain 12 points and 'adeals/es' attempt at 8 points both resulted in penalizations.

P	O	O	L	S		A	B	E
E		P	I	E	S		I	N
A	H		T		T	E	T	
	E	R		D	O	R	E	A
C	R	O	S	S	W	O	R	D
	S	T	O	O	N	S		E
T	E	E	N		S	E	R	A
E			S	O		S	O	L
R	O	D		R	E		E	

(Dictionary: *The Oxford English Dictionary*)

4 SQUARE BASHING (see page 146)

The ultimate is a 15/nil whitewash and as few games even utilize all fifteen squares so such an achievement can be considered a true rarity.

Facing a competent opponent, Russell Byers became the first and, so far, only person known to have forced this remarkable result. The consequent word grid is a true wordsmith's production containing as it does some amazing words, which, when challenged, all proved to be valid. The adjudicator failed to find one of the words, AFLAJ, in the dictionary only to be informed by Russell that it does not appear in the reference work in the correct alphabetical position but as the plural of its anagram, FALAJ!

```
A D D A X E R I C O W L S T U M P A N I C
F       Y       H       T       L       R
L       L       E       E       E       E
A       E       S       E       A       A
J O R A M E A N S E V E R A P I D R E A M
O       I       T       O       R       O
U       S       I       A       O       N
S       T       N       S       O       T
T E S T Y O U N G H O S T R A M P E R C H
E       A       H       A       E       E
R       C       A       P       A       A
A       H       Z       I       C       R
I N E P T O R I I N F E R O A C H A B I T
```

(Dictionary: *Chambers English*)

5 SEVEN UP (see page 155)

Played to strict rules which limit the 'Wimbledon words' to those invalid for replaying on the grid (i.e. the subjects are proper nouns) and ending the first stage once a player has a minimum of 50 letters to his or her credit the best result to date is Tom Wright's 74 points produced from five 7-letter plays. This beat the previous record of 73 points from six 7-letter plays made by Julie Titchener.

(Dictionary: *Chambers English* supplemented by *Pears Advanced Word-Puzzler's Dictionary*)

6 WORDS (see page 98)

As sheer luck can produce victory in just one guess so the only worthwhile record is that of the lowest average.

However, to produce a true average involves the tedium of the loser continuing to guess until his or her word is revealed. For its competitions the Scarsdale Chapter has adopted a formula which reflects a fair approximation to a true average and dispenses with the necessity to continue once a victory has been obtained.

Based upon the fact that regular players rarely need to exceed twenty guesses to achieve victory even when facing the most obscure of words so the formula assumes that it takes, on average, four guesses to discover each individual letter ($4 \times 5 = 20$). Thus, if Jack finds Jill's word in fourteen guesses and at this stage, Jill has found only three of his letters the 'score' is:–

JACK   14

JILL   14 plus the number of *undiscovered* letters multiplied by 4. This is $14 + (2 \times 4) = 22$

The Chapter plays to any dictionary currently available and these include *Funk & Wagnalls Standard, Collins English* as well as *Pears Advanced* consequently such 'horrendous' words as QCEPO (a type of skin infection) can be encountered. It took Dawn Hawkins just eleven guesses to discover that word and she has the Chapter's leading average based on this formula with 11.6

7 SHELLING PEAS (see page 170)

The contest is unique in that the reader cannot compete if he or she wishes to draw a comparison with a known result. Therefore, if you wish to match the prowess of your associates with that of the Scarsdale Chapter replay the identical task faced by the founder members at their inaugural meeting.

The author set the sixteen strong company the test of adding the letter P to the following words:–

IT

AT

TO

AY

ALE

TOE

DEAL

EDITOR

STEREO

The average score was 19 points with a range from net 13 (gross 22) to Russell Byers' 26 points. No player found the PEPPERPOTS of STEREO and only Russell and Ivy Dixon-Baird (25 points) scored with EDITOR. Obsolete words were allowed (only one was played) and the description of the game details 64 points available from extant words.

(Dictionary: several were available in the event of dispute and advanced planning – by consulting the *Oxford English Dictionary* for obsolete words – revealed that PIPT, TAPP, TOPP, POPT, AELP, APLE, APPEL, LAPE, LAPPE, PALPE, POPET, TOPPE, PLADE, DAPLE, DAPPEL as well as the previously detailed PAPY and TORPIDE were possible to give a potential 92 points known maximum score.)

8 ACID DROP (see page 83)

The easiest of all targets – merely record against your opponents one complete hanging.
  Using such as:

> A deaf husband and a blind wife are always a happy
>   couple.
> God sends nuts to those who have no teeth.
> Everyone speaks well of the bridge which carries him
>   over.
> Never choose your linen or women by candlelight.

all taken from a dictionary of proverbs in the hope that they were unknown to the opposition no team of the Chapter's players has failed to decipher a statement. Furthermore, no team has suffered the indignity of a hanging.
  The playing format has one team of (say) four players choosing their proverb whilst their opponents choose another. Once the teams have made their selections one player from each side

changes places and issues the challenge on behalf of the team. This ensures that all are engaged in competitive activity and there is no delay to the fun.

Section Three
The Appendix

All words are nouns unless otherwise specified.

Definitions are limited to the senses in which the word is relevant to a particular game. Dated references such as (17th/18th cent) which occur after a definition mean that the word was current at that time but is now considered obsolete. Regional references such as (Cornwall and Devon) denote dialect usage. Additional detail of this sort is given only if relevant to a particular game. Capitalized entries, such as **ABJECT** and **ABODE**, provide unusual meanings for well-known words. These are for the games of **Dutch Auction** and **Newby's Bluff**. No additional detail is given with these entries, but all the facts – however remarkable – can be confirmed in the *Oxford English Dictionary*. Serious wordsmiths can discover even more meanings for the capitalized entries if they consult the *English Dialect Dictionary*.

'Jack and Jill's dictionary' may be presumed to be either of two great works, the *Oxford English* or *Webster's International*.

abactor one, in historical times, who stole sheep or cattle by the flock or herd

abas a Persian weight used in weighing pearls and the equivalent of an eighth of a carat (18th cent)

abassi a Persian silver coin worth somewhat less than an English shilling of the same period (18th cent)

abba a bishop of the Coptic Church. A Christian Church which separated from the mainstream in 451 A.D. It is centred on Egypt.

abdest the Muslim rite of washing the hands before prayer

abelgate an envoy of the pope whose specific task is to bring to a newly created cardinal his insignia of office

ABJECT a castaway: a degraded person *verb* to exclude: to lower

ablaqueate *verb* to loosen or remove the soil from the roots of trees to enable their fibres to spread out (15th to 18th cent)

able-whackets described as being 'very popular with horny-fisted sailors' it is a mariner's card game in which the loser is beaten over the palms of the hands with a handkerchief tightly twisted like a rope

ABODE delay: a prediction *verb* to prognosticate

ACCESS an attack of fever: an addition, increase or growth: an arrival upon the throne

ACCIDENT an unfavourable medical symptom: an event: a phenomenon: an irregular feature in the landscape

ACCOMPANY *verb* to cohabit with: to congregate: to fill a place with people

accoucher a male midwife

acephali a race of men without heads believed to exist in the newly-discovered lands but, by 1753, such belief was considered '*ill warranted*'

achatour the term 'purveyor' had, by the reign of Edward III (1327–1377), attracted such odium that a law was passed forbidding its use as a description for the officer of the royal household charged with the duty of supplying provisions. Henceforth he was called achatour, though the term lapsed after several centuries of use.

ACHE the letter H: wild celery: parsley

actioner the worker who makes the action of an instrument of such as a gun or a piano (Note: when playing ODDJOB limit yourself to either gun or piano.)

ACTOR an agent or manager: a public prosecutor: an author

ADAMANT a diamond: the magnet: a non-magnetic object

adamate *verb* to love dearly (17th cent)

ADAM'S APPLE a variety of the orange: a variety of the lime: a variety of the grapefruit

addax a sandy coloured antelope of the Sahara

ADDER the Devil: a dragon: any snake: a slowworm: a newt: a dragonfly

ADDRESS the action of making ready: an appliance: attire *verb* to put on a garment: to stand erect

adeps lard

adeptist skilled alchemist (17th cent)

adjutrice a female assistant (17th cent)

Adullamite one of a small number of M.P.'s who detached themselves, during the 1866 parliament, from the Liberal party which formed the government of the day. The

Adullamites became a small third party.

ADVANCE one who has been raised to office   *verb* to profit: to boast: to increase

ADVENTURE a marvel: an accident: fortune or luck   *verb* to happen

ADVERT *verb* to turn towards: to take notice: to give warning of

advice prudence or wisdom: opinion or judgement: the way in which a matter is regarded

ae *Scottish adjective* one

aedile a magistrate of ancient Rome having responsibility for such as public buildings, shows and police

ael a grandfather or forefather (the term is essentially a 13th to 16th cent word but existed in the legal phrase, **writ of ael** in the 19th cent)

aer an obsolete form of **air, ear, ere** and **ore**

aet a Shetland form of the word **oat**

afare *verb* to depart (A Middle English word)

AFFAIR bearing, deportment: action, performance: rank, dignity

afgod the Old English word for a false god, revived in the late 18th century

AGAIN *adverb* in the opposite direction   *preposition* in full view of: in welcome of: in competition with: in resistance to: instead of: in anticipation of

agapet the masculine equivalent of a nymphomaniac (18th cent)

AGATE in the process of drawing gold wire, an instrument used for burnishing: a very small person: a printer's type called ruby in England but agate in the USA

aggresteyne a disease of the tail feathers of hawks shown when ' . . . *ye see your hawk hurt her feet with her beak and pulleth*

her tail then she hath the aggresteyne.' (15th cent)

agistor an officer who receives, and has to account for, payments from those whose animals have been allowed to graze in the royal forests

aglopened *adjective* frightened (15th cent)

agonistarch one who trained the combatants for the ancient Greek games

ai the two-toed sloth

ain a Scottish form of the adjective **own** – common in such expressions as **ain folk**, own kind or own people

AIR confidential or secret information: violence, force or anger: a cloth laid over the chalice in the Greek Orthodox Church: a facial expression *verb* to set to music: to evaporate   *adverb* before: early or soon

ALBUM rent paid in silver: the whites or leucorrhoea, a vaginal discharge: in ancient Rome, a tablet on which public notices were recorded: a visitor's book

alcalde a magistrate of a town, a sheriff, in Spain or Portugal

aldress the wife of an alderman or a mayor (17th/early 18th cent)

ale dame a woman who runs an ale house (late 17th cent)

ale draper a term now found only in the dialects of such as Yorkshire and Lincolnshire for an inn keeper

alienist literally a 'mad doctor', a mental pathologist

alker a sort of mediaeval custard. A recipe of 1381 says, '*For to make rice alker, take figs and raisins and do away with the kernels*'

ALLAY an addition of fresh hounds to a hunt: the dilution of such as wine: an alien element:

the degree of purity of gold or silver: a metallic compound *verb* to allege: to mix metals: to debase: to temper such as iron or steel: to defeat by argument

allegator one who alleges or confirms (17th cent)

all-night man a body snatcher, one who disinterred corpses by night in order to sell them to medical students for dissection (19th cent)

ALLOWANCE applause: voluntary acceptance: a remainder: permission

almacle an olive which, from ripeness, has fallen from the tree (16th cent)

almirante the Spanish word for an admiral

ALMOND a tonsil: a kind of pigeon: an oval with pointed ends: the plate over the entrance to the shell of a whelk: a delicate pink colour

almug an extant nearly 400 years old error for its anagram, **algum**. It even had its own variant form: **almaggin**, and the twin spellings of algum and almug both refer to a tree mentioned in the Bible. It is probably a kind of sandalwood.

alnager for many centuries, until the office was abolished during the reign of William III (1689–1702), the alnager was a sworn officer appointed to examine and attest the measurement and quality of woollen goods. The measurement was by the ell (in England 45 inches, in Scotland 37.2 inches) and the value was attested by the affixing of a leaden seal.

alopecist one who undertakes to cure or prevent baldness

ALP a bullfinch: an elephant: a goblin or fairy of varying degrees of maliciousness within the British Isles, but demonic in Germany

alpe alternative spelling of **alp** in the sense of a bullfinch

althingman a member of the Icelandic parliament

alurk *adverb* 'His head in shape as by nature's work, not one hair amiss or lieth alurk.' This quote of 1572 illustrates, by denial, alurk's meaning as out of place or awry.

amah a wet nurse in India etc.

AMBER the name of a river in Derbyshire: a bucket: a dry measure of four bushels: either of the plants, the St. John's wort or the All Saints' wort *verb* to perfume with ambergris

amboht a handmaid (circa 1200 A.D.)

amblygon a triangle or other obtuse-angled figure

amlet an omelet (18th cent)

amethodist a quack doctor (17th cent)

amildar in India, a native factor, manager or agent especially a collector of revenue

amit the amice or white vestment draped around a priest's shoulders

amma a truss

AMOUNT *verb* to cause to rise: to increase: to go back in time: to result: to signify

AMUSE *verb* to gaze in astonishment: to detain: to beguile, cheat or deceive: to divert the attention of a military enemy from one's true purpose

amyke a friend (15th cent)

amyllier 'On olives and amylliers and all kind of trees, the popinjays perch.' Popinjays are parrots but no one knows what type of tree is an amyllier. All one can say for certain is that it is a type of tree which a popinjay would select in A.D. 1400.

anana the pineapple

anatine *adjective* of, pertaining to, or resembling a duck

ANCHOR the pin of a buckle: a hermit: an architectural ornamentation shaped like an arrowhead *verb* of tree roots, to hold fast like an anchor

ANCIENT a standard bearer: a flag: a superior in age: an ancestor: a written work by a classical Greek or Roman author: that author *adjective* designating an office formerly held, the equivalent of ex- as in **ancient colonel** (ex-colonel): venerable: in legal terms, designating that land (now in royal or other possession) held by the crown in the days of Edward the Confessor or William the Conqueror

andabate a Roman gladiator who fought on horseback and wore a blindfolding helmet (In the 16th cent this term was used figuratively for one who was hoodwinked)

andagram an anagram of a word plus an additional letter. Basically, it is a device of a cryptic crossword compiler who sets a clue such as 'Sedately around the capital of Russia for a weighing machine (9).' The answer is this specialized type of anagram which combines a basic word, SEDATELY, *and* the letter R (the capital letter of Russia) for STEELYARD. However, the andagram concept features in a number of games including Shot Putting and Maxwell Caulfield's Gramps, to name but two.
(The word andagram was coined by the author for *Pears Advanced Word-Puzzler's Dictionary* and clearly stated to be such. Andagram has since been quoted in various newspapers and magazines but, technically, it cannot be construed as being a 'proper' word until at least one basic, standard, dictionary decides to accept it. Until such time the word itself is invalid for any word game – even those which are andagram games!)

andersmeat a meal taken between dinner and supper (late 16th/ early 17th cent)

andrew a valet, a gentleman's servant (late 17th cent)

ane a Northern dialect form of the word **an**

anestri the plural of **anestrus**, a period of sexual dormancy

anil the indigo plant: the dye therefrom

anile *adjective* old-womanish

animal magnetist a hypnotist, based on the belief that he used an invisible force (animal magnetism) to achieve his results (18th/19th cent)

anker a measure of wine or spirits which varies in different countries. The Rotterdam anker, for example, is that of the old English anker of 10 pre-imperial gallons of wine (the equivalent of 8 ½ imperial gallons). The anker is, or was, used in Russia, Holland, North Germany, Denmark and Sweden.

anteman valet or an usher (17th cent)

ante-supper a 17th century Earl of Carlisle was one of the originators of this vanity, a display of food laid out prior to supper but not consumed

anthine honey, oil or wine flavoured with flowers but a 17th century writer warned against consuming such if it appears reddish, as it will prove unwholesome (17th/18th cent)

anthos the flower, rosemary. It was given this epithet to signify its being the flower *par excellence*. (16th to 18th cent)

antimasquer during the intervals of a 17th century performance of a masque (an early type of pantomime) an antimasque was staged. This was a crude burlesque of what had already gone before and the players were called antimasquers.

antilopine *adjective* of or pertaining to an antelope

antiparle a conference (early 17th cent)

antiphoner a book containing sentences to be sung by a choir

antiplastic *adjective* denoting that a particular medicine impoverishes the blood

antisera a plural of **antiserum**, a serum containing antibodies

antsier the comparative of the slang adjective, **antsy**, meaning eager, impatient, restless

ao the personification of light in Maori legend

aps a dialect form of both **asp** and **aspen**

asterin a pigment obtained from the flower, China aster, and isolated as crystals of chloride

apan the 10th century form of the word ape was **apa**. The plural was apan

apiarian *adjective* pertaining to beehives or beekeeping. (It is also a less common term for an apiarist or beekeeper)

apomel a decoction of a honeycomb and vinegar boiled together (17th/18th cent)

APPARITION appearance in history or pre-history: that which appears: an illusion or sham: the festival of the Epiphany: the first re-appearance of a heavenly body: that seen in the mind's eye

apple squire a pimp (16th/17th cent)

apprest preparation, provision (Shelling Peas note: This obsolete word can be supplemented by TAPPERS together with the 26 anagrams listed under AEPRST if expanded from STARE in *Pears Advanced Word-Puzzler's Dictionary*)

APPROVE *verb* of land, to make a personal profit by increasing the value or rent: to show to be true: to put to the test of experience: to display: to corroborate or confirm: to exhibit to advantage

APRON the diaphragm of an animal: the skin covering the belly of a roast duck or goose: the abdomen of a crab: a strip of lead which conducts rainwater on a building towards its gutter: a piece of lead on an historic naval gun which covers the touch hole: at the base of a sluice, a platform which intercepts the fall of water so preventing the erosion of the bottom

aproner a barman or a waiter (17th cent)

apron rogue a mechanic (17th cent)

apron squire a pimp (16th cent)

aps the aspen tree, a former standard English term still found in most southern English dialects

apteyker a Yiddish word for a pharmacist

araba a heavy screened wagon used by Tartars

arear *verb* in the rear (also an obsolete verb used by such as Holinshed in the sense of to raise)

ARBOUR a lawn: a flower garden: a herb garden: an orchard: a vine or similar tree or shrub trained on a trellis: a covered alley or walk

archegay an iron-pointed wooden dart thrown as a weapon

archet a violin bow (18th cent)

arenose *adjective* sandy

arfname an heir (11th to 13th cent)

argenter a banker or money changer (15th cent)

arghhood cowardice (13th/14th cent)

argology idle speech (17th cent)

Arianism the heretical doctrine of the 4th century presbyter, Arius

ariole a soothsayer (14th to 16th cent)

arisard an ancient female costume comprising a long robe or tunic girdled round the waist

ARM the leg of a hawk: might, power: a ray of a starfish: a main branch of a tree *adjective* poor, needy *verb* to put one's arm round: of a horse, to press down its head and bend its neck such that it rests the branches of the bridle upon its brisket

armarian a monastic librarian charged with the specific duty of keeping the books free of insects

armyworm a caterpillar which is a pest in both Australia and the USA

aromatary a dealer in spices for perfumes (17th cent)

arman a confection consisting of honey of roses, breadcrumbs, nutmeg powder and cinnamon used for restoring appetite in horses

arn a Scottish word for the alder tree

ARREST a mangey tumour on the sinew of a rear leg of a horse: a small bone of a fish: a judgment, decree or order (of a French supreme court): an abiding place

arrha a sum of money given as a pledge that the balance will be paid on completion of the contract. The plural is **arrhae**.

ARROW the name of a small constellation in the northern hemisphere: the penis: the flowering stem of a sugar cane: after pruning, that stem of a vine or tree allowed to become the main stem *adjective* cowardly *verb* to wound: to fire a long pointed missile having feathers for balance in flight

arsefoot a bird mentioned in a 16th century work and subsequently identified by one writer as a dabchick and by another as a penguin

arsemetricke a 16th century spelling of **arithmetic**

ARTICLE the number 10: any multiple of 10: a clause in a will: a moment of time between successive periods: a joint connecting two parts of the body *verb* to make specific accusations against: to charge with specific offences

Askapart one of a race of hardy warriors, the Askaparts, who dwelt in Arabia and also the personal name of a giant killed by the mediaeval knight, Sir Bevis of Southampton. The Askaparts featured in romantic writings from the 15th to the 18th centuries.

aspalax an eastern European mole

ASSAY *verb* to taste food and/or drink before the same is offered to the lord or prince: to attack, assault or assail as a test of the opponent's mettle: to enquire: to try on clothes: to try by getting the 'feel' of a thing: to sound out: to test by practice: to learn by experience: to test by temptation

asself *verb* to adopt or appropriate, to take to one's self (The inflected forms include **asselfing**)

ASSEMBLE *verb* to unite two things or persons: to indulge in sexual intercourse: to meet in battle

assent opinion: accord *verb* to

agree mutually: to send for: to send forth (these last two known only from the use of the past participle in forms such as '*the lords were assent*')

astromancer an astrologer

atblench *verb* to escape (13th cent)

ATLAS a large size of drawing paper: the bone which supports the skull: an Eastern silk-satin *verb* to carry on one's shoulders: to prop up

ATTEND *verb* to kindle: to wait or tarry: to look forward to: to associate one thing with another: to remain for

ATTIRE the full set of antlers of a deer or moose: a headdress: personal ornamentation *verb* to prepare venison for the table: to equip a horse for war: to put in order: to dress a woman's hair

AUNT a prostitute: a gossip: an old woman: in Cambridge, Oxford University and, in Oxford, Cambridge University

auntler a 15th/16th cent spelling of **antler**

AUTHENTIC one considered to be an authority: an original *adjective* automatic: entitled to obedience or respect: legally qualified

AUTHOR an ancestor: one having authority over others: one who instigates: one who sires *verb* to state or declare: to originate or cause

AUTO a play: (NEWBY'S BLUFF, the following two meanings are normally written in full as **auto-da-fé** or **auto-de-fé** but auto is an accepted form) a sentence passed by the Spanish Inquisition: the public burning of a heretic

autology the scientific study of oneself

avener one employed as the chief officer of a stable of horses

AVER a carthorse: an ox used as a beast of burden: an old or worthless horse: money *verb* to assert the truth of a statement: to assert the existence of

award custody *verb* to guard: to parry a blow: to furnish

AWE a floatboard of a waterwheel: anger, rage: that which inspires fear: the month of August *verb* to reverence: to influence by such as profound respect

AXES whilst this particular word is not its plural, a singular form is another word for the hog deer: the teeth on second cervical vertebrae: central props which sustain any system: straight lines from eyes to objects of sight: main stems or roots (Note: The singular for each of the above is axis. In the case of the hog deer, the phrasing changes to such as 'a herd of' or 'a pair of' or, like deer, the singular is its own plural)

axile *adjective* coinciding with an axis

ay *interjection* ah! oh! *adverb* every, always (Shelling Peas, the extant words are PAY, PYA, YAP, YAPP and PAPPY. Deduct 2 points for PAPY, an obsolete form of poppy, unless you intend to set a competition at advanced level. PYA and YAPP are defined elsewhere.)

aynbrekher a Yiddish word for a burglar

baboo an Indian clerk literate in English

backbear the arborial equivalent of being caught in possession of stolen property. It is the act of carrying on the back, an illegally killed deer. The laws concerning this are so ancient that even Old English grammar is featured in the legal terminology. Instead of a man being described as a 'backbearing thief' he is called a back-berend thief.

backet in Scotland, a shallow wooden trough for carrying such as ashes, coals, mortar or salt

backlet a backyard (Gloucester, Somerset, Devon and Cornwall)

BACKSIDE the under surface of a leaf: a privy: the opposite

backstress a female baker (16th cent)

BACON the blubber of a whale: a clown: a live pig: a dead pig: the surname of an author known as Doctor Mirabilis: a different author, this one produced a work on Henry VII but some claim he produced a work on Henry VIII

badderlocks a Scottish term for an edible seaweed described as being ' . . . *the best of all algae when eaten raw*'

badelyng unlike *fesnyng* which has survived in the phrase a *fesnyng of ferrets*, this 15th century collective noun for a brood of ducks has, unfortunately, become obsolete

badger a term, still extant in various dialects, for an itinerant dealer who acts as a middleman between such as a farmer or a fisherman and the consumer

badling an effeminate man (11th to 18th cent)

badmash a rascal

baff-end in the coal mines of Northumberland and Durham, a piece of wood 15 to 18 inches long, 5 to 6 inches wide and 1 to 2 inches thick. It is used for driving behind cribs or tubbing to bring them into proper position.

bagasse the waste material in sugar making. It is disposed of in a huge square, redbrick furnace called a bagasse burner.

BAGPIPE a locust's organ of sound: a long-winded monotonous speaker: a distiller's glass retort shaped like an Irish musical instrument *verb* of a sail, to bring it to the mizen-shrouds

BAIL custody, power: in Australia, a framework restraining a cow's head whilst she is being milked: a crossbar: the wall of the outer court of a castle: a pole separating horses in a stable: a bulwark of a boat: a ship's bucket *verb* to confine: to hoop: to secure or guarantee

baisemain writers from Spenser (1596) to Smollett (1748) have used this term for a kiss on the hands

BALD *adjective* corpulent: streaked with the colour white: trivial, paltry *verb* to depilate

balductum a posset of hot milk curdled with wine or ale (16th cent) (in the 15th cent it was spelt **balducta**)

baldystrot a pimp or a procuress, a 1483 spelling of a word which had various forms including **bawdstrot** in *Piers the Plowman* (1360). It is not recorded outside these dates.

BALE a funeral pyre: a bonfire: a set of three dice: mental agony: death: evil *verb* to dance

baleys a bundle of twigs used for flogging (13th–16th cent but still extant in Shropshire as a verb to flog or birch)

BALK an isthmus: a blunder: a defeat: a grave mound: a crossbar in a kiln: the stout rope at the top of a fishing net: the beam of a balance: a disappointment: a ridge between two furrows: a piece missed out in ploughing *verb* to miss by error: to lie out of the way: to signal to fishing boats which direction the shoal has taken: to plough up in ridges

ballistier the soldier who fired a ballista, a type of catapult which hurled such as rocks (early 17th cent)

ballmine a kind of iron ore found in rounded lumps or nodules (a Staffordshire term)

balzan a horse with four white feet (17th cent)

BAN a military governor in certain of the Balkan states: a curse *verb* to curse: to chide: to call forth: to summon by proclamation

banchiere the Italian word for a banker

bandle an Irish linear measure of two feet

bandster one who binds sheaves after reaping

BANK a shelf: a batch of treasury notes: a long bench: a coalface: the seashore: the brothel quarter, suppressed in 1546, on the south side of the Thames: a row of keys on an organ

banxring a Javanese species of tree shrew which resembles a small squirrel except that it has a longer nose and no whiskers

barapicklet in Welsh the word is **bara pyglyd** which means 'pitchy bread' and could refer to the colour of this centuries-old traditional product. It is a Welsh light bread made of fine flour kneaded with milk and is produced in the form of small cakes.

BARB a man's beard: in certain orders of nuns, a piece of white linen worn from under the chin midway to the waist: on a shield, a design of a sepal of a flower: a North African breed of horse noted for its speed: a dun-coloured variety of pigeon *verb* to shave or trim a beard

barbara a technical term in the study of logic for a proposition such as:- All trees are plants, all oaks are trees, therefore all oaks are plants.

baresark a wild Norse warrior of historical times

BARGAIN a small farm: a battle: a transaction that entails unpleasant consequences *verb* to contend or fight

BARK a cylindrical receptacle for candles; a rowing boat; a xebec; the human skin; the husk of a fruit or grain: the cry of a squirrel

BARKER the spotted redshank: a tanner: a pistol

barlafumble in wrestling or similar play, a call for a truce by one who has fallen (Scotland, 16th to 18th cent)

barmaster a judge having authority to settle disputes amongst Derbyshire lead miners

BARON a freeman of a Cinque Port who, until the 18th century, had the feudal duty of bearing a canopy over the head of the monarch on coronation day: until 1832, an M.P. of a Cinque Port: in foreign usage, a saint: a judge of the Court of Exchequer: in law and heraldry, a husband

barrat a general term covering three different groups of woe. Deception, fraud, fraudulent dealing and trouble, distress, sorrow, grief, pain were two 13th to 16th century groups. Contention, strife and fighting was a 13th/14th century group of senses though the word, **barratress** (a virago, an amazon or female warrior) was used in the 16th century.

BARROW the badger: a basket in which wet salt is left to drain: a castrated boar: an infant's long sleeveless garment: in the days of King Alfred, a mountain: subsequently, a hill: by the Middle Ages, a hillock: today, a mound or heap

bartoner the husbandman or farm manager of a manorial farm retained in the lord's possession

Bascuance a 17th cent term for the Basque language

BASE the skirt of a woman's outer petticoat: the smallest kind of cannon used during the 16th/17th centuries: an apron: a socket: a children's game of pursuit: a fish, the perch

baselard in 1381, Sir William Walworth, the lord mayor of London, stabbed the famous rebel Wat Tyler in the neck with a baselard. It is a dagger worn at the girdle.

baser an executioner who used an axe (14th cent)

bashaw of three tails in the Ottoman empire the more horsetails carried on the standard of an imperial official the greater his rank. A bashaw, or pasha, with three tails was the highest ranked.

BASIL sheepskin tanned in bark: an iron fetter for a prisoner's ankle: a large brass cannon capable of firing a 200lb shot

BASS the inner bark of the lime or linden: shale with a dark stain: a kiss: straw: a flexible basket *verb* to kiss

baston in 1366 a law of Richard II gave a convict freedom on license providing he was accompanied by the baston, a man carrying a red staff and employed by the warden of Fleet Prison. This legal provision lasted for a number of centuries.

BAT a pack-saddle: a walking stick: a sun-dried brick of clay and straw: a lump: shale found between coal seams *verb* to flutter like a hawk

batful a 16th/17th cent *adjective* having a sense of fertile. The superlative form occurs in a quote of 1607, '*The Beggars Belly is the batful'st ground that we can sow in.*' The comparative form, **batfuller** does not appear to have been recorded in a literary work.

BATH a Hebrew liquid measure of approximately 6½ gallons: a mass of molten material in a furnace: the prepared liquid in which a dyer immerses cloth: baptism: the water of baptism

BATTERY the plank closing the bottom of a coal shute: a combined series of prisms: an embankment: the platform on which artillery is mounted: a wound or bruise: the beating of drums

battlewright a warrior (14th cent)

baxter a baker. Today, in Scotland, it applies to a person of either sex though it ceased to have that meaning in southern England around 1400. In England it continued as a term for a female baker until approximately 1550.

BAY an arm of an American prairie surrounded on three sides by trees: a rounded projection of land jutting into the sea: the second branch of a stag's set of antlers: the sound of birds singing: the small fruit of the laurel: the original 16th century fabric, baize, then lighter and finer: a reddish brown colour: a horse of that colour: an embankment to retain water: a recess in a range of hills: an opening in a wall *verb* to bathe

bazil a 17th cent form of **basil**, the herb, and an 18th cent form of **bezel**, the cutting edge of a chisel

bdellatomy the practice of piercing a leech to drain it of blood whilst it is still sucking the wound of a patient. This is to ensure that it continues to perform its medicinal purpose and not cease when satiated.

BEAM the main trunk of a stag's horn: the shank of an anchor: a ship: the radius of a circle: the wooden cylinder of a loom: a tree (in this sense the word expired by the time of the Norman Conquest but is still retained in the names of such trees as **hornbeam**, **whitebeam** and **quickbeam**)

BEAR a pillowcase: barley: pressure: a rough mat for wiping boots on: a wave of the sea   *verb* in Backgammon, to remove a playing piece at the end of the game

BEARD the freshwater shrimp: the fish, hake: an oyster's row of gills: the barb of a fish-hook: the coarser parts of a joint of meat: the sharp edge of a board

bear leader a travelling tutor (18th cent)

BEAT a bundle of flax due to be steeped in water: either of two particular blows struck in fencing: the rough moorland sod due for burning   *verb* to burn that sod: to bat the eyelids: with the addition of the word GOOSE, it is to put one's hands under the armpits to keep them warm (i.e. *to beat goose*)

bed broker a pimp (16th cent)

bedsister a 13th century term then spelt **bedsuster**. It is a mistress or concubine, viewed in relationship to the lawful wife of a man.

bedstaff a stick used in a bedroom but no one is sure what it was used for! Dr. Johnson explained it as, '*A wooden pin stuck anciently on sides of the bedstead to hold the clothes from slipping either side.*' However, no historians agree with his opinion and tend to have more robust explanations for its use!

beglerbeg the governor of a province in the Ottoman empire

BELL the catkin of the hop containing the female flowers: the body of a helmet: in an iron hopper with a large central opening, that pulled into it from below which closes it: the cry of a rutting stag: a bubble in a liquid   *verb* of hops, to develop to this fertile stage: to bubble: to roar: in NEWBY'S BLUFF use the expression *to bell the cat*, for DUTCH AUCTION say *to (this word) the cat* is to perform a hazardous feat and is taken from the fable of mice debating amongst themselves as to who would hang this particular object around the neck of the cat to warn them of its approach

bellyetter sometimes hyphenated as **bell-yetter**, a bell founder

bellyter a beggar (16th cent)

belsire the masculine equivalent of a **beldame** in the ancestral sense; he a grandfather, she a grandmother (14th to 17th cent)

belswagger a pimp (16th to 18th cent)

BEN the winged seed of the horseradish tree: the parlour: a mountain peak   *adverb* within   *preposition* into or within the inner part   *adjective* inner

BEND a long draught of liquor: two parallel lines drawn across a shield: a sash: a fetter or other device to render a person or a limb in restraint: a scroll in decorative work: the childbirth confinement of a woman: a moral restraint: a metal clamp used to strengthen a box: a knot in a rope: half of a complete cow's hide: a glance of the eye: a leap or bound

bendwith the shrub, wayfaring tree, the twigs of which are used to tie up such as faggots (15th to 18th cent)

BENEDICT a newly-married confirmed bachelor: an honest report: an exorcist   *adjective* mildly laxative: blessed

BENEFIT a good deed: a winning lottery ticket: a lottery prize: a churchman's living: a natural gift: a kindness

benet one of four lesser orders in the Catholic Church inferior to a priest. He has the specific function of exorcizing evil spirits.

BENT a grassy plain or heath: an old stalk of various grasses: a bundle of reed grass formerly used in London to adorn chimneys: a curved form such as a bow   *adjective* determined: braced for action

berger a French word for a shepherd

Bergmann a German word for a miner

berman a porter (circa 1000–1300 A.D.): a miner (17th cent)

bermother water of nettles was recommended for the bermother, when ' . . . *she pusheth upward*' according to 16th century advice. Bermother is the womb or uterus.

bernard a **barnard** or decoy used by a gang of swindlers (16th/17th cent)

BERRY a collective noun for rabbits (NEWBY'S BLUFF players may add that the traditional term is *A berry of conies*): a burrow: a gust of wind: an egg of a lobster: a hillock: Dryden's term for a theatre with a sense of either burrow or hillock (it is not clear which) as a place where poor folks congregate   *verb* to thrash: to beat such as a path: to swell: to gather fruit of this type

BESTIAL a wooden tower used in a siege: the Scottish legal and technical word for a farm: an animal (NEWBY'S BLUFF, add that the plural is **bestials**)

betty a male housewife

bibliopole a bookseller

BICKER a wooden bowl or dish capable of holding liquid: historically, a drinking vessel of any material: a sprint: a fight involving missiles   *verb* to flash or gleam: to sprint: or archers or users of slingshots, to skirmish or fight: to assail with missiles

bidstand a highwayman, a term current during the stagecoach era

BIG a nipple: barley: a boil   *verb* to inhabit: to build: to pile up   *adjective*   rich, wealthy

bigate a Roman silver coin having a design of a biga, a two-horsed chariot

biggand a builder (14th cent)

biglot *adjective* bilingual

BIKE a nest inhabited by wasps, hornets or wild bees: a beehive-shaped stack of corn: a swarm: a motley crowd of people: a well-provisioned storehouse   *verb* to swarm like bees

BILL the booming cry of the bittern: a medical recipe: an ancient Anglo-Saxon type of broadsword: in the 16th/17th centuries, a three-edged weapon comprising a concave ax with a spike at the back and a spear tipped head to the shaft: a letter written by a pope: a written petition: the human mouth: the human nose: a prayer: a label: a publicly read announcement   *verb* to hoe: to peck: to caress

BILLY the masculine equivalent of a **tittie**: a highwayman's cudgel: an Australian bushman's teapot: a comrade (NEWBY'S BLUFF, a billy and tittie are a brother and sister)

BIN a manger or similar container for fodder *adverb* within, inside *preposition* within, into: during or in the course of

BIND the quantity of 250 eels: the quantity of 14 gallons of salmon: a thin stratum of shale: a curved line connecting two identical musical notes to indicate continuity not repetition of that sound: confinement at childbirth: the honeysuckle

BING in Yorkshire, a pile of potatoes: in Derbyshire, 8 hundredweights of lead ore: in Staffordshire, the best lead ore: in Shropshire, a railed off part of a cowhouse containing fodder: historically, a pile of anything – even dead bodies: in an alum works, a pile of alum thrown together in order to drain: generally, the kiln of a furnace using charcoal in the smelting process: a bread basket: any sort of bin

BIRD the young of a wolf: the young of a snake: the young of a pelican: the young of an eagle: a young man: a maiden (Note, in the sense of maiden the use is very ancient and it was over 300 years old when Shakespeare used it. Originally, like rabbit and cony, a bird was the young of the fowl and was extended as the young of the above named. For a lad, the sense became obsolete in the 16th century.)

BISHOP the ladybird: a watchman: a sweet drink of wine, oranges or lemons and sugar: mulled, spiced port: a high priest of the Jews: a child's smock: a woman's bustle

BIT the womb: a fire bucket: fourpence: a cow's mouthful of grass: death's sting: the point of a pickax *verb* to restrain

BIZARRE a carnation striped with three or four colours: the streaked gillyflower *adjective* of tulips, yellow and marked with purple or scarlet

blackcoat a parson

BLACKGUARD a particular blend of snuff accidently created by the Dublin snuff merchant, Lundy Foot, when he was only a boy: a collective term for the lowest grade of domestic servants in an historic royal or noble household – it comprised the scullions and kitchen knaves: an individual soldier dark in appearance or character: a collective term for the rabble which scraped a menial living following an army: a street arab who cleans shoes *verb* to abuse or revile in offensive terms

blackmanger a 14th century spelling of **blancmange** which, in those days, was a dish of chicken minced with cream, rice, almonds, sugar, eggs and the like

BLEACH soot, ink, lampblack or any other substance used for blacking: a skin disease *verb* to blacken

BLESS to brandish such as a weapon: to beat or thrash: to exerocise an evil spirit by making the sign of the cross

BLINK a trick or stratagem: in the plural, branches thrown in the path of a deer to make it change its course: in the plural, feathers thread on a line to scare birds away *adjective* of milk, slightly sour *verb* to avoid: to deceive: to evade, shirk, ignore: to blindfold: to turn such as milk or beer sour: to glance or let it fall a glance

BLOCK the object of aim in a game, such as the peg in quoits or the jack in bowls: a whetstone: a bargain: a falcon's perch: a contrast to straw in old epigrams such as '*Ye stumbled at a straw but leapt over a block*' (DUTCH AUCTION, substitute '*blank*' for *block*): a person credited with the intelligence of a log

blockman a coastguard (16th cent)

BLOOD gargut, a disease of pigs: an aristocratic rowdy: a clan: the supposed seat of sensual appetite: red coral   *verb* to let sap flow from a tree

blood hunter an 18th century equivalent of a murder squad detective

bloodstrange the small herb, mousetail especially *Myosurus minimus* the little mousetail

bloodsupper one who is bloodthirsty (16th cent)

blowen a slang term for a prostitute

blucher as Field Marshal Gebhard Leberecht von Blucher arrived late in the day to assist Wellington at the battle of Waterloo so, of three classes of horse drawn cabs admitted to 19th century railway stations, the bluchers were the last in line. The more priviledged cabs given precedence. But, a blucher is more widely known as a strong leather half-boot also named after this famous Prussian military commander.

BLUE the colour of thin milk: the colour of the flame of a candle in the presence of ghosts, the Devil or as a portent of death *verb* to blush

blue dahlia the same as a blue moon, anything rare or unheard of

bluehead the marshworm, a popular bait with anglers

blueman a negro (14th/15th cent)

bluenose both a purplish coloured potato grown in Nova Scotia and a nickname for a Nova Scotian

blue pipe the lilac (17th cent)

blunger today, it is a mechanical device. But, formerly, it was a long flat wooden instrument with a cross handle at the top and used for blunging. Blunging is the mixing of such as clay and powdered flint with water in the primary stages of pottery making.

blunker a Scottish term for one who prints cloths

BLUNT a re-pointed needle: a strong-pointed needle suitable for binding shoes or making stays: ready money   *adjective* barren: unpolished   *verb* to dilute

BLUSH a collective noun for boys (A blush of boys): a blink: a glance or look

bo a Japanese Buddhist monk

BOB a 14th century coin worth in the region of a penny halfpenny: a deception or trick: a knot of lobworms used as bait for eels: a pendant earring: a small bunch of flowers: a weight on the tail of a kite: a lump of potter's clay   *verb* to strike with the fist

bodylet certain words are called nonce words and this is one of them. It is a word coined purely for the nonce (for the particular occasion) and, though subsequently recorded in dictionaries, fails to become standard English. It occurred in the following sentence of a book published in 1870, '*The savage also wears necklaces and rings, bracelets and anklets, armlets and leglets – even, if I may say so, bodylets.*' An ornamental bangle for the body.

BOG something to be feared   *adjective* proud, saucy verb to provoke: to defile with excrement

BOMBAST raw cotton: cotton wool   *adjective* padded

BOLD a dwelling or building *adjective* of grain, plump: of wind, fierce: of a coast, rising steeply from deep water *verb* to grow strong or big: to make a fire strong or fierce

bombero a Spanish word for a fireman

bonagh a career soldier (17th cent)

bonder a Norwegian peasant farmer

bone-ace a card game, popular in the 17th and 18th centuries, in which every third card dealt to a player is turned up. The highest card wins the bone, or half the kitty. It is also the name of the ace of diamonds, which is the highest individual card.

bone-polisher the cat-o'-nine-tails

boneshaw sciatica (14th to 18th cent)

bongrace a curtain worn, in the 16th and 17th centuries, on the front of women's bonnets to protect their complexions from the sun. Today, it is an archaic term for such as a wide-brimmed straw hat which provides shade.

boniface the landlord of an inn

BONNET the second stomach of a cow: a thimblerigger's accomplice: a snare for fish: an additional piece of canvas attached to a sail: one in league with an auctioneer to raise the bidding: the cowl at the top of a ventilating shaft: a balaclava of chainmail: a nightcap worn in bed: a Scotch cap

bonze a Japanese Buddist clergyman

bonzess a female bonze

Boobrie a mythical gigantic waterbird of the Argyllshire lochs. Its voice is like the roar of an angry bull; its neck is nearly three feet in length; its beak is seventeen inches long and hooked like that of an eagle

whilst the rest of it resembles an enormous black duck. Its diet consists of sheep and cattle which it devours ravenously.

bookwright a maker or author of books (ODDJOB note: Select either)

BOOT a medicinal cure: the right of a tenant to essential timber from a landlord's estate: help or rescue: penance: compensation: the repair of a decaying structure such as a bridge: that plundered: a piece of armour for the leg: a leather case for a violin

boot-catcher an 18th century servant at an inn who pulled off guest's boots

boothaler (boot-haler) a brigand or a highwayman (17th cent)

BOROUGH a manor house: a fortress: a suburb of a city

borough-English the custom, long established in the home counties, of the youngest son inheriting all the lands and property. Also known in Somerset, it is rare in the midlands and unknown north of the Humber.

boroughhead a headborough (q.v.)

BORROW *verb* to sail close to land: to release by paying a ransom: to defend: to assert confidently

borsholder a headborouogh (q.v.)

BOSS a bundle of straw used as a seat: a fat woman: a small cask: a water conduit issuing from a corpulent figure: a plasterer's hod: a bulky animal: a mass of rock protruding through strata of a different kind *adjective* hollow: empty: powerless *verb* to kiss: to ornament with metal studs

BOTTLE a dwelling or building: a bundle of hay or straw: the honey bag of a bee

bottle boy an apothecary's assistant

bottle holder in the days of bareknuckle fighting, the second or assistant to a pugalist

BOTTOM the cocoon of a silkworm: the soil in which a plant grows: a ball of thread

BOUGH the gallows: the shoulder of an animal *verb* (pronounced *baux*) of a dog, to bark

BOUGHT an enclosure for sheep at milking time: a square seat in a church: a bend in the coastline: a coil formed by the body of a snake: the fold of a cloth *verb* to link: to bend or fold: to enclose sheep (inflected forms are **bought, boughted** and **boughting**)

BOUNCE the dogfish: an explosion: a boastful falsehood

BOUNDER one who owns a tract of land containing tin ore: one who marks out limits: a landmark

bouquinist a dealer in second-hand books of little value

bovicide literally one who slays cattle but humorously used for a butcher

BOW a herd or cattle: an Indian musical instrument comprising a series of bells: the provision of a benefice granted by the pope

bowler the workman who shapes the bowl of a spoon

box keeperess a female attendant on those occupying a box at the theatre

brachetour a brewer (16th cent)

BRAG a disease of cereals better known as smut: a large nail: the bray of a trumpet

BRAID a whim: an attack: a deception

BRAKE a brewer's wooden mill for crushing such as hops: an implement rather like a pair of scissors used for stripping bark from trees: a thicket: fern: a crossbow: a pump handle: a horse's bridle: a cage: the rack, an instrument of torture: a baker's kneading machine: a toothed instrument used for crushing flax

BRANCH a child: a chandelier: a horn worn as part of a woman's headdress in ancient times

BRAND a torch carried by Cupid: a blight which turns leaves brown: destruction by fire

BRASH an attack: a sudden burst of rain: loose broken rock found under the topsoil *adjective* of timber, fragile or brittle

BRAT the flatfish, turbot: a thin bed of impure coal: a child's pinafore: the skin on a rice pudding: a woman's apron: a jacket for a sheep's back

BRAVE a hired assassin: finery: an exclamation having a sense of Excellent! or Capital!

BREAD pollen: a pie crust: a morsel of food

breadwright a baker (13th cent)

BREAM *verb* of pigs, to copulate: to clean the hull of a sailing ship by applying heat to the coating of pitch thereby releasing the accumulated rubbish for brushing off *adjective* used as a combining form with the word **backed** to describe a horse having a high ridged back

BREECH the roe of the codfish: a term of ridicule for the coins of Cromwell *verb* to flog on the buttocks

BREEZE a gadfly: small cinders: a rumour

brehon an ancient Irish judge (the Brehon law was abolished by James I)

brekekekex the noise made by a frog

BREW yeast *verb* of oysters, to produce spawn: to dilute with water

BRICK a lamprey which has a number of very long and narrow black transverse markings: in heraldry, a design in the shape of a building: an oblong loaf of bread

BRIDE the dark crimson underwing of a moth: the string of a bonnet *verb* to mince or act in a camp fashion

BRIDGE a tripod for holding a pot over a fire: a landing stage or jetty: a narrow ridge of such as shingle across the bottom of a channel

bridle cull a slang term for a highwayman (18th cent)

BRIEF a motto: the action of trimming the edges of all but the significant playing cards so that, by touch, one can isolate such as an ace and thereby cheat: a letter from the Pope on a matter of discipline

BRIGHT a beautiful woman *adjective* of a person, charming: of a sound, shrill

BRIM a vicious woman *verb* of pigs, to copulate: to develop fruit

brine smeller one who inspects an area in the search for a new salt mine

brinjarry a travelling grain and salt merchant in India

BRISK a wanton: a fop *adjective* of tone, unpleasantly sharp

BRIT the young of the sprat: the young of the herring: the young of the mackerel *verb* to cut to pieces

brollachan a mythical being of the Scottish Highlands. It has recognizable human eyes and mouth but the rest of it is completely shapeless and beyond description. It can only speak two words and these are the Gaelic for 'myself' and 'thyself' and its mother is a malicious dangerous spirit. Rustic Highlanders tend to have problems when they entertain

this creature – especially from mother who exacts any revenge needed for her offspring.

broomdasher a dealer in such as faggots and brooms (a dialect word after the style of haberdasher)

broom squire one who makes rustic brooms or besoms from natural materials gathered in such as the New Forest

BROTHEL a man who is a worthless good-for-nothing: a prostitute: a madam or other keeper of a house of ill-repute

BROWN a copper coin: a brunette: an unbleached state *adjective* of a sword, burnished or glistening

browze the third and inner covering of the nutmeg, the others being the shell and the mace (18th cent)

BRUTE a Welshman: a hero *adjective* of a surface, unpolished

bruzzing the sound made by a bear (17th cent)

BUBBLE a round ornament of gold or leather worn by children of a freeman of ancient Rome: a hollow bead of glass formerly used for testing the strength of spirits: a dupe *verb* to cry or blubber: to cheat, to humbug

BUCK a large basket used for trapping eels: the male of the goat: a native Indian of South America: a species of polygonum, the seed of which is used as cattle fodder: the T-shaped end of the beam of a plough *verb* of rabbits, to copulate

bucrane a decorative sculpture on a building of the skull of an ox

buddler one who washes such as lead ore in Derbyshire, tin ore in Cornwall or silver ore in the U.S.A. in a shallow inclined vat called a buddle

BUDGE court rations: a leather bag: a sneak thief: a push or shove: lambskin with the wool dressed outwards to create a fur: a weapon similar to a spear *adjective* pompous *verb* to put together in a clumsy fashion

BUFF the reindeer: a breathing hole in a helmet: nonsense: the dress of a catchpole or petty officer of justice who made arrests for debt: a blow or stroke: endurance (the sense in which it applies to the game of Blind Man's Buff): the blindfolded player in that game *verb* to stutter: to explode into a laugh: by sudden force, to cause to burst: to swear to: to stand firm

BUFFET a footstool: a sideboard *verb* to muffle bells by the tying of padding to the clappers

buffo a comic actor, a singer in comic opera

BUG a scarecrow: a hobgoblin: a self-important person

buggess a native Malayan soldier in service with a European colonial power

bukshee a paymaster-general of the army in a colonial Indian state

bulbitate a particularly unpleasant natural accident defined, in 1623, as '*To befilth one's breech.*'

BULK the one who bumps or otherwise distracts a victim whilst the pickpocket robs him: a stall: a pile of fish due for salting: the belly

BULL a bubble: a flavoured water drink produced from the act of putting water into such as an empty spirit barrel: a main bar of a harrow

BULLET the piece of paper on which a voter puts the name of his candidate: an official military order that board and lodging should be provided for the bearer: in plural form, the game of bowls

bull whacker a driver of a bullock cart in the old Wild West

BUMBLE a bullrush: a small round stone: the bittern: a confusion: an idler: a bandage used for blindfolding *verb* of a bittern, to utter its cry

bumbo a drink comprising rum, sugar, water and nutmeg

BUMP the cry of the bittern: a kind of floor matting: a material for candlewicks or coarse sheets

bumtrap a slang term for a bailiff (18th cent)

BUN a squirrel: the stalk of flax: the tail of a hare

BUNG a pickpocket: a purse: one who superintended the serving of grog on a ship

bungo a Central American boat carved out of a single trunk and 40 feet in length

burio a Scottish word for a hangman (16th cent but, as **burrio**, it continued to the 19th)

BURN water from a well: warm water used for washing: a burden

BURROW a halo of light around the moon: a heap: shelter

buscarl a mariner of historical times

bush laywer a tough and tangled plant, the New Zealand bramble

bush ranger in Australia, an escaped convict who took refuge in the bush

BUTT a surface of coal exposed at right angles to the face: a cart of rude design: the thicker part of an animal's hide: a hassock: a headland: a hillock: a ridge between the furrows created in ploughing: a small piece of land detached from the rest: on the side of a ship, the end of a plank: an end, aim or object: the length of a shooting range: a terminal point: a block from which an anvil is cast: a catkin: the base of a leafstalk: the trunk of a tree: any flatfish native to British waters *verb* in angling, to point the base of the fishing rod directly at the catch in order to obtain a more rigid hold: in surveying, to mark out limits: to aim a missile: to dive head first

BUTTER a blacksmith's paring knife: in play, one who cheats: in a sawmill, a machine for squaring ends

butter badger a badger (q.v.) who deals in butter

butterbag a Dutchman (17th cent term of contempt)

BUTTON a thimblerigger's accomplice: one in league with an auctioneer to raise the bidding: an oblong piece of wood loosely screwed in the centre and used as a door fastening: a knob at the top of a cap: a leather ring through which the reins of a horse pass: anything of little value: a pimple *verb* to fasten a door with a button (DUTCH AUCTION. Delete 'a button', substitute a precis of the definition): of a cauliflower, to come to a head prematurely

BUTTONS sheep's dung: an animal's testicles: the plant, tansy

BUXOM *adjective* obedient: humble: flexible *verb* to yield to

BUZZ a bur or rough seedcase: a large bushy wig: a downy land beetle favoured as an angler's bait: an artificial fly in a similar shape: a whim: bombastic writing *verb* to pick a pocket: to drain a bottle to the last drop: to mutter *interjection* the equivalent of 'hey presto!': a command for silence

BUZZARD the worst of its kind, but only in the expression '*Between hawk and buzzard*', which expression is used for a person or thing that is average (a hawk being the best sporting bird, a buzzard the worst): a stupid ignorant person: any of various night-flying insects such as a large moth or a cockchafer

buzzgloak a slang term for a pickpocket

bybloemen the tulip is divided into four main varieties; the bizarres, the roses, the selfs and the bybloemens. The bybloemen varieties are white, shaded with violet or dark purple.

Byron the solution to the saying is *A rose by any other name would smell as sweet*

byrthynsak the old Scottish law of byrthynsak held that a man would not be hanged for such as sheep stealing providing that he was capable of carrying in a sack upon his back a weight equivalent to the stolen animal or animals

ca a Scottish word for a pass or defile between hills and also for calf. The plural is **caas**.

cachekow one who impounds cattle, a bailiff (Scottish 16th cent)

cad ignoring various other meanings, ODDJOB players have the specific occupation of a builder's labourer

cadger ignoring both the common meaning and the fact that it also means one who carries hawks, ODDJOB players have a specific occupation. An itinerant dealer having a horse and cart (in earlier days a packhorse) who trades rural produce such as eggs, butter and chickens in the town and small items from shops in the country.

cadilesker a chief judge in the Ottoman empire

caduceator a herald, a messenger (17th/18th cent)

cafard a hypocrite, an imposter

calepin a dictionary (16th to 18th cent)

calf's snout the flower, snapdragon

camelopardel a giraffe with the horns of an ibex (an heraldic device)

cannet a duck without feet or a beak (an heraldic device)

canstick *Kit with the canstick* is a 16th century form of *Jack o' lantern* or *Will o' the wisp* and Shakespeare referred to 'brazen cansticks' in *Henry IV Part One*. A candlestick (16th/17th cent).

cantatrice a female professional singer

capelocracy shopkeepers as a class

caphar an 18th century toll imposed by the Turks on Christian merchants taking their wares from Aleppo to Jerusalem

cappyhole a 17th/18th century Scottish schoolboy's game of attempting to throw a marble in a hole

carcel the French lamp, a lamp in which the oil is pumped to the wick by clockwork

carcoon a clerk in British imperial India

cassy a straw basket of Orkney and Caithness suspended from the shoulders with a strap

castane the 14th to 16th century word for a chestnut still extant in the form of the adjective, *castanean*, of or pertaining to a chestnut

castock in Scotland and northern England, a cabbage stalk

catathleba a fabulous monster about which very little is known. In a work circa 1300 A.D. the following mention is made, '*Another beast there is, of evil kind, catathleba is her name.*' (For fun, you can add that the anagram of this word is

THE BAAL CAT after pointing out that Baal is an evil false god mentioned in the Bible.)

catbrain a Staffordshire term for a soil of rough clay mixed with stones

cate a viand or delicacy

catechu any of several tannin-based astringent substances obtained from the bark, wood or fruits of various eastern trees or shrubs. They are used in medicine, tanning, calico printing and dyeing.

cathead often hyphenated as **cat-head**, it is either of two virtually horizontal beams projecting either side of the bow of a ship. A ship's anchor is catted, or raised, to be cathead by means of the **catpurchase**, a rope, pulley and tackle arrangement having such individual names as **catrope**, **catblock** and **cathook**.

catsilver mica (16th to 18th cent)

catstick in the game of tip-cat, a small piece of wood tapering at both ends and called a cat is made to spring from the ground and be driven as far as possible with the aid of a stick called a catstick

cattleist an artist who paints pictures of cattle

cauliflowering nobody knows what this means. Southey wrote, in 1799, '*Some barber's leathern powder bag wherewith he feathers, frosts or cauliflowers (people).*' in 1845, Lord Campbell wrote ' . . . *and to cauliflower their wigs*' Based on this evidence it is presumed that the verb, to cauliflower, means to powder.

cavalet a hollow stick used, in France in the 16th and 17th centuries, to blow the fire

cavallard in both Texas and Louisiana a local term for a band of horses or mules

ce a musical syllable, the equivalent of **re** (bebization scale) or of **mi** (bobization scale)

cebratane a wooden blowpipe for shooting clay pellets at birds (17th/18th cent)

cecils minced meat, breadcrumbs, onions, anchovies, chopped parsley and seasoning rolled into balls the size of a turkey's egg and fried. Recommended for serving with cold beef.

centress a female **centre**. In the Fenian Movement, an Irish republican organization founded in the U.S.A. in the 19th century, a centre is a leader and the **head centre** is the chief. The Fenian Sisterhood has **centresses** and a **head centress** respectively.

cepotaph a tomb in a garden

cervalet a musical instrument which resembles a short, thick sausage and has a bassoon-like tone

cestus is both a girdle worn, in ancient times, by a bride and a type of Roman boxing glove. The ancient Romans wore this contrivance of leather thongs loaded with strips of lead and iron in their sporting contests. In the sense of girdle, the correct plural is **cesti** and, in the sense of a glove, the correct plural is the same as the singular, **cestus**.

ch an aphetic form of **ich**, one of the obsolete forms of the pronoun I. Ch has *never* existed as an independent word. It has only ever been used as part of a compound form in southern dialects such as that of Shropshire. In these dialects speakers say such as **chad** (I had), **cham** (I am), **chud** (I would), **chard** (I heard), **chave** (I have) or **chill** (I will). They never say such as 'CH-AD' or 'CH-UD' or any similar sound implied by considering ch as a word in its own right. To pretend otherwise is as logical as pronouncing scrabble as 'SCR-ABBLE' as the letters SCR prefixing a word have, in many cases, arisen phonetically. The prefixing letters, SCR, also appear in major dictionaries as a separate entry in just the same fashion as does the non-word, ch. It is just rather unfortunate that ch is treated in one particular word play contest as being a real word. Obviously, if the rules of the game permit it, you would be at a disadvantage if you denied yourself access to it but, at least it is not valid for any game invented by the author. His games are limited to real words. **Cham**, **chud**, **chard** etc. are perfectly acceptable for these games. Ironically, however, the reference work used to 'legitimize' ch will not provide access to such as **chud**, a real word!

cha the beverage, tea

chadfarthing an ancient duty of a farthing levied by the Church on all houses at Easter to pay for holy oils and waxes. Known by various names – such as **waxifarthing** – the specific term for the diocese of Lichfield was chadfarthing after St. Chad to whom Lichfield Cathedral is dedicated.

chairship the period of the reign of an individual pope (17th cent)

chairwoman a 17th/18th century form of **charwoman** a charlady

chal fellow, person, man (a gypsy word now assimilated into English though normally restricted to a Romany context)

channel bill a huge Australian cuckoo, over two feet in length

chapeless *adjective* designating the want of a chape or sheath

chapwoman a female dealer or hawker

Chartaline an adjectival trade name designating a blanket made of thick paper. An 1883 newspaper advert claimed that it was as warm as two pairs of woollen blankets.

chasteling a eunuch (16th cent)

chevisancer a moneylender (16th/17th cent)

chi the feminine of **chal** (q.v.)

chicker *verb* of a cricket, to utter its cry

Childermas 28th December, the festival of the Holy Innocents slaughtered by order of Herod

childwite in old law, a fine paid to the lord of the manor for making one of his bondwomen pregnant. In 1603, for example, any man who sired a bastard in the manor of Writtle, Essex, was fined 3 shillings and 4 pence.

chimney publican one who undertook the collection of the chimney tax and paid a fixed fee for the proceeds which became his. The chimney tax of two shillings per annum for each fire hearth in a dwelling was imposed during the reign of Charles II and repealed during the reign of William and Mary

chuckfarthing an old game, popular since the 17th century, of the pitch and toss variety. Players threw coins at a mark. The player whose coin came nearest then collected all the coins and attempted to toss them into a hole. All which fell in the hole became his.

ci a Middle English word for a dog. The plural is **cwn**.

clamjamphrie rubbish, anything of little value (Scotland and northern England)

clarence a horse-drawn carriage with seating for four. Named in honour of the Duke of Clarence who later became King William IV (1830–1837).

claude a 16th century form of **clawed**, the past tense of the verb, claw

clay-eater one of a number of dwellers in the Southern States of the U.S.A. who existed on turpentine-whiskey and rid their craving for food by eating an aluminous earth. Even the negro slaves of the period looked upon them with contempt.

clibby *adjective* sticky, adhesive (Cornwall and Devon)

clinamen an inclination or bias

clipsome *adjective* of a waist, suitable for embracing

clive *verb* to climb (14th cent)

cloamer a potter (17th cent)

closer the worker who joins together the uppers of boots or shoes

co a Scottish word for a shed

coal whipper one who, prior to greater mechanization in the late 19th century, raised coal from the hold of a ship by means of a pulley

cockpenny a traditional payment with a history of several hundred years. At Shrovetide the schoolmaster of such northern schools as Manchester Grammar, Clitheroe Grammar and St. Bees received from each pupil one penny. It is supposed to be in lieu of a cock for the sport of cockfighting and cash payments have been made since at least 1524. Whilst the custom continued until the late Victorian period it is no longer in existence.

cock rose any wild poppy with a red flower (Scotland and northern England)

codder ODDJOB players choose one of the following:– a saddler or leather worker in

Lincolnshire: a gatherer of peas in the London rural areas: a seaman on a cod fisheries trawler based in the U.S.A.

codonostome the mouth of a jellyfish

coistrel a groom, specifically the servant in charge of a knight's horses

colporteur a hawker of books and newspapers especially one employed by a religious society to travel and distribute Bibles and tracts

colt evil a disease which causes swelling in the penis of a horse

compter a debtor's prison. The Poultry compter of London existed from the 15th century until it was pulled down in 1817. London's other 15th century compter, the Bread Street compter, was demolished in 1555, its successor was the Wood Street compter which gave way, in 1791, to the Giltspur Street compter. This lasted until 1854. Similar city prisons of this type existed in such places as Exeter and Southwark.

conacre the word is derived from corn acre and is a traditional Irish system of land tenure. A small parcel of land, fully prepared for sowing, is let for a season. The crop belongs to the person who paid the rent but, if the rent has not been paid in full, the crop is detained until the monetary transaction is complete.

conceytate pregnancy (15th cent)

conder a pilchard fisherman's lookout man. Stationed on a high place – such as a cliff top – he signals to the fishing boats the direction taken by shoals of such as herrings or pilchards.

conjee *verb* to starch (collars, shirt fronts etc.) with rice water

conjobble *verb* to discuss

conniption hysterical excitement (An American vulgar noun of the 19th century, it was used adjectivally in the classic British comedy film, *The Wrong Box*, in memorable lines which had a character suffering a 'conniption fit')

consewe the word occurs only in the phrase, **capon in consewe** and a recipe of 1430 gives these instructions:- '*Take a capon, seeth him in water, quarter him, scatter thereupon sugar and send it in with almonds*' A similar contemporary recipe for **capon in consy** has the bird cut into small pieces, stewed and coloured with saffron. Though both phrases suggest a sweet sauce is the meaning it would seem that consewe is merely the mode of cooking.

contabile the Italian for a bookkeeper

contrude *verb* to push or thrust together (17th cent)

conygarth cony is the correct name for the rabbit and is still the legal and heraldic term. A rabbit is the young of the cony – as leveret is the young of the hare. A garth is a small piece of enclosed ground and a warren is a garth specifically used for breeding game. A conygarth has these animals as they were originally held when first imported after the Norman Conquest, in small enclosed plots of land. Strictly, the maze of burrows excavated by the wild rabbits should be called cony buries as a conygarth is a true rabbit warren.

coo-in-new the white beech, a timber tree of New South Wales, Australia

copart *verb* to share (17th cent) (Not to be confused with **co-**

part, the hyphenated noun designating one of two or more conjoint parts of a whole)

copshen in the 18th century herrings were described by such terms as 'fat herring', 'shotten herring' (one that has spawned) and copshen. A copshen was a herring without a head.

corbicula commonly called 'the basket', it is that part of a back leg of a bee in which it carries pollen

cordax an indecent dance performed in old Greek comedy

cordiform *adjective* heart-shaped

corpse candle a flame seen gliding delicately in a churchyard or over a grave and believed to be either an omen of death or the route which a subsequent funeral will take

corvy an ancient military defensive device rather like a modern day crane. It was mounted on the defender's wall and consisted of a beam of timber furnished with grappling irons. It was used to demolish such as stones piled against the walls by the attacking force in their attempts to scale the ramparts. It could also be used to pick up any individual beseiger who came too close.

corylet a copse of hazel (17th cent)

cosp in the Cheshire dialect it can mean either end of a spade. The blade or the crosspiece at the top of the handle.

cost-castle a 17th century children's game consisting of picking up objects whilst running

cott a variant spelling of **cot** in the sense of a small house

cottabus a fashionable amusement of the young men at ancient Greek drinking parties. An individual would throw the remaining measure of wine in his goblet into a metal dish, at the same time invoking the name of his mistress. If all fell in the dish with an agreeable sound it was taken as a sign that he stood well in her favour.

couple beggar a 17th century priest who performed marriages which scandalized society (i.e. an aristocrat with one of low birth, so coupling to a 'beggar')

course-a-park a 17th century rural game in which a girl called out the name of a boy who then had to chase and catch her. Contemporary accounts suggest that the girls enjoyed being caught.

court cream insincere flattery such as that of a courtier (17th cent)

covert-baron a married woman

cowan one who builds dry-stone walls (Scotland)

crappit-heid a Scottish delicacy consisting of the head of a haddock stuffed with oatmeal, suet, roe, onions and spices

crepuscle twilight

cricket-a-wicket an old game about which very little is known. It appears that around the period 1590–1610 people enjoyed making noises rather like those of a grasshopper.

crit a colloquial short form of **criticism** and perfectly acceptable for word games in either the singular or plural form

cro '*It is statute be the king, that the cro of any earl of Scotland is seven times twenty kye*'. In the ancient Celtic laws of Scotland, the cro was the compensation made for a man according to this rank. In the case of a Scottish earl it was 140 cows.

crocus a quack doctor (a slang term of long medical usage and conjectured as being an ironic reference to the Latinized surname of one Dr. Helkiah Crooke who wrote medical textbooks in the early 1600's)

croker in the 16th century, one who cultivated or sold saffron. (Saffron, which is used to flavour or colour food, is the dried stigmas or terminal aspect of the female part of the flower, crocus)

cronk in Cumberland, the cry of the raven: in the U.S.A., the cry of the wild goose

crwth an ancient Celtic musical instrument consisting of four strings played by bow and a further two strings which were plucked

cu a fairy dog of great size

cub a surgeon's assistant at St. Thomas's Hospital, London. The term was used until 1738.

cubbel a 13th century word for what is now called a clog. A clog is the equivalent of an anchor, it is a large block of wood or the like chained to the leg of a beast to prevent its straying.

cubeb the berry of a Javanese climbing plant resembling a grain of pepper and used in both medicine and, having a pungent spicy flavour, in cooking

cubert unfortunately, it is not known if there has ever been a skeleton in the cubert – though it is perfectly possible. The phrase, *skeleton in the cupboard* or *in the closet*, was revived in the mid 19th century by Thackeray and a cubert is a 17th century form of the word, cupboard.

culex a gnat, the plural being **culices**. In technical terminology, *Culex* is the genus which includes the common mosquito but the Latin word, culex, has been used in English for the gnat since at least 1483

when it was described as '. . . *a little beast which hath six feet and two wings*' Gnats and mosquitoes were considered, in the 19th century, to belong to the same genus. Scientifically, they are now considered far removed from each other. This confusion between gnats and mosquitoes can still be found in the 1988 edition of *Chambers English Dictionary* which gives *Culex* as being the genus of the gnat. Other dictionaries – such as *Funk and Wagnalls* – have the technical term correctly applied to the mosquito.

Curtana the name of the sword of mercy, the only non-pointed sword carried in the coronation of an English monarch. Also known as St. Edward's sword, it is carried in the front rank of the regalia with the sword of justice and the third sword to the right and left of it respectively. These are carried drawn, whereas the sword of state (which appears later in the procession) remains in its scabbard.

dalt a foster child (Scotland)

damasax a Danish ax, a type of battle ax having a very long blade and, normally, a spike at the back

darker a labourer paid on a daily basis

dataller a labourer (CALL MY (domestic) BLUFF. A casual worker engaged on such as road works and paid on a daily basis. Essentially a Lancashire term but not a dialect word.)

dauke the wild carrot (15th/16th cent)

dayeseye literally the 'day's eye', an early form of **daisy** which makes its being a symbol of the sun more easily appreciated. The sun is a powerful shield against magic and it is sometimes said that the custom of children wearing daisy chains is to protect them from being carried off by the fairies.

dead tongue the plant, water hemlock, which has a paralysing effect upon the organs of speech

dead wed a mortgage (14th to 17th cent)

dearborn a type of American light four-wheeled cart, once common in the country districts around St. Louis and New Orleans and named after its inventor

death hunter an undertaker

deemster (for ODDJOB choose the archaic term only, for CALL MY (domestic) BLUFF all is valid) an archaic term for a judge: on the Isle of Man, one of two judges having jurisdiction for either the north or the south of the island and who take an oath to execute the laws '*as indifferently as the herring backbone doth lie in the midst of the fish.*'

deese a herring hang or place where herrings are dried   *verb* to dry herrings (both senses, Sussex)

deesse a goddess (16th/17th cent)

defensor a magistrate of a provincial city of the Roman empire after 365 a.d.

demerlayk described in 1400 as 'the devil's craft', it is magic or occult practices (12th to 15th cent)

dempster (for ODDJOB choose the obsolete term only: for CALL MY (domestic) BLUFF all is valid) a judge (13th cent): an official of a Scottish court who, for many centuries, pronounced the sentence delivered by the judge: an alternative word for an Isle of Man **deemster** (*q.v.*)

Dendrobatidea in South America, the native Indians obtain a poison for their arrows by heating certain frogs over a fire. This causes the highly toxic substance to gather on the frog's skin. Known as arrow-poison frogs, some live in trees and many of the males guard the few eggs which are laid on moist land. After hatching, the tadpoles live on daddy's back for a week finally swimming away in the pond he visits each night. Dendrobatidea is the technical term embracing all species of the arrow-poison frogs.

departer a refiner of gold or silver (17th cent)

derfly in Malory's *Morte d'Arthur* this adverb is used in a sense of grievously or terribly in the line '. . . *and, therefore, derfly am I damned for ever.*' It had various meanings of which forcibly or violently had the longest life, occurring in literature from 1200 to 1605. It was both an adjective and an adverb related to the Old English word, **derf**, which meant trouble or tribulation.

derrick a hangman (17th cent)

derverye madness (15th cent)

destour a Parsee chief priest

desultor a circus performer whose speciality is leaping from one horse to another

develler a boxer or pugilist (Scotland)

devil's books playing cards

dewbit a light pre-breakfast snack (Dorset)

dewblown *adjective* of cattle, swollen with the over indulgence of fresh moist grass or clover

dexter a dyer (Middle English)

dey a woman in charge of a dairy

(NOT a 'dairy-maid' as noted by one particular dictionary)

diamoron a compound of syrup and mulberry juice used as a gargle for a sore throat (15th to 17th cent)

didymate *adjective* of plants or animals, paired or twinned

die-wise *adjective/adverb* in the form of a cube

diffode *verb* to dig such as a hole or a ditch (17th cent)

digenesis the phenomenon better known as **alternate generation** and exhibited by such an animal as the sea fir. One generation exists as a tree-like creature anchored to the frond of a large seaweed. Small buds of tissue develop on its 'branches' which float free as tiny male and female jellyfishes which breed sexually. Their offspring is the asexual sea fir.

dighter ODDJOB choose from:– a composer: an author: a director: a ruler: a preparer (senses 11th to 16th cent) a winnower of such as corn (sense still extant in modern dialect)

dildo described, in 1697, as ' . . . *a green prickly shrub, that grows to about 10 or 12 feet high, without either leaf or fruit. It is as big as a man's leg, from the root to the top, and it is full of sharp prickles, growing in thick rows.*' Dildo is a 17th/18th century term for the cactus

dilligrout a particular type of gruel or pottage and a mess of this pottage had to be served to the king on his coronation day by the lord of the manor of Addington, Surrey. Failure to perform this service would have resulted in that lord's forfeiture of his manor.

dimber *adjective* pretty

dimber-damber a leader of a gang of thieves

dimp *verb* to mark with dimples

dinders a term local to Wroxeter, Shropshire, for the small coins found on its Roman sites. A dinder being a Roman denarius.

dinmont a young ram, one which has had its first shearing but yet to receive its second

dinus vertigo

diopter a type of ancient theodolite

dioptre a diopter

Dirty Allan the skua, a seabird described as 'a gull turned into a hawk'. It steals both eggs and chicks, kills such as fulmars and puffins, robs gannets and kittiwakes of their prey and will even eat carrion. The skua feeds its young by disgorging the contents of its stomach.

disper a Winchester College slang term for a portion of food. Such portions being variously described as **fat flab**, **cat's head**, **long disper**, **middle cut**, **rack** and **cut**

disporteress a female jester (15th cent)

disselboom in South Africa, the pole of a wagon

ditton a phrase or expression especially a motto or proverb (16th/17th cent)

dobson in the U.S.A., the larva of an insect akin to the mayfly used as an angler's bait

doddy a cow or bull without horns

dog hanging a wedding feast at which money is collected for the bride

dog poison the plant, fool's parsley

dog's guts the bummalo, a fish best known as Bombay duck

dog's mouth the snapdragon

dog's trick a catnap whilst seated

dolly mop a drab or slut

Dom a cathedral church: a title of dignity in Portugal or Brazil

domba an Asiatic tropical tree, the seeds of which yield a thick dark green strongly-scented oil used both medicinally and for burning in lamps

domeykite a greyish-white arsenide of copper named after Domeko, a Chilean chemist and minerologist

donge a mattress (15th cent)

dongola in Canada, a canoe race in which the paddling is performed by teams of equal numbers of men and women in each boat

Dooinney-Oie pronounced *dunya-oi*, this is the friendly 'night man' of Manx legend. He is a spirit who gives warnings of storms either by blowing a horn or appearing in the misty form of a man and speaking the warning direct.

doomster until the practice was abolished on 16th March 1773, the additional title given to the public executioner when he formally pronounced the death sentence in a Scottish court. Others could perform the function of the doomster, but rarely did so.

doppy a gold coin of the period when Italy comprised various independent states. Its value varied in these states and was worth between eleven shillings and fourpence and a guinea.

drakestone a flat stone skimmed across the surface of water in a series of rebounds against that surface

dree-draw an illegal fishing implement. It consists of three hooks joined back to back, weighted with lead and fastened to a line. The line is stretched across a river and each end is held by a man.

dremels a dream (14th cent)

dreper one who dreped – a murderer (15th cent)

dribber one who dribbed – fired his arrows which fell short or wide of the mark (16th cent)

drifter ODDJOB choose between:– a fisherman on a boat using a driftnet: a lead miner working a horizontal seam

drink-a-penny the little grebe or dabchick

droil a servant who performs any menial task, a drudge (16th/17th cent)

dropper a distiller (18th cent slang)

dropstone either a stalactite or a stalagmite (a 16th/17th cent popular term as these are caused by the action of the dropping of water)

drovy *adjective* a word long in use before Chaucer wrote, in 1386, ' . . . *an horse that seeketh rather to drink drovy or trouble water than for to drink water of the clear well.*' It meant turbid or cloudy but is now only found in such dialects as that of Cumberland, with a sense of muddy.

drowsen an oatmeal pottage, common in the West Country in the 17th century, and made by boiling oatmeal with the dregs from beer barrels

drudge pudding a menial who worked in the kitchen (18th cent)

drungar a Byzantine admiral

drunkenwort tobacco (17th cent)

drwry between the 13th and 16th centuries the word, **drury**, had various spelling forms and meanings. Now, the word is known only as a surname or else brought to mind with London's famous Drury Lane. Historically, a drury or drwry had associations with love – often illicit sexual love. It meant love, love making, courtship, a love token and a sweetheart.

dryfat any large container – box, tub, barrel etc. – for the storing of non-liquid items (16th/17th cent)

dryine a serpent with an odious stink reputed to dwell in hollow oaks (16th/17th cent)

dso see **zho**

duck-billed cat the Mississippi paddlefish, a primitive fish related to the sturgeon and possessing a prolonged snout which is extended as a flat sword. As the snout is sensitive and easily damaged and the fish swims with its mouth open to gather its planktonic food so the purpose of this strange appendage is still speculative.

dulbert a blockhead, a stupid person (Scotland and north England)

dunpickle the marsh harrier, a bird of prey

dustpoint a 17th century boy's game after the fashion of quoits. A series of holes or 'points' were scraped in dust and a throwing contest ensued whereby participants had to lodge a stone in each hole.

dustyfoot a travelling pedlar

dyspathy the opposite of **sympathy** – aversion, antipathy or dislike

dziggetai a Central Asian wild ass

dzobo see **zho**

dzomo see **zho**

ea a drainage canal in the English Fenland (as **Ea**, the Babylonian god of the waters)

each uisage pronounced *ech-ooshkya*, this is the fiercest and most dangerous of all the mythical Highland water horses. It is a spirit which can assume many different guises and, as a horse, it can be mounted but the rider is incapable of dismounting. Once it has a victim it dashes into the sea or a loch and there devours all but the liver of the rider.

earnit a dialect form of the noun, **earthnut**

earthgrine an earthquake (13th cent)

earth horn a contrivance said to produce a subterranean noise and supposed to have been used by the English at the Battle of the Standard (22nd August 1138) in order to discomfort the Scots by terrifying their cattle

ee an eye (Scotland) – the plural of which is **een**

egg-hot a hot drink made of beer, eggs, sugar and nutmeg (an old Berkshire recipe)

cgglcr a farmer or dealer in poultry (Oxfordshire)

eik the greasy perspiration of a sheep

eirack a hen less than a year old (Scotland)

eirmonger an egg dealer (14th cent)

eisell vinegar (12th to 17th cent)

ela pronounced *E la*, it is the highest note of the mediaeval music scale, the gamut, which ranged from lower G in the bass to upper E in the treble

electrix the wife of an elector, a prince of Germany entitled to take part in the election of an emperor of the Holy Roman Empire (Note, but do not reveal, the standard term is **electress**. This is a 17th century word)

elephanta a violent storm which occurs at the termination of a monsoon

elet a very old word now found only in Wiltshire dialect, fuel

elfcake enlargement of the spleen attributed to the malice of an elf and described as '*hardness of the side*' (16th cent)

elf cup a small stone perforated by friction at a waterfall and placed under a stable door as a protection against witchcraft

elmen *adjective* of or pertaining to the elm tree: made of its timber: composed of elm trees

elp an early word for the elephant

elroquite an apple-green to grey coloured silicate of aluminium and iron. The colour coming from chromium.

em the letter M which, by occupying a square, is the standard by which printers measure a line of type

embroyn *verb* to befoul or cover with filth (16th cent)

eme an uncle (a very ancient word now only found in dialects such as that of Yorkshire)

emmet but an anthill

emptings pronounced *emptins* but often written as **emptyings**, it is yeast (now only U.S.A.)

en half of an **em** (q.v.)

encheater a treasury official who superintended the collection of revenue from that confiscated (a 14th century equivalent of **escheator**)

end-away *adverb* successively, one after another (Sheffield area)

end-gatherer one, little better than a beggar, who made a meagre living collecting refuse wool

endiaper *verb* to dapple, variegate

endraper *verb* to weave into cloth (15th cent)

enfermer the superintendent of an infirmary (14th century and, therefore, monastic)

engastriloque a ventriloquist (18th cent)

ent a term in metaphysics to describe the existent or the existent unity

enter-deux in 1589 Anne of Denmark was married to King James VI of Scotland at a ceremony with an enter-deux. An enter-deux is a proxy bridegroom acting on behalf of and with the full approval of the intended husband. Anne thus became the legitimate queen of Scotland and, in 1603, when he became James I of England she was equally England's lawful queen. They were the parents of King Charles I.

enterlove *verb* to love mutually

enterpart *verb* to share in (14th cent)

entia the plural of **ens**. An ens is a term in philosophy for something which has a physical existence as opposed to an attribute or a quality.

ephah the dry equivalent of the Hebrew bath. The bath being a liquid measure of approximately 6½ gallons. The ephah was used for non-liquid items and varied between 4½ to 9 gallons.

epistaxis bleeding from the nose

epopt one initiated into the ancient Greek Eleusinian mysteries

er *interjection* expressing hesitation

eranist a meal to which each contributes his or her share

erendrake an ambassador (9th to 13th cent)

ern an obsolete verb of a river, to flow. Also a dialect form of **earn**.

ers the plant, bitter vetch

esne a domestic slave of the Anglo-Saxon era

estrain *verb* to bind tightly (15th cent)

eta a member of the Japanese lowest social class

ethel ancestral land or estate

evejar all different languages since ancient Greek times have named this bird to reflect the completely erroneous belief that it sucks milk from domestic animals. Its English name of goatsucker is a typical example, but it is better known as a nightjar.

evviva a shout of applause meaning long live

ewdendrift snow raised and driven by the wind (Scotland)

ewder vapour or smoke (Scotland)

exine a variation of **extine**, the outer membrane of a grain of pollen

exta the entrails of a victim studied by a soothsayer in order to make his predictions

eye baby the mirror image of oneself seen on the eye of someone else

eyewright one who treats ailments of the eye

eyey *adjective* full of holes

fairess a white witch (17th cent)

faki a schoolmaster in Africa

falcon gent a 15th century form of **falcon gentle**, the female of the peregrine falcon

famblecrop the first stomach of a cow (East Anglia)

fanfan a pet dog

fantigue Dickens spelt it **fanteeg**. In Shropshire it is spelt **fantaig**. In Worcester – **fanteague**. Some even spell it **fantique**. It is a state of anxiety or excitement, especially one in the form of a fit of ill-humour.

fap *adjective* drunk

farcost a type of inferior ship of the Middle Ages

farcy humour a **farcy bud** or a **farcy button** are examples of a farcy humour. The bud is a small tumour and the button is a similar tumour but with thickening of connective tissue and these are typical manifestations of the equine disease, farcy. In short, any sign of farcy afflicting a horse.

fardlet a little bundle (14th to 16th cent)

fardry a face which has been painted with cosmetics (15th cent)

farsang an ancient Persian measure of distance, approximately 4 miles

farthingbag the second stomach of a cow (Shropshire)

Fastgong pronounced *fasgun*, an old Norfolk word similar to the Cumberland and Scottish terms of **Fastens even**, **Fastens een** or **Fastens eve** – the eve of Fastens or Lent. Shrove Tuesday

fastland the mainland

fastship meanness, minginess or parsimony (13th cent)

fat hen pronounced *fal-hen*, any of various goosefoot plants capable of being eaten as vegetables

fatiloquist a fortune-teller (17th/18th cent)

fawney rig a petty fraud involving a brass ring, gilded to look like pure gold. The confidence trickster 'discovers' it in the path of the dupe who, believing the 'finder' to be a simpleton, buys it from him at what seems a bargain price.

fax still extant in such words as **Fairfax** or **Halifax**, it is Old English for the hair of the head

fayer a cleaner (various dialects)

feaberry apart from **feaberries**, the plural is **feabs**, **fabes**, **fapes** or **thapes**. An unripe gooseberry (Norfolk).

fearbabe a bugaboo or night time terror of such pathetic belief that only the merest child could possibly take it seriously (16th/17th cent)

featherwife a woman who prepares feathers for practical use

feeblose *adjective* somewhat feeble

feedman a soldier who received a wage for his service (15th to 18th cent)

felapton a universal negative such as '*Virtue should not be renounced*' coupled with a universal affirmative such as '*All virtue has its woe*' produces the particular negative conclusion that '*Some woe, therefore, should not be renounced.*' That example of a felapton, as this particular mood in logic is termed, dates back to 1551.

fellmonger a dealer in sheepskins

felonry the convict population of early modern Australia

ferash an Indian domestic servant having the specific duties of pitching tents, spreading carpets and similar physical activities, a handyman

ferblet an obscure 14th century adjective believed to mean effeminate

ferflax a material, described in the *Daily News* 10th May 1889, as a mixture of iron and vegetable fibre shreds

ferrup a meaningless word found in such expressions as '*What a ferrup!*' '*What the ferrups*?!' '*By the ferrups!*' where one might use less polite terminology in other company

fetchlight a flame seen gliding delicately in a churchyard or over a grave and believed to be either an omen of death or the route which a subsequent funeral will take (Wales)

fex sediment, waste, dung (16th cent)

fiant from the twelfth year of the reign of Henry VIII to the present this word has been used to describe a warrant addressed to the Irish chancery under the Great Seal. However, in the plural, it can also mean badger dung!

figdust finely ground oatmeal used as fodder for a caged bird

figsue a posset of figs and bread boiled in ale (Cumberland)

file ODDJOB choose either a whore (14th cent) or a pickpocket (17th/18th cent)

filibeg a kilt

fimble the male plant of hemp, the female being a carl hemp

finewed (pronounced *fin-ewed* or *vin-ewed*) *adjective* mouldy (now only Cornwall but Shakespeare and other writers used it)

fingersmith a midwife

fishing frog the anglerfish, any of various ugly marine fishes which have a sort of 'fishing rod' on their heads

fitsides *adverb* equal, a match, quits and only used in the Scottish phrase *to be fitsides with* (a named person)

fixfax the thick tendon in the neck of sheep or cattle (Cumberland)

fiz an alternative but perfectly acceptable way of spelling **fizz**

flagger a prostitute

flamb *verb* to baste (Scotland)

flatman one employed on a flatboat such as a canal barge

flickle *Little and little, the cat eateth the flickle* appeared in a book of proverbs and epigrams in 1562. Flickle is a rare form of **flick** which, in turn, is a form of **flitch**, now found only in dialects such as that of Lancashire. A side of bacon.

flidder in Whitby they have a saying, '*He sticks like a flither.*' On the Isle of Man it is called a **flitter**. In Scarborough, the flitter or flither is called a **flidder**. A limpet.

flimper in order to flimp, a flimper needs a victim with a pocket watch, an accomplice and a crowd. The accomplice pushes the victim in the back, the flimper steals the watch whilst the crowd adds to the confusion and facilitates the escape. A thief.

flockmeal *adverb* the opposite of piecemeal – by the piece. This ancient word, which was first recorded circa 893 A.D., lasted until the 17th century and means by the flock or group in reference to people, or by the heap or group regarding objects.

flodge in Lincolnshire, a small pool or puddle

fo a dialect term for the measure of eight square yards

fog-race a 17th century jocular term for progress

foldboat a small collapsible boat of rubberized sailcloth

forbysen a Middle English word for a proverb

foremaid the senior female assistant in a 16th century shop

forfex a pair of scissors

forgett a side piece of a finger in a glove

formicant *adjective* crawling like an ant

forsado a galley slave (16th/17th cent)

fostal the track of a hare. The plural of this 15th century word being **fostalx**

fostrild a nurse (13th century)

foujdar in British imperial Bengal, a judge hearing criminal cases

fox-evil alopecia, the disease of the scalp which results in hair falling out

frampold *adjective* bad-tempered peevish

frass the excrement of larvae

fraterer a monk in charge of the dining room (15th cent)

fripier a dealer in old clothes

friseur a hairdresser

frister a sweetheart (17th cent)

Frome a town in Somerset

fruitwife a bawd

frutex any shrub

fuff the spit of a cat

fufu a West African dish of peeled yams which are boiled, pounded and shaped into balls

fuk a type of sail on a 15th/16th century boat

fulker a pawnbroker (16th cent)

fullhead a castrated stag

fumade a smoke pilchard

funambulator a tightrope walker

funduck an 18th century spelling of **fonduk**, a North African inn or hotel

furca a gallows

furner a baker

fuster a maker of saddletrees (14th/17th cent)

fuzzock a fat, unwieldy woman

ga the bobization equivalent of the musical syllable **fa**

gabeller one who collected the salt tax in France prior to the Revolution

galer one, in historical times, who collected the manorial duty on fish

galopin a boy who performed various household duties such as running errands turning meat on a spit or acting as a page

gam a noun of assemblage for whales

gambist a peformer on the viola da gamba

gamp an inferior nurse

gan a slang word for the mouth

ganneker a publican (14th/15th cent)

garbler one who removed refuse from spices either as an official or as a merchant

garreteer a literary hack

garthman one who owns or works in an enclosure (either freshwater or saline) containing fish

genetor a cavalryman (15th/16th cent)

gentleman-at-large one who is unemployed

goedesian a land surveyor (17th cent)

gester a professional singer or reciter of romances (14th/15th cent)

getter a coal miner

giller one who guts and cleans fish

gilt a thief

girl a maid servant

glimmerer either a woman who entered a house on the pretext of obtaining a light for her own domestic fire and took this opportunity of pilfering or a person who begged for a living claiming to have lost all by fire (16th–18th cent)

glottographer a glossographer or writer of commentaries

glutman a low-ranking customs officer (18th cent)

glyptographer one who engraves on precious stones

gomashta in India, a clerk in a native language

gombeen man/woman a moneylender

goujat an army valet

gozzard a gooseherd, one who tends a flock of geese

grabby a foot soldier (cavalry slang)

grass captain in Cornwall, one who oversees the operation of separation of ore from rock above ground

grass nurse a wet nurse (18th/19th cent)

greffier on the Channel Islands, a registrar, clerk or notary

gregory a hangman (named after Gregory Brandon, London's hangman during the reign of James I)

grinter one in charge of a granary (Scotland 15th to 17th cent.)

grubbler a grubber in any sense but (for ODDJOB) construe as one who digs ditches or performs similar menial tasks

gubernatrix defined by Cockeram in1623 as 'she who ruleth' hence (for ODDJOB) assume the persona of Mrs. Thatcher or any other woman of power

guffy a soldier (sailor's term)

gul a rose, introduced from the Persian to the English language by Byron in his expression 'gardens of gul' which phrase was subsequently taken up by Hood and Ruskin. (If you are still bemused by the wordsmith puzzle see entry for Byron)

guster a professional or official food taster (Scotland 17th cent)

gy a Scottish form of **guy** in the sense of a guide

hace a Scottish form of the adjective **hoarse**

hackbutter a soldier equipped with a hackbut, an early type of portable firearm

halurgist one who works in salt

halver a fisherman entitled to set a half-net in order to trap fish as the tide ebbs

hammerer apart from the general sense it is a specific term for a geologist

handman a manservant

hangster a female public executioner, a hangwoman (15th cent)

harl a fibre of such as hemp: a barb of a feather

harle a **harl** in either sense

haubergier a maker of coats of chain mail (15th cent)

havener a harbour master

haxter female, a prostitute: male, her bully or protector

headborough an old title which gradually decreased in significance until it came to mean the petty constable of a parish, the sense in which **boroughhead** and **borsholder** also applied

headswoman a midwife (East Anglia)

heaver apart from general usage, specifically a docker

hellier a slater or tiler

herden coarse flax or hemp

heretoga the leader of an old English army

hermenuet an interpreter

hewster a dyer (17th cent)

hieromonach a monk-priest of the Greek church

hillman apart from general usage, a specific term for a worker in a slate quarry

hillwoman apart from general usage, a forewoman in a rag and bone yard

hippodame one who tames horses (the earlier form of the current **hippodamist**)

histrion an actor

hog reeve an officer of a New England community charged with the prevention or appraising of damages caused by straying pigs – the post is now nominal

hoppo a Chinese customs and excise officer

house farmer also called a **house jobber** or **house knacker**, he or she is a property developer who converts dwelling houses into tenements and, essentially, charges the highest rent possible with the minimum of attention to duties such as repair and maintenance

howdy a midwife (this Scottish word probably arises not from a greeting such as 'How do you do' but from the word **hold** in its sense as benevolent or kind)

huer a Cornish pilchard fishermen's lookout man who, stationed on a high point on the land, directs the boat or boats towards the shoal of fish

hurrier either (for ODDJOB) a miner concerned with the movement of coal from the face or else an 18th cent term for a haberdasher

hurter apart from other meanings, one who gathers hurtleberries in Surrey

ide a European carp-like fish

io a large Hawaiian hawk

ism any faddish or ridiculous theory or doctrine

jazy a type of wig, originally made of a worsted material

ka the spiritual self in the ancient Egyptian religion. In the context of one of the games it is used as a Scottish word for a jackdaw.

kar an alternative spelling of the Scottish adjective **car**, meaning left or sinister

ket raw flesh, carrion: rubbish (senses now retained only in dialect) – a matted, hairy fleece of wool (Scotland)

keta a species of salmon found in the Pacific

knat a species of sandpiper also known as a knot

ky cows (a term formerly in general usage but still retained in the north and in Scotland)

lat an isolated pillar

lep a Scottish form of the word **leap** in its sense as a basket

lepa the fragments which adhere to the hands of the one who offers a pinda or ball of rice to deceased ancestors in a Hindu ceremony

loppy *adjective* limp

lota a polished brass water pot

lunk a stupid person

mait the Scottish form of the noun, adjective and verb **mate**

manred an obsolete word with various meanings including sexual intercourse

mel honey

nae a Scottish and Northern form of the word **no**

nar a Scottish and Northern adverb with a sense of near or nigh

nat a Burmese spirit or demon

nea a Scottish and Northern form of the word **no**

neg an obsolete form of **nag**, in the sense of a horse

nerita a species of sea snail (the plural is either **neritae** or **neritas**)

ness a headland

O interjection expressing such as pain, lament, surprise, appeal or entreaty according to intonation. Apart from other meanings, simply as the interjection it is both a noun and verb.

ob a familiar of a Hebrew witch

oe a small island

oi an exclamation

oink the sound of a pig

om a type of mantra or passage taken from a Hindu religious work and uttered as an incantation

oo a Scottish word meaning either wool or we

ora a Danish coin introduced to Britain by the Vikings

Ottoman empire now reduced to the modern republic of Turkey, it once included various eastern European countries as well as Arabic lands such as Egypt. It was founded by 1288 by Osman I (Ottoman) and was ruled by sultans until 1922 when Mohammed VI abdicated and, for a further two years, Abdul Mejid II was the caliph.

outen *adverb/proposition* outside, away, distant etc. (formerly standard English but still retained in some dialects)

ouuen an earlier, modern English, form of **oven**

oy a grandchild (Scotland)

oye an oy

pa a Maori fortified village (plural **pas**)

padle the lumpfish, a clumsy sea fish: a hoe or similar scraping implement (both senses Scottish)

palp *verb* to touch, feel

paple a Scottish form of the verb, **popple**

papple a Scottish form of the verb, **popple**

pe the seventeenth letter of the Hebrew alphabet also a Portuguese and Brazilian measure of length

pel a stake at which swordsmanship was practised in the 14th century

pela china wax, a white wax obtained from an insect

peridot olivine, a green-coloured gem

peto the wahoo, a dark-blue edible fish (note that one of its anagrams, **tope**, is also a fish)

pire *verb* to look narrowly at something especially in order to see that which is indistinct (formerly standard English and still found in such dialects as Northumbrian)

plap *verb* to fall with a flat impact

ple an early form of the word **plea**

popple *verb* to bubble, to boil up like water

pote a stick or rod used for poking, thrusting or stirring also a flat piece of wood used to open up old thatch in order to insert new thatch

proteid either a protein or a species of salamander

psa *interjection* expressing contempt, impatience, disgust

pteropid *adjective* belonging to or having the characteristics of the flying fox family

pya a species of plant, the tubers of which supply arrowroot

qadi an alternative, but perfectly

acceptable, spelling of **cadi**, a Muslim civil judge

qat (prounced *kat*) an Ethiopian bush which yields a narcotic

qi Chinese philosophy, the physical life-force

qu the half-farthing, a coin of Victorian times, though the term itself is a bookkeeper's word dating back to the 16th cent. when no such coin existed. The convenient transfer of description is of recent origin used only by players of word games as a shorthand description of a very useful word that is, technically, obsolete.

quean a harlot

rander a person who slices meat into strips or long slices

rae an alternative way of spelling **roe** in the sense of a deer

ranite a variety of zeolite, a hydrous silicate found in the cavities of igneous rock

rata a large New Zealand tree bearing crimson flowers

ratine an alternative spelling of **ratteen**, a thick twilled woollen cloth

rea a Portuguese coin, the plural of which is **reis**

ren a Middle English word meaning a run or course

resiant an archaic word for a resident

resinata a Greek white wine with a resinous flavour

ret *verb* to soak such as flax in order to soften it

retin *verb* to recoat with tin

retsina a resin-flavoured Greek wine

rin a Norfolk word for brine and a Scottish form of **run**

rit *verb* to cut with a sharp implement, to tear, to scratch: to slit a sheep's ear (formerly

standard English and still extant in Scotland and northern England)

rivalship emulation

rom an adult male gypsy

seeer one who sees in a normal sense, as opposed to one who sees psychically

sen a Japanese bronze coin

serry *verb* to form in serried ranks

SET *As a noun these are just some of the meanings*: a mining lease: pressure as a power employed by shipwrights: a fixed look with the eyes: the attempt by a woman to gain a man's affections: an absolute cessation: the position taken by a dog in pointing towards game: the way in which something is put in writing: a fixed habit: the direction of a current: a person's build: an adjustment of a waver's loom: a square in the pattern of a tartan: a tartan's pattern: the hang of a ship's sails: the position of a limb: the elevation of a gun: the slight lateral deflection in opposite directions of the alternate teeth of a saw: the amount of that deflection: the area of a hunt: a twig used for grafting: a bedding-out plant: a seed potato: the kitty or stake in a game of dice: a pleat in a ruff: a square paving stone: the burrow of a badger: a political party: the number of couples required for a square dance: a pair of bagpipes: a definite number of copies of a bill of lading: a spell of weather: a suite of apartments let as lodgings: a frame for supporting the sides and/or roof of a mine: a team of six horses: a coal train *As a verb these are just some of the meanings:—* to seat: to put a hen to sit on eggs:

to make a bird perch: of a rabbit, to be resting: to suit: to sink: to plant a crop: to graft: to deposit: to wager: in dominoes, to play first: to imprison: to place a person in the pillory: to hit a person: in geometry, to mark off a line of a definite length: to cause to be: to put singers at the correct pitch: to muzzle a horse: to bestow a name: to invest: to apply a remedy to: to bestow pain: to add one thing to another: to fix in one's mind: to rest one's eye upon: to imprint: to put a specious appearance upon a thing: to prescribe: to appoint a festival to be observed: to lay down a law: of God, to fix a time for: to introduce a fashion: to start a hymn for others to follow: to make an appointment: to lease: to take a mining lease: to lay a snare for animals: to sew: to settle an affair: to insert a stitch: to put into the oven: to write a book: to translate: to cast a horoscope: to dispose of land: to adjust the teeth of a saw: to tune an instrument: to pleat a ruff: to suppose: to care so much for: not to care for: to prepare for dyeing: to cause a flower to develop into fruit: to establish a particular breed of sheep: to puzzle: to escort a person: to punt a boat: to besiege a place: to watch for the purpose of robbing: to launch: to restore to health: to put a horse in a stable: in hunting, to bring to bay: to pretend to be: of a bullet, to expand on impact: of a cart, to tip up: *The word is also an adjective and even an obsolete Scottish conjunction having a sense of though, although*

sith *conjunction* seeing that

somewhere! This is where you find the answer to the last of the Things. As it said – ' . . . in the Appendix, somewhere!' It is, therefore, a double challenge, both discovering it here and solving it. The solution to the puzzle is the question – HOW LONG DID IT TAKE YOU TO FATHOM THIS OUT?

sopper one who sops

spae prediction, prophecy: omen

spitz any of various breeds of dog of the samoyed or Pomeranian type

st *interjection* either used as an exclamation demanding silence from a person or people or else a command to an animal to depart or a command to attack

stang a sting: the pipefish: an eel spear: the tongue of a Jew's harp

stearin fat in solid form

suq a local market in various Arabic countries

tae Scottish form of **toe**

tai the Japanese sea bream

taim an early form of the word **them**

taj a tall conical hat worn by a dervish

tanier an alternative way of spelling **tania**, a farinaceous tuber akin to the eddoe

tave *verb* to sprawl: to strike out with arms or legs: to strive, toil, labour (Formerly standard English now only found in such dialects as that of Yorkshire)

te a variant spelling of **ti**

ter an obsolete form of the words **tar** and **tare**

theat a Scottish word for one of the ropes which tie a horse to the plough

thein a variant spelling of **thane**

theine caffeine (originally thought to be an alkaloid exclusive to tea)

thig *verb* to solicit gifts

thimblerigger one who performs a

swindling trick by which such as a pea is shifted by sleight of hand from one to another of three inverted thimble-shaped cups

ti the musical syllable in the tonic sol-fa

tirane an obsolete form of the noun, **tyrant**

toon the Indian mahogany tree

torpide an obsolete form of **torpid**

traise *verb* to betray (became obsolete after 16th century)

whipper and hougher often referred to as the hougher, he was an inferior official appointed by the corporation of Newcastle-upon-Tyne during the 18th and 19th centuries with an annual salary of £4.6s.8d. His duties as a hougher being the cutting of the sinews of pigs which plagued the city's streets by straying and, as a whipper, the punishment of felons. He was also the public hangman.

wor a variant form of the literary Scottish adjective and adverb **war** (or as Burns and Scott prefer, **waur**) meaning worse

xa an obsolete modern English form of the word **shah**

xebec a small Mediterranean sailing vessel

xenon a heavy inert gas

xi the fourteenth letter of the Greek alphabet

xiph an obsolete name for the swordfish

xylyl the hypothetical radical of the volatile colourless liquid, xylene

yah an exclamation of disgust, aversion or defiance. It is also a verb to utter such a cry and is, in addition, a dialect form of the adverb, **yea**.

yapp a style of limp leather bookbinding with overlapping edges

yate a eucalyptus tree of southwestern Australia: a gale (In this sense formerly standard English but now only found in such dialects as that of Cumberland)

yed both a noun and verb meaning (to) fib, contend, wrangle. Formerly standard English, it is now retained only in literary Scottish.

yee an obsolete form of **eye**, **ye** and **yea**

zax a pointed hammer for trimming slates

zeta the sixth letter of the Greek alphabet: a room in a building but the specific designation varies according to user but normally signifies that it is subject to externally produced heat or cooling by such means as pipes. An alternative designation is that of a room above a church porch.

zho a hybrid beast of burden from a cross between a yak and a Ladakhi cow. Zho is either male or female and it can also be spelt **dso**, **dzo** or **zo**. The male is a **zhobo** and the female is a **zhomo**. The same suffixes of -**bo** and -**mo** can also be applied to the other spelling forms i.e. **dzobo** or **dzomo**

zo see **zho**

Bibliographical Postscript

The copyright of any material quoted in *Pears Word Games* is deemed to lie with the person or publication named in any particular commentary.

The inventors of games are given where known and sincere apologies are extended to anyone whose credit has been overlooked. This will be corrected in any future editions of this book.

Back issues of the journal of recreational linguistics, *Word Ways*, are available on microfilm from University Microfilms (A Bell and Howell Company), 300 North Zeeb Road, Ann Arbour, Michigan 48106, USA. New issues from Word Ways, Spring Valley Road, Morristown, New Jersey 07960, USA.

The Scrabble enthusiasts magazine, *Onwords*, is published by Allan Simmons, Onwords, 10 Church Lane, Wormley, Herts. EN10 6JT.

The journal of the American Cryptogram Association, *The Cryptogram*, is published by the A.C.A., P.O. Box 6454, Silver Spring, MD 20906, USA.

All three magazines are available only on a subscription basis and enquiries should be addressed as given above.